RAIN FORESTS

Dwight Holing and Scott Forbes
Editors

John Gattuso
Series Editor

Discovery Communications, Inc.

Distribution
United States
Langenscheidt Publishers, Inc.
46–35 54th Road, Maspeth, NY 11378
Fax: 718-784-0640

Worldwide
APA Publications GmbH & Co.
Verlag KG Singapore Branch, Singapore
38 Joo Koon Road, Singapore 628990
Tel: 65-865-1600. Fax: 65-861-6438

Printed by Insight Print Services (Pte) Ltd, 38 Joo Koon Road, Singapore 628990.

Cataloging-in-Publication Data for this book is on file with the Library of Congress, Washington, D.C.

An aye-aye, a member of the lemur family found only on Madagascar, uses its large ears to detect insect larvae in wood and a long, bony finger to pry them from their burrows.

R *ain Forests* combines the interests and enthusiasm of two of the world's best-known information providers: **Insight Guides**, whose titles have set the standard for visual travel guides since 1970, and **Discovery Communications**, the world's premier source of nonfiction entertainment. The editors of Insight Guides provide both practical advice and general understanding about a destination's history, culture, institutions, and people. Discovery Communications and its website, www.discovery.com, help millions of viewers explore their world from the comfort of their homes and encourage them to explore it firsthand.

About This Book

This book reflects the contributions of editors and writers with extensive knowledge of the world's rain forests. Series editor **John Gattuso**, of Stone Creek Publications in New Jersey, worked with Insight Guides and Discovery Communications to conceive and direct the series. Considering the worldwide scope of the project, Gattuso called on two people, one in each hemisphere, to shepherd the text through the editorial process: **Dwight Holing**, a San Francisco Bay Area writer and editor with numerous books and articles to his credit as well as an extensive travel history in rain forests from Alaska to the Amazon, and **Scott Forbes**, an editor and writer based in Sydney, Australia, and the editor of *Discovery Travel Adventures: Australian Outback*.

Most people associate rain forests with the tropics, but temperate rain forests are found as far north as the Alaskan panhandle, a place that writer, photographer, and biologist **Tom Walker** has visited countless times over the years on various journalistic assignments and whale-watching expeditions. Walker lives in a log cabin that he made himself near Denali National Park, and though he jokes about being "self-unemployed" since 1972, he's produced more than 10 books and numerous magazine articles. **Lawrence W. Cheek**, a frequent contributor to this series, makes his home near the rain forests of Washington's Olympic Peninsula. Cheek has written nine books, all of them about a much drier region – his native Southwest. He moved to Seattle in 1996, assembled a closet full of Gore-Tex, and began writing about the natural history of the Pacific Northwest. "I was rain-deprived for most of my life," he says, "so I love hiking in the rain forest in even the heaviest downpours."

If there's a soggier place than the Olympic Peninsula, it's Waialeale, an extinct volcano on Kauai – the oldest of the Hawaiian Islands – that has the dubious distinction of being the wettest spot on Earth. As Honolulu-based **Rita Ariyoshi** explains, however, the rain is a minor inconvenience compared to the beauty of the island's celebrated Na Pali Coast. Award-winning author **David Rains Wallace** takes readers on a tour of another island forest – Puerto Rico's El Yunque – as well as Monteverde Cloud Forest, which is perched like a "sky island" in Costa Rica's Tilarán Mountains. He also writes about the evolution of rain forests and their inhabitants, a topic he has explored in several works over the years, including *The Monkey's Bridge*, a *New York Times* Notable Book for 1997.

Elsewhere in Central America, writer and photographer **Robert Friel** explores the rain forests of Belize, a place he's gotten to know both personally and professionally as a travel journalist, scuba diver, and adventurer. Farther south, readers are guided through Peru's sprawling Manu Biosphere Reserve by **Susanne Methvin**, a freelance writer and an avid conservationist with more than 20 years experience leading

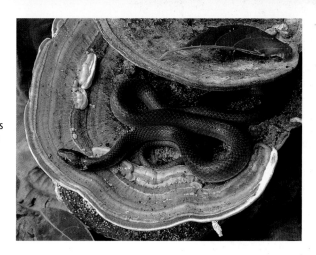

nature tours for Mountain Travel–Sobek in El Cerrito, California. **Glen Martin**, the environmental beat reporter for the *San Francisco Chronicle*, covers two fascinating but threatened ecosystems: Brazil's Atlantic Forest and the temperate rain forests of Chile's Lake District. He also writes about the struggles of indigenous people to maintain traditional ways of life in the face of powerful outside pressures.

Across the Pacific, **Amanda Burdon** covers the Wet Tropics of her native Australia. Formerly an associate editor with *Australian Geographic*, she now works as a freelance writer, specializing in environmental, travel, and social topics. "One of the wonderful things about the Wet Tropics is the sheer mystery of it," she says. "The whole place seems to be celebrating life." Fellow Aussie **Margaret McPhee** has written extensively on the wilderness areas of the Australo-Pacific region. Here she confines herself to a destination she has long wanted to explore: New Zealand's Fiordlands National Park.

British-born **Christopher P. Baker**, an award-winning travel writer now living in Oakland, California, covers the wildlife and cultures of Papua New Guinea. Bangkok-based **Morris Dye**, a former travel editor at the *San Francisco Examiner*, writes about Borneo and northern Vietnam. After several years as a senior writer with *Australian Geographic*, travel and nature writer **Pip Moran** is now based in Taiwan, where she launched her journey to Thailand's Khao Yai National Park. The experience gave her a fresh perspective on both the rigors and pleasures of a rain-forest adventure, the subject of her chapter on how to prepare for your trip.

Born in Britain and raised in South Africa, **Philip Briggs** first visited the gorillas of Bwindi in 1988 and has returned several times in the course of researching three editions of his Uganda travel guide, one of nine guidebooks to his name. Like most tourists who visit the gorillas, he describes having an "almost mystical" sense of recognition. "One of them regularly broke off from chomping on bamboo to study us, its soft brown eyes staring deeply into ours, as if seeking out some sort of connection." An institution in publishing, both as a writer and publisher of the Bradt Travel Guides, **Hilary Bradt** has an ongoing love affair with Madagascar. Since her first visit in 1976, she has returned more than 20 times as a tour guide and an author, writing four books about the island – and the Madagascar chapter of this book.

Michael Matz's chapter on conservation issues is informed by his experiences as an environmental journalist for *Greenwire* and a writer for Conservation International, as well as his present position at the Exploratorium, a museum of science, art, and perception in San Francisco. He also tackled the monumental task of assembling Travel Tips and the Resource Directory.

The editors and writers woud like to thank Emily Russell, Douglas B. Trent, and Marianne van Vlaardingen for research assistance, the many park rangers, naturalists, and tourism officials who reviewed the text, and Judith Dunham and Nicky Leach for editorial assistance. Thanks also to the members of Stone Creek Publications' editorial team: Sallie Graziano, Edward A. Jardim, and Nicole Buchenholz.

Centipedes (opposite), like this one from Peru, kill earthworms and other prey with poisonous fangs. Their bite can be quite painful to humans.

A pseudoboa (above), known in Spanish as a *coral macho*, waits for its prey on a colorful bracket fungus.

The helmeted hornbill (below), a native of Borneo, is known for its prominent casque, the enlarged upper surface of its bill.

Dense vegetation (following pages), including large, round leaves of *Gunnera insignis*, better known as poor-man's umbrella, crowd a waterfall on Poas Volcano in Costa Rica.

Table of Contents

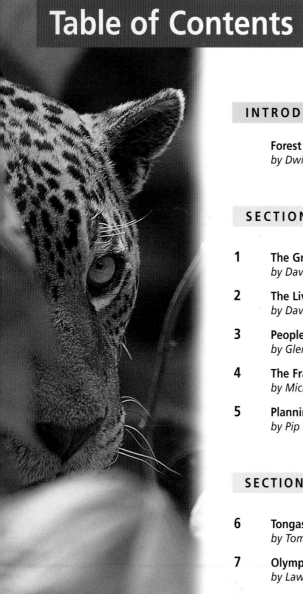

MAPS

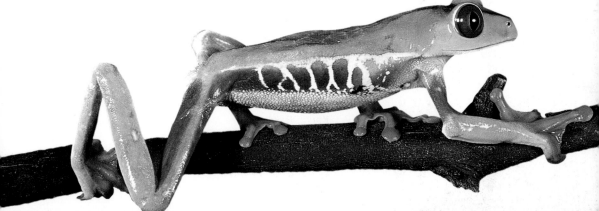

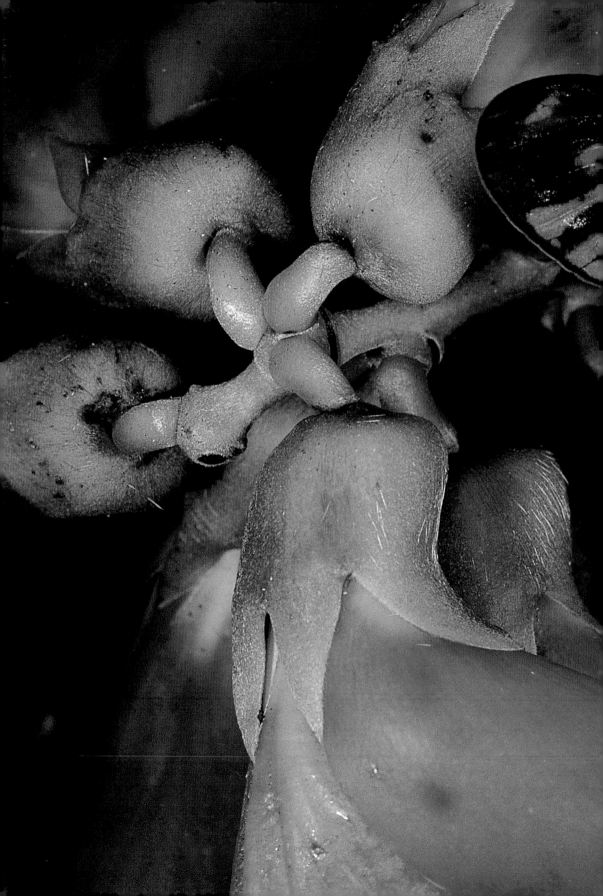

n the moments before the violet of a tropical sunrise gives way to graphite and then cobalt, the quiet of a velvety night is pierced by the ringing call of a bellbird. Louder than any barnyard rooster, the bird's revelry touches off a sunrise serenade of buzzing insects, croaking frogs, and howling monkeys. Early morning light ripples across an emerald sea of treetops whose tangled limbs clutch at one another like desperate lovers. Overhead, a boisterous flock of macaws streaks across the sky, leaving feathery trails of scarlet and blue in their wake. Beneath the unbroken canopy, a swollen river the color of tea moves as silently and sinuously as an anaconda. At water's edge, a gold and black-spangled jaguar laps thirstily before retreating into the jungle to rest after its all-night prowl. The air turns warm. Clouds billow. And then comes the rain. It falls unrelentingly, then falls again. ◆ Welcome to another day in the strange, beautiful, and increasingly imperiled world of the rain forest – the most alive place on Earth. Here in nature's living laboratory dwell over half of all living things, from delicate orchids that grow in air and butterflies as large as your outstretched hand to three-toed sloths that dangle motionless from trees and countless plants, insects, and birds that don't even have names yet. ◆ Rain forests come in two basic types – tropical and temperate – but there are thousands of different variations, from the cold and misty ancient fir and spruce forests of south-east Alaska to the hot, humid, and utterly remote highlands of Papua New Guinea. A combination of climate, location, and a host of other environ-mental factors has created a seemingly endless array of ecosystems

Complex, mysterious, and achingly beautiful, rain forests capture the imagination and stir the soul.

A poison arrow frog climbs a heliconia plant. Indians in South America use the poison of some species to tip their darts and arrows.

Preceding pages: Butterfly, Tambopata River, Peru; Olympic National Park, Washington; orangutan, Borneo.

A cecropia leaf (left) lies on the forest floor. From the moment a leaf hits the ground, insects, fungi, and bacteria begin to break it down.

Squirrel monkeys (bottom) spend most of their lives in the canopy. They live in large troops in the tropical forests of Central and South America.

A Yanomami girl (right) from Venezuela holds a pet parrot. There are about 50 million indigenous people in the world's rain forests.

matched only by the dizzying diversity of plants and animals that live in them. Because rain forests occur on six continents and in dozens of countries, there is a tantalizing menu of destinations from which the traveler eager to quench a thirst for knowledge and adventure can choose. Consider the options you'll find detailed in the pages that follow: searching for resplendent quetzals in the cloud forests of Costa Rica, floating through the jungles of Papua New Guinea, bathing in the spray of waterfalls in Thailand, dodging saltwater crocodiles in Australia's Wet Tropics, or hiking among thousand-year-old trees in Chile's spectacular Lake District.

No matter what the locale, sight, or activity, all rain-forest travel has something in common: the inescapable truth that wherever you visit, the destination is unique, rare, and, undoubtedly, endangered. No matter how wild, remote, or expansive, all rain forests – from the tiniest patch of Atlantic coastal *mata* in Brazil to the sprawling jungles of Borneo – are exceedingly fragile. Sadly, habitat loss due to logging, agriculture, and increased urbanization is threatening our planet's natural nurseries.

Because rain forests are so delicate, traveling to them is often fraught with a sense of urgency. Part of the hurry has to do with experiencing an ecosystem before it disappears. Even more important, however, is the realization that your visit can actually serve as a tool for conservation. By traveling in a rain forest and supporting the local economy as an eco-tourist, you can directly help in its protection.

The sense of fulfillment that comes from knowing that your trip can make a difference is just one of the many rewards that rain-forest travel brings. So come. Embark on a journey that's almost guaranteed to change your view of the natural world. Witness the mystery and magic of life. Feel the awe. Sense the wonder. And discover all that awaits you in the rain forest.

◆

Preparing for the Field

◆

Ready yourself for adventure by learning about the natural history of rain forests and their inhabitants, the cultures of their indigenous peoples, and the conservation challenges that threaten their survival.

To understand what makes a rain forest different than other forests, it's first necessary to dispel a few misconceptions. As you might expect, the most essential ingredient of any rain forest is moisture. Rain forests develop only in areas that receive more than 80 inches (203cm) of precipitation annually, but the distribution of precipitation over the course of the year is as crucial as the amount. Northeast Thailand's Korat Plateau, for example, gets almost as much rain as southern Thailand's Malay Peninsula, but most of the rain on the plateau falls during the monsoon season. The plateau is dry for months at a time and lacks organisms that characterize the classic rain forest of the peninsula a few hundred miles south. In fact, many tropical forests aren't rain forests at all. Some lose their leaves during the dry season and look like temperate forests in winter, although the weather may be quite balmy. ◆ Nor are all rain forests found in the tropics. Although we usually

Rain forests are the greenest places on Earth. No ecosystem harbors a greater variety or quantity of plant life.

associate rain forests with the warmth and exuberance of tropical climates, some occur in temperate zones. The largest rain forest in the United States, for example, is in southeast Alaska and gets much of its moisture in the form of snow. And while they are much cooler than their tropical counterparts, temperate rain forests produce an even greater density of organic matter. ◆ Tropical rain forests occupy the wide equatorial belt between the tropics of Cancer and Capricorn. South and Central America (called the "neotropics") contain the largest expanse; the rest occurs in Africa, Southeast Asia, and the Australo-Pacific region. Thousands of tree species inhabit them, including the kinds usually associated with "jungle" –

Rain forest cloaks the sheer walls of the Nanue River valley on the Big Island of Hawaii.

Preceding pages: A strawberry poison arrow frog sits atop a caiman, Bocas del Toro Islands, Panama.

A bromeliad (left) collects rainwater, soil, and fallen leaves, and provides a habitat for a variety of small creatures like this poison arrow frog.

Mushrooms (bottom) and other fungi don't photosynthesize like green plants but extract nutrients from organic matter such as decaying leaves or wood.

Mist (right) veils the cloud forests of Uganda's Virunga Mountains.

Epiphytes (opposite, bottom), plants that grow on other plants, cluster around a tree trunk in the El Yunque forest of Puerto Rico.

Earth's largest – gigantic conifers like Douglas fir and araucaria. Small epiphytes such as ferns, lichens, and mosses are also abundant.

Tropical and temperate rain forests weren't always so widely separated. Fifty-million-year-old fossils from places like Wyoming and Patagonia show that tropical figs and palms once grew in today's temperate zones, and that they grew close to temperate firs and redwoods. Evidently, the Earth's climate was much warmer, and temperate rain forests grew in cool highlands while tropical rain forests occupied warm lowlands. A similar arrange-

palm, mahogany, and fig, to name a few.

The biological diversity encompassed by tropical rain forests is staggering. Compare Borneo with Great Britain, for example. The tropical island has no less than 2,500 native tree species while Great Britain has only 35. Eighty tree species have been recorded in a single acre of the Amazon. Smaller plants such as shrubs and epiphytes (plants that grow on other plants) are even more multifarious. Some

20,000 orchid species live epiphytically; various other plant groups include another 10,000 epiphytic species.

The other main category, temperate rain forest, occurs in the mid-latitudes of the Northern and Southern Hemispheres. The largest expanses grow on the Pacific coasts of North and South America; they also occur on Pacific islands such as New Zealand and Tasmania. Plant diversity is lower here than in the tropics, but tree species include some of the

ment still prevails in the tropics, where high-altitude cloud forests dominated by temperate trees such as oaks and pines grow above lowlands where palms and rubber trees are found. A cloud forest may look much like an adjacent lowland forest, lush with orchids, vines, and tree ferns, but will have completely different plant species.

Rain, Rain

The abundance of moisture that nourishes rain-forest plants also presents challenges to their growth. Torrential rains wash nutrients into streams or leach them so deeply into the soil that roots can't reach them. Plants compensate by forming a dense mat of roots near the surface to absorb nutrients quickly. Another problem is that continually wet leaves are fertile breeding grounds for tiny organisms such as fungi, algae, and lichens that impede the leaves' photosynthetic function. Tropical trees get around this difficulty with a characteristic leaf shape – oblong, with an elongated "drip tip" that conducts water off the leaf's surface.

Given the density of vegetation, access to sunlight poses another challenge and is determined largely by a plant's height. Old-growth forests are organized by strata – shade-tolerant herbs and shrubs at ground level, sub-canopies of small trees, canopies of large trees, and scatterings of giant trees, called emergents, above the canopy. Temperate emergents such as Douglas firs are among the planet's largest trees, growing more than 300 feet (90m) tall. Tropical ones such as African and American ceibas or Asian dipterocarps reach more than 200 feet (60m) tall, and may have sizable trees growing on their branches.

Plants that grow on trees add a further dimension to a rain forest's structure. Epiphytes such as orchids, cacti, and bromeliads grow in soil that accumulates on tree branches, having arrived as seeds on air currents or in animal droppings. Mistletoe sends roots into its host and lives parasitically on the tree's sap. Strangler fig seeds sprout on branches, then grow roots downward to the forest floor. Vines such as philodendrons, aroids, and rattans sprout on the forest floor, climb upward on trees, then spread and flower when they reach the canopy. The accumulated growth of epiphytes and vines may break branches or shade out host trees, but hosts also take advantage of their "guests." They grow special roots on their own branches that draw nutrients from the soil and moisture that gather around epiphytes.

Life at the Top

Most plant growth and reproduction occurs in the canopy, where solar radiation provides energy for photo-

synthesis. Scientists have just begun to understand how complex and vital this leafy realm is. The majority of insects and other canopy invertebrates have yet to be identified and probably number many millions of species. The myriad ways in which animals interact with the giant trees – as pollinators, parasites, seed dispersers – may never be fully understood, but the evidence of those interactions is plain in the flowers and fruits that fill the treetops.

Rain-forest reproduction has no single season – different species flower at different times of the year. Some species blossom at long intervals, such as the dipterocarps of Borneo, which undergo mass flowerings about every five years. Another Asian tree seems to flower only after nearby lightning strikes fill the air with ozone. In neotropical rain forests, a sizable tree species of the genus *Tachigalia* flowers and fruits once in its lifetime, then dies, leaving a break in the forest canopy for its seedlings to grow in. Plant activity is less exuberant in temperate rain forests, but evergreen trees photosynthesize throughout the year, and some plants flower in winter.

The canopy's brilliance can make the shadowed forest floor seem lifeless by comparison, but this is an illusion. Protected from ultraviolet rays and drying winds, biological activity is intense in the humid calm. Trees live in symbiotic relationships with fungi called mycorrhizae that coat their roots and transfer water and nutrients into their cells. Mycorrhizae in turn are

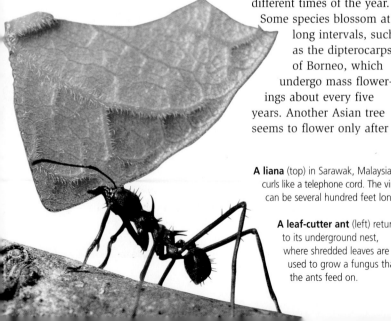

A liana (top) in Sarawak, Malaysia, curls like a telephone cord. The vines can be several hundred feet long.

A leaf-cutter ant (left) returns to its underground nest, where shredded leaves are used to grow a fungus that the ants feed on.

Fog Drip

At least a third of the precipitation received by a rain forest comes not from rain or snow but from condensation. The reason has to do with the surface area of plants. A large coniferous tree in a temperate rain forest, for example, can have more than 60 million needles, with a combined surface area of about 40,000 square feet (3,700 sq meters). As fog or clouds pass through the tree, moisture gathers on the needles and drips off. Even after months without rainfall, the ground under the tree will be moist while nearby clearings are dry and dusty.

The same process is at work in the tropics. A study in a Colombian cloud forest, for example, showed that nearly half of its annual precipitation came from fog drip. In many places, condensation produces enough moisture to sustain highland rain forests through months of drought, while lowland forests without fog lose their leaves and turn brown.

The process is more than a scientific curiosity; it has a profound impact on climate. Without the moisture produced by fog drip, local precipitation can be reduced by a third or more, which not only affects human communities (particularly during the dry season, when condensation feeds mountain streams) but impedes the forest's ability to regenerate.

part of a complex ecosystem in which bacteria, protozoans, invertebrates, and other tiny organisms number in the billions per cubic foot of soil. Tropical soil ecosystems break down fallen leaves and wood so fast that little organic humus accumulates. A colony of one species, the leafcutter ant, can remove a large tree's foliage in days, carrying the leaves to huge underground nests, where they use them to grow a fungus that they eat. In temperate rain forests where decay is slower, humus accumulates at depth, with a corresponding abundance and diversity of soil organisms.

Rain forests give an impression of agelessness,

and for good reason. Some trees live for hundreds of years – thousands in the case of temperate conifers. Tree seedlings can wait in the shade for decades until a windfall lets the sunlight in and allows them to grow toward the canopy.

Rain forests are also capable of adapting to change. During the last ice age, they receded in response to glacial cold and dryness, but also occupied new lands as growing ice caps lowered sea level. Hurricanes, volcanic eruptions, and wildfires destroy millions of acres, but forests begin to regenerate rapidly under natural conditions, although old growth takes centuries to return. In the

tropics, thousands of "pioneer" plant species specialize in colonizing open areas, including trees such as balsa, which can grow 15 feet (4½m) in one year. In temperate rain forests, angiosperms like oaks sprout from stumps, and some conifer seedlings grow best on burned soil.

Most important, perhaps, rain forests help perpetuate the benign climate in which they flourish by absorbing carbon dioxide (a so-called greenhouse gas) and producing oxygen during photosynthesis. They also absorb and transpire water that would otherwise run off the land. It's all a part of a self-regulating, self-sustaining ecosystem that scientists are just beginning to understand.

The Living Ark

chapter 2

The extraordinary diversity of rain-forest plants has fostered a corresponding variety of animals. As many as 20 animal species may live in association with a single plant. A study conducted by the U.S. National Academy of Sciences found that a typical, four-square-mile (10-sq-km) patch of rain forest is home to some 125 mammal, 400 bird, 100 reptile, and 60 amphibian species, as well as 750 kinds of trees. Species of insects and other invertebrates dwarf these figures: researchers have counted more than 2,000 types of invertebrates in one Amazonian tree. Remarkably, the species found in a tree a few hundred miles away are almost completely different. ◆ This wealth is not always obvious. First-time visitors to rain forests may be disappointed at the apparent scarcity of exciting wildlife, and, in fact, the density of animal populations in a rain forest is smaller than that of a coral reef or savanna. A little patience will reveal surprises, however. In the rain forest of the Malay Peninsula, skinny eight-inch (20-cm) lizards seem unremarkable until one of them suddenly disappears from a tree

Rain-forest animals have had to devise a wide range of strategies to compete in their densely inhabited environment.

trunk and lands on another tree 50 feet (15m) away. This is the famous *Draco volans*, one of the world's only aerial reptile species, which glides through the air on flaps of skin located on its flanks. In Central America, slightly larger lizards, basilisks, also seem unremarkable until one suddenly gets up on its hind legs and runs across the surface of a stream. These lizards have flaplike toe scales and are light and quick enough to be supported by the water's surface tension. ◆ Often, the very diversity and ingenuity of rain-forest animals is what makes them seem scarce. Because of their

Fewer than 20,000 orangutans remain in the wild, a reduction of as much as half in the last decade. The loss is due largely to habitat destruction caused by logging, mining, and agriculture in the rain forests of Sumatra and Borneo, their only remaining homes.

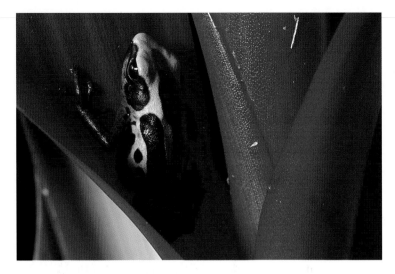

guessing, some mimics are edible, some aren't.

Rain-forest attackers can be amazingly stealthy, particularly parasites. In Asia, tiny land leeches drop onto passing animals and, while secreting a natural painkiller to conceal their presence, suck the host's blood. A neotropical botfly, *Dermatobia hominis*, lays its eggs on female mosquitoes; when the mosquitoes bite animals, the eggs drop off and hatch into grubs that burrow under the animal's skin. Again, the hosts are oblivious, although the grubs later cause discomfort as they grow large enough to emerge and pupate.

Flying Frogs and Beautiful Birds

environment's complexity, they tend to spread out, and many are experts at concealment and camouflage. Competition for food is so intense that a conspicuous animal is prone to become a quick meal for another. Cryptic individuals survive to pass on the trait. Asian stick and leaf insects, for example, resemble foliage right down to leaf veins, thorns, and spots of fungus. A neotropical nightjar, the potoo, hides by mimicking a vertical dead branch.

Showy rain-forest animals are generally fast-moving, like birds, or inedible, like poison arrow frogs. Common in neotropical forests, these rainbow-colored frogs secrete skin toxins that range from moderately poisonous in the Central American strawberry frog to lethal in the Colombian *Phyllobates terribilis*. A single thumbnail-sized individual of this species can pack enough poison to kill a thousand people. Sometimes edible animals mimic inedible ones, like the numerous yellow-and-black butterflies that resemble the toxic heliconiid family. To keep predators

The most common characteristic of rain-forest animals, however, is adaptation to life in the trees. Most phyla have evolved species that thrive in the canopy or subcanopy, ranging from the worms, insect larvae, and tadpoles that throng pools in epiphytic plants to the monkeys and apes that obtain water from

those pools. Not only lizards but frogs and snakes have taken up gliding in the forests of Southeast Asia. Several species of the color-ful frog genus *Rhacophorus* glide from tree to tree using their webbed toes, which allow them to steer a bit. *Chrysopelea* tree snakes glide by spreading their ribs and flattening their bodies. Gliding rain-forest mammals include squirrels, marsupials called honey gliders, and Malaysia's flying lemurs. All are light enough that the lift provided by their outspread body surface temporarily defies gravity.

Birds, the ultimate treetop dwellers, reach their greatest diversity in tropical rain forests. A relatively small country like Costa Rica, for example, has more than 840 species, compared to about 650 bird species in the continental United States. Prominent among its vast array of rain-forest species are motmots, toucans, jacamars, woodcreepers, and antbirds. In New Guinea and Australia live the most splendid rain-forest birds of all, the birds of paradise. When the males spread their iridescent feath-ers during mating displays, they resemble giant flowers more than birds, and they make strangely unavian clapping, hissing, and tolling sounds. More than 40 species are known, ranging from starling- to raven-size. Among the most extraordinary is the male King of Saxony bird of paradise, a seven-inch-long (18-cm) creature with 18-inch

(45-cm), sky-blue head plumes that it erects during displays.

Bats are also hugely diverse in rain forests. Costa Rica alone has more than 100 kinds – half of its mammal species. They feed on insects, fruit, nectar, blood, frogs, fish, birds, and other bats, and range in size from the false vampire bat, a predator with a 30-inch (76-cm) wing-span, to the disk-winged bat, which weighs little more than an ounce and roosts in rolled leaves. Bats may be amazingly abundant in some rain forests. An estimated two million wrinkle-lipped bats inhabit a single small cave near Thai-land's Khao Yai National Park. When they emerge for a night's feeding, they sound like the wind rushing through the trees.

The arboreal animals of temperate rain forests are not as diverse as their tropical counterparts but are equally ingenious. Flying squirrels are common in North American forests and feed on the fruit-ing bodies of soil fungi, better known as truffles. They help to perpetuate tree seedlings by spreading the fungal spores in their droppings. Another rodent, the red tree vole, builds nests high in hemlocks and Douglas firs and feeds on the needles. Generations of voles may inhabit a single giant tree. Among the birds that nest in temperate rain forests are marine species like the marbled murrelet, which lays its eggs high in Douglas fir or redwood trees.

Arboreal wildlife diversity is a product not only of

The vivid colors of a poison arrow frog (opposite, top) warn predators to stay away.

The basilisk (opposite, bottom) is known as the Jesus Christ lizard for its ability to dash across water.

Camouflage (above) serves both predator and prey. A spectacled caiman (top) lurks beneath the cover of water plants; a Panamanian moth (middle) is virtually invisible against a backdrop of leaf litter; and a blunt-headed tree snake (bottom) relies on its coloring to hide from predators during the day and prey at night.

today's botanical complexity but of the evolutionary past. Asia and Africa have similar mammals such as apes and monkeys because they have been connected for most of the past 50 million years.

The New World tropics – the neotropics – were isolated for most of that time, and their monkeys are quite different than those of the Old World. For example, many neotropical monkeys have prehensile tails,

a trait wholly absent in the monkeys of Africa and Asia. In Madagascar, primitive primates called lemurs are the main climbers. In Australia and New Guinea, non-human primates are absent, and marsupials such as possums and even kangaroos inhabit the canopy.

Tree dwellers of quite different ancestry may develop similar appearance and behavior through the process of convergent evolution. The prehensile-tailed kinkajous of neotropical rain forests resemble monkeys, lemurs, or possums, but are actually relatives of the raccoon. Neotropical toucans – long-billed birds that feed largely on fruit – look and act somewhat like the unrelated hornbills of the Old World. The New World's dazzling hummingbirds are unknown in the Old, where a similarly long-billed group, the sun-

Deadly Trade

In 1998, a biologist who set out laser-triggered cameras to survey animals in Thailand's national parks got a surprise. Although the cameras did capture tigers, deer, bears, and elephants, they also photographed just as many poachers.

Despite protective measures, rain-forest contraband is still widely sold. A recent study of Chinese medicinal stores in seven American cities showed that more than half carried products made with parts from endangered species. Boundaries between legal and illegal traffic are porous. Of 14 Asian elephants performing in an American circus in 1999, 12 had been rounded up in the wild despite U.S. laws meant to prevent this practice.

In some countries, animals are now more commonly seen in markets than in the wild, and conditions can be brutal. Bears are boiled alive in some Asian restaurants. In the pet trade, most animals die during capture and transport. Even professional care often fails. According to animal-welfare activists, the circus that featured 14 Asian elephants had lost four to accident, disease, or unknown causes in the previous 18 months.

Tourists are major consumers of wildlife products, but can help to curb poaching by following the guidelines of TRAFFIC, a trade-monitoring program run by the World Wildlife Fund and World Conservation Union. In general, souvenir buyers should be wary of reptile skins and other leathers, birds and feathers, ivory, furs, and plants such as orchids. It is illegal to import such products into the United States and many other countries; the items may be confiscated by the customs service, and, in many cases, a heavy fine imposed.

A green vine snake (top) takes aim at a passing insect. Its usual prey is birds, frogs, and small mammals.

Pickled snakes (below) are sold as medicine at a Vietnamese market.

The bare-tailed woolly opossum (opposite) of northern South America is largely arboreal but will make ground forays in search of a meal.

birds, occupies the forest's flower-feeding niche.

Under the Big Top

Convergent evolution has also fashioned diverse forest-floor dwellers into similar shapes. In the neotropics, large rodents called pacas and agoutis pad about under the trees, feeding on fruits and herbs. Tiny deer called muntjacs fill a similar ecological niche in Southeast Asia, while small antelopes frequent the African forest floor. A variety of wild pigs inhabits Old World forests; in the New World, the similar, distantly related peccary occupies the same niche. Every tropical rain forest has characteristic kinds of large, ground-dwelling birds – guans in the neotropics; pheasants in Asia; guinea fowl in Africa; megapodes in New Guinea. In the temperate rain forest of New Zealand, flightless birds such as kiwis and large, nocturnal parrots called kakapos nest in ground burrows, and seabirds like ancient murrelets nest underground in the rain forests of the Pacific Northwest.

Invertebrates found on the floor also occupy similar ecological niches worldwide. Ants and termites are vital to plant decomposition and recycling. Termites process dead wood with the help of microorganisms in their digestive systems. Some ants use dead leaves to grow edible fungi in underground nests. Many species of beetles, the most diverse insects, specialize in recycling

dead matter. Scarabs, for example, form dung into balls that they roll through the forest. They then lay their eggs in the balls and bury them. When the larvae hatch, they feed on the dung, safe from predators. Other beetles bury dead creatures for the same purpose. Nothing on the ground stays unused for long.

Rivers of Life

Rain forests always incorporate streams and, often, extensive wetlands. Indeed, tropical rain forests have the world's greatest diversity of freshwater animals. The Amazon Basin has more than 3,000 freshwater fish species,

and the smaller Congo and Mekong Basins have a corresponding richness. Most of the hundreds of colorful fish species in aquarium stores come from these areas. Tetras and guppies, for instance, are American, gouramis and barbs Asian. Rain-forest waters also support freshwater dolphins, giant otters, manatees, many crocodilians, and the planet's largest snakes – the anacondas of South America and the reticulated pythons of the Old World. Even usually marine animals such as sharks, rays, sawfish, and tarpon inhabit them. Again, convergent evolution has fashioned similar animals from different origins. In the

White bats (left), found only in Central America, bite leaves so that they fold over, making a protected spot to roost.

Chameleons (bottom) don't change color to camouflage themselves but to communicate aggression, sexual receptivity, and other "feelings."

Scarlet macaws (opposite), now endangered in much of their range, perch near Peru's Tambopata River.

neotropics, the world's largest rodents, capybaras, live in riverbank herds. Pygmy hippopotamuses occupy a similar niche in Africa.

Freshwater wildlife is less diverse in temperate rain forests, but its abundance can be even more impressive, as with the salmon runs of southeastern Alaska and British Columbia. Seven species of Pacific salmon swim up the rivers of the Pacific Northwest to spawn and may pack themselves so tightly into tributaries that the streambed is totally obscured.

Not all rain-forest wildlife is specialized for restricted areas. Colorful and noisy parrots occur in almost every tropical rain forest, although they are more diverse in the neotropics and Australia than in Africa or

Asia. As the New Zealand kakapo demonstrates, parrots even occur in temperate rain forests, not only in the Australian region but in South America, where parakeets fly happily in icy drizzles as far south as Patagonia. Many songbirds winter in tropical rain forests, then migrate to temperate ones. Rufous hummingbirds feed at Alaskan huckleberry flowers in June and at Mexican salvia in January. Bright yellow-headed hermit warblers nest in Pacific Northwest conifers, then wander as far south as Panama in winter. Some wide-ranging mammal species, such as the American puma and gray fox, live in both tropical and temperate rain forests.

Wildlife Hot Spots

Finding animals *is* trickier in rain forests than in savannas or grasslands. Populations of large mammals tend to be sparse, and an elephant, rhino, or bear can move through thick underbrush with surprising quiet. Even monkeys and apes can travel silently

through the treetops when they want to, although they seem to enjoy making noise. With some luck, however, it is not too difficult to see wildlife. Animals congregate around food sources such as fruiting trees, and concentrations are often easy to find. Many canopy-dwelling creatures, such as macaws and howler monkeys, have extraordinarily loud calls. The usually silent large mammals of the forest floor can sometimes be located by their smell, which lingers in moist rain-forest air. For example, the tapir, a shy inhabitant of American and Malaysian rain forests, has an unmistakable odor like that of the distantly related horse.

With a modicum of attention and knowledge, a walk in a rain forest will never be boring. If the forest floor is quiet, there is usually something going on in the treetops or along a waterway. At sunset, a new cast of characters appears as fireflies light up, bats come out, and strange little primates like neotropical night monkeys or Indonesian tarsiers become active. Nocturnal calls are strange and sometimes hauntingly beautiful, like the quavering whistle of the neotropical tinamous, ground-dwelling birds that resemble grouse but are more closely related to rheas.

Wildlife diversity assures that each visit to a rain forest will be different, and you may even encounter a species unknown to science. That is the true wonder.

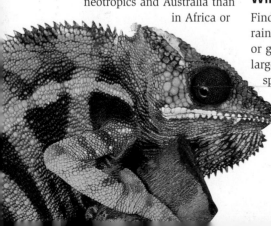

No one knows rain forests better or is more dependent upon their survival than the indigenous people who inhabit them. About 1,000 tribes totaling some 50 million people live in or near the world's rain forests, and while these groups are quite different from one another culturally, they do have a few things in common: they live in small groups usually no larger than a few hundred people, they practice a "mixed economy" of hunting, gathering, and light agriculture, they are at least partially nomadic, and they share a profound knowledge of their environments accumulated over a tenure of hundreds and sometimes thousands of years. Sadly, most of them also lead a rather tenuous existence, plagued as they are by the intrusions of the outside world. Disease, deforestation, dislocation, and a host of other ills **Indigenous people struggle** have already taken a heavy toll, reducing the **to maintain traditional** indigenous population of the Amazon **ways despite encroachment** Basin, for example, from about six million **on their lands and cultures.** at the time of European contact to 250,000 today. A good many groups have endured the hardships, however, and are beginning to fight back and even reclaim lost ground by reintegrating fading traditions into the new lives they have been forced to adopt. Although the stuation remains grim, there is some cause for optimism. ◆ Making a living in a fragile ecosystem like a rain forest is no simple matter, but traditional people have learned to extract the resources they need without taxing the environment's ability to regenerate. While it's true that rain forests contain a greater density of living tissue than any other terrestrial ecotype, most of it is of little utility to humans. It is locked up in the trunks and canopies of the

A Kayapó man of the upper Xingu River in northern Brazil wears a parrot-feather headdress. The tribe has managed to retain much of their traditional culture despite the presence of loggers and miners.

The Yanomami (left and below) live in communal huts.

A Quichua Indian in the lowlands of Ecuador roasts a handful of larvae (opposite, top), considered a delicacy by some Amazon tribes and a good source of protein.

Black-and-white dancers (opposite, bottom) attend a sing-sing, or celebration, in the New Guinea Highlands.

great trees, in vast mats of mycelia beneath the forest floor, and in swarms of insects and other arthropods that are too minute, too venomous, or simply too unpalatable to eat.

What's more, many foods are only available seasonally. Fruits, nuts, and edible greens come and go. Depending on species and season, fish may be abundant or scarce. And large animals – including staple quarry such as monkeys in Amazonia or antelope in the Congo – are distributed thinly through the forests and require a great deal of time, effort, and skill to hunt.

As a consequence, rainforest societies are frugal societies; virtually nothing is wasted. They also tend to be nomadic ones. People need to range widely to find the food they need. And while many tribes depend on farming for such staples as manioc, plantains, maize, or yams, rain-forest soils are generally thin and of poor quality. Slash-and-burn plots can't be farmed long before they are exhausted, forcing the cultivators to move on.

Forest Gardens

Among the current masters of such agriculture are the Yanomami of the Amazon Basin, who have learned to garden in the forest without damaging it. The Yanomami are of an ancient lineage, having inhabited Amazonia for at least 11,500 years. Their numbers have fallen drastically in the past few decades; today, no more than 20,000 survive in their traditional homeland, which incorporates about 50 million acres (20 million hectares)

in Brazil and Venezuela.

In spite of it all, most surviving Yanomami have clung tenaciously to their traditional way of life. Living in communal villages characterized by "yanos," or large, doughnut-shaped thatched structures, they tend their garden plots assiduously, clearing new areas for cultivation as soil fertility decreases.

The Yanomami grow about 80 percent of their food; plantains are the staple, augmented by manioc, peach palms, and maize. They cultivate a great variety of other plants as well, for both food and medicine. Yanomami gardens may look helterskelter, but they are exquisitely designed to produce the greatest quantity of crops in the smallest space, with the least amount of effort. Plants are intermixed, mimicking the diversity of the surrounding forest. This minimizes insect damage, as bugs are unable to target favorite plants. Crops mature on a staggered basis, assuring a constant supply of food.

Though the plots are quickly reseeded by the forest, perennials and trees continue to produce food for 50 years or more. Late-stage gardens may be undetectable by outsiders, but the Yanomami know their locations and return periodically to harvest them.

The Yanomami obtain their remaining provender – fruit, game, fish – from the forest. They are also an enthusiastically entomophagous people. In other words, they eat insects, larvae,

and arachnids, including termites, grubs, and large spiders, which are considered a great delicacy.

Gamekeepers

Across the Atlantic, in the vast Congo Basin, is another of the planet's great tropical rain forests. Among the people who inhabit this region, which sprawls across parts of Cameroon, Gabon, and the Democratic Republic of Congo, are Pygmies, a generic term applied to tribes such as the Baka, Twa, Efe, and Bayaka who share diminutive stature, relatively light skin compared to their Bantu neighbors, and consummate skill as hunters and gatherers.

While many Pygmies leave the forest seasonally to work on Bantu plantations, they still engage in traditional subsistence pursuits for much of the year. And though relations between the Bantu and Pygmies are often strained – even hostile – they exist in

essential symbiosis with one another. In return for bush meat, medicinal plants, and labor, Pygmies receive finished goods such as knives and machetes as well as agricultural commodities and salt.

The Pygmy approach to living in harmony with the forest is different than that of the Yanomami. Agriculture plays a subsidiary role. In the quasi-permanent villages scattered throughout the Congo Basin, little is grown other than a few banana

trees, coffee plants, and occasional plots of maize or hemp.

Most of their food comes from the forest. Game is somewhat more abundant in the Congo than the Amazon, and Pygmies pursue everything from termites to forest elephants. They also rely heavily on wild flora, consuming more than 500 types of plants, nuts, and fruits. To the visitor, the great forest of the Congo Basin appears devoid of seasons beyond the arrival and departure of monsoonal rains, but Pygmies know better: there are numerous seasons, each determined by the availability of particular foods rather than a change in weather. The maturing of specific fruits, the spawning of certain fish, the arrival of migratory birds – Pygmies know the cycles of each and make forays into the forest accordingly.

Among the most highly prized wild foods is the *peke*, or wild mango. Pygmies process the seed kernels of the fruit into a highly nutritious paste that is extremely rich in oil, making it a particularly valuable addition to a diet otherwise deficient in fat.

Another important delicacy is wild honey, which is available at the end of the rainy season, when African honeybees exploit a brief abundance of nectar and pollen. To collect the honey, tribal members first locate the hive by uncannily tracking bees in flight through the kaleidoscope of forest foliage. They then climb as high as 120 feet (37m) into the canopy to reach the hives, cutting footholds in the wood with small axes and securing themselves to the trunks with liana belts.

The hunt, however, is central to Pygmy culture. Much time is spent in hunting camps away from the villages. Such camps may incorporate several families and move every week or so, depending on the availability of game. Pygmies are singularly skillful hunters, relying on traps, nets, and poison-tipped arrows, and they take a great variety of game, ranging from small antelopes like duikers to elephants.

Pygmies live in loosely confederated family groups, and are generally easygoing. They can be formidable when provoked, however, and they view encroachment of traditional hunting grounds as a particularly heinous offense. While the Yanomami preserve the forest by cultivating it as a garden, Pygmies protect it by acting as gamekeepers, patrolling and hunting their ancestral territories, taking only animals sufficient for their needs, expelling poachers and other interlopers.

A Dani tribesman (top) stages a mock battle at his village in the remote Baliem Valley of Irian Jaya. The Dani were first contacted by westerners in 1939.

A Huaorani Indian (left) of Ecuador uses a strap made of vines to climb a tree. The Huaorani have struggled to prevent oil companies from intruding on their territory.

Pigs and Palms

The Penan of Borneo illustrate yet another approach to exploiting forest resources without damaging them. The Penan inhabit the deeply forested uplands of the Malaysian state of Sarawak and are traditionally nomads. Today, only about 400 or so tribal members still hew to the old ways, searching the forest for their daily necessities.

Like Pygmies, the Penan are egalitarian and socially motivated by kin ties, and are intimate with every aspect of the forest that sustains them. One of their sayings sums up their knowledge of the envi-

Penan hunters (left) aim a blowpipe with deadly accuracy. Their poison darts can drop a wild pig weighing more than 150 pounds (68kg) in a matter of minutes.

Penan children (bottom) are taught by example rather than discipline; sharing is highly valued.

ronment: "The earthworm may go hungry and the mouse deer get lost in the forest, but never we Penan."

Their forest yields saps that serve as glue for bird traps, bark and vines for twine and ropes, and aromatic gums for trade. The Penan

can identify more than 100 fruiting trees and precisely predict when each species will bear fruit or nuts. They utilize about 50 medicinal plants, at least eight different plants for blow-dart toxins, and 10 plants for fish poison. Wood from different trees serves various needs. Some are ideal for blowpipes, others for musical instruments or canoes.

Their staple, however, is the wild sago palm, which yields large quantities of starchy, edible pulp from which sago flour is made. The Penan harvest these palms with great care, felling the trees in such a way that new suckers are stimulated, assuring future harvests.

And in a way, the Penan are swineherds. Though they hunt opportunistically, their primary quarry is the bearded pig, a large wild hog. It is their main source of protein, and its meat figures prominently in their feasts and religious ceremonies.

The Penan assure a good population of pigs by protecting dipterocarps, huge trees that produce vast quantities of the fruit eaten by the animals. To the Penan,

international pressure on the Malaysian government to abandon the project has been intense; at this time, the outcome is unclear.

The Yanomami have struggled against similar incursions into their territory by thousands of "garimpeiros," wildcatting miners drawn by the discovery of gold and tin ore.

The garimpeiros have been repeatedly repulsed by both the Brazilian government and the Yanomami but still return, driving off the wildlife, poisoning the water with the mercury that is used to separate gold dust from ore, silting rivers with high-pressure hoses that strip away soil, and sometimes murdering the Yanomami outright.

The pollution and homicide are bad enough, but the most destructive aspect of the garimpeiro invasion is microbial. Malaria, tuberculosis, and viral respiratory diseases have winnowed Yanomami populations severely. Child mortality has skyrocketed, and the birthrate has plummeted. A study sponsored by the American Anthropological Association in 1993 reported that malaria and other diseases were killing the Yanomami at a rate of 13 percent per year.

Though wise beyond measure in the techniques of surviving in the jungle, the Yanomami have been less successful in influencing government policy. Recently, however, some charismatic Yanomami leaders have ventured from the rain forest

healthy stands of mature dipterocarps mean a larder full of pork, and they view the felling of these mighty trees by the loggers that are encroaching on their territory with particular horror.

Invasion and Resistance

That's why in 1987 a group of Penan formed a human blockade on a logging road in the Tutoh River region, the first of many such protests that focused international attention on the frenzied pace of logging in Sarawak (the annual loss reached three percent in the 1990s, about twice the rate of logging in the Amazon) and the harm it's doing to the indigenous population. The Penan are also resisting Bakun Dam, a massive hydropower project on the Balui River that would flood 173,000 acres (70,000 hectares) of deep rain forest and displace 10,000 people. Though relocations of Balui River residents have proceeded sporadically,

A Quichua boy (left) collects and cooks edible tree snails.

Diversity is a hallmark of forest cultures. This Huli man (opposite) represents only one of 30 or more tribes that attend the annual Highlands Show in New Guinea. More than 700 languages are spoken on the island.

Traditions are passed from parent to child among Peru's Javiro Indians (below), but, like many forest people, their world is changing quickly.

and are now eloquently making their case in the arenas of both national law and international public opinion.

Similar struggles are being waged by innumerable other tribes: the Kayapó of Brazil against mining, logging, and dam-building in their territory, the Huaorani of Ecuador and U'wa of Colombia against oil exploration, the Amungme of Indonesia against an ongoing mining operation, and dozens more.

It's hard to remain optimistic. Very little good news is coming out of the Amazon, Africa, or Southeast Asia; realists must accommodate themselves to the essential bleakness of the situation. But while the predicament facing them is dire, it is by no means hopeless. Though the people of the forest remain determined to practice their ancient ways of life, many are also employing modern tools in their struggle: cell phones, fax machines, the Internet, and the media. Their stories are getting out and eliciting strong responses.

If the rain forests are to be saved, they must be understood. By categorizing taxa, by measuring rainfall, nutrient flows, and gas respiration, we can develop a pretty good sense of the constituent parts of a forest. But we won't really understand the sum of those parts until we see the rain forest through the eyes of the people who live there. And that's why indigenous people are the most important inhabitants of the forest. They are our interpreters. We need them to explain exactly what it is we are losing.

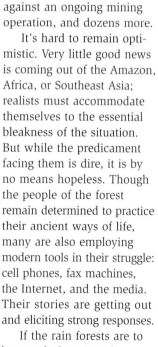

The Fragile Web

n the time it takes you to read this chapter, more than 600 acres (243 hectares) of tropical rain forest will have been destroyed. By this time tomorrow, 100 species will have become extinct as a result of tropical deforestation. In a month's time, 2.8 million acres (1.1 million hectares) of tropical rain forest will have disappeared, and within a year the total loss will be equivalent to an area almost as large as the state of Arkansas. If this devastation continues to increase at current rates, the razing of all of the world's tropical rain forests will have been completed by the middle of this century. ◆ The situation is little better in temperate regions. In the United States and Canada, for example, more than half of the coastal rain forests that once ranged from Northern California to Alaska have been felled. Even today, rates of clearance remain high: in the Great Bear Forest of British Columbia, one of the world's largest temperate rain forests, 300 acres (120 hectares) disappear each day. ◆ The ramifications of these losses extend far beyond the mere cutting down of trees. Rain forests provide essential habitat for roughly 50 percent of the world's plant and animal species, and sustain the traditional lifestyles of about 50 million indigenous people. They play a critical role in global climate regulation and watershed protection, and they harbor countless plant species that may yield treatments for diseases such as cancer and AIDS. ◆ International awareness of this major environmental issue has grown in recent years. Governments, conservation organizations, and rain-forest communities have developed a range of innovative strategies to protect these precious habitats. Moreover, millions

Conservationists have realized that to halt the ongoing destruction of rain forests they must directly address its causes.

A farmer burns rain forest on Madagascar.
Forest soil is nutrient-poor and prone to erosion, compelling farmers to clear fresh patches after only a few years of cultivation.

Ravaged landscapes (left) bear the scars of improvident use. Logging roads and skid trails fragment the rain forest of Borneo (top). Erosion at a copper mine gouges a hillside in the New Guinea Highlands (bottom).

ever deeper into the forest. In many regions, this cycle is accelerated by rapid population growth.

Shortsighted government policies have exacerbated the situation. Some South and Central American governments, for example, subsidize the clearing of forests in order to earn much-needed foreign currency from cattle ranching. Other countries, like Indonesia, have implemented government programs that relocate millions of people from crowded cities to remote rain forests in a misguided attempt to limit urbanization.

Of particular concern in recent years is the logging of virgin forests. International timber companies have dramatically increased the scope of their operations, often by taking advantage of weak government regulations. Loggers not only remove trees; they also build roads, thereby opening up once-inaccessible areas to poachers and settlers and dividing forests into smaller tracts. This fragmentation has particularly serious implications in tropical regions where plants and animals are highly interdependent. Some tropical trees – fig trees are just one example – rely on just one type of insect (a kind of wasp) for pollination; if the insects disappear, so do the

of people around the world now believe they have a moral obligation to preserve what is left of our natural heritage and regard rain-forest conservation as one of the most important aspects of this global stewardship. Yet, as the above figures attest, the situation remains critical.

A Relentless Assault

The reasons for the destruction are many and complex. Most often, forests are cleared to make way for human settlements or to provide farmland or pasture. But they are also harvested for timber and

cleared to facilitate the construction of dams and the extraction of oil, gas, and metals.

Powerful political and socioeconomic forces drive the destruction. Poverty and inequitable land distribution are major factors. In developing countries where most of the arable land is owned by an elite few, the poor often have no choice but to slash and burn forests in order to grow food and eke out a living. In the tropics, soils formerly swathed in forest tend to be deficient in nutrients, and cultivation soon renders them infertile, forcing farmers

trees. Logging can thus set off an ecological unraveling that may ultimately lead to disaster.

The massive fires that ravaged the tropical rain forests of Indonesia, Brazil, and Mexico in recent years provide a disturbing illustration of this unraveling effect. Decades of logging and clearing had left behind large swaths of bare ground. Covered in highly flammable debris, these cleared patches acted as kindling, while the use of fire to clear adjacent areas of forest set off the conflagrations. Researchers estimate that the 3.7 million acres (1.5 million hectares) of the Brazilian Amazon severely damaged by logging operations each year render another 66.7 million acres (27 million hectares) vulnerable to fire during the dry season.

Debt for Nature

How do you persuade the governments of developing countries to allocate funds to nature preservation when their people are living in poverty and their economies are crippled by ballooning foreign debt? In searching for an answer to this thorny question, Washington-based Conservation International came up with a strategy known as a "debt-for-nature swap." This involves the environmental organization purchasing all or a portion of the debt owed by a developing country from the creditor at a heavily discounted price. In exchange, the debtor country agrees to make some kind of commitment to the preservation of its natural ecosystems. Normally, this comes in the form of a trust fund that will cover the costs of running parks and reserves, but it may also include legislation to protect particular areas.

The first debt-for-nature swap took place in 1987, when the Bolivian government agreed to fund and protect the Beni Biosphere Reserve in return for the alleviation of $650,000 worth of debt. Since then, Conservation International has sponsored no fewer than 18 swaps in six countries.

Small wonder that other nations and organizations are lining up to participate. Both the World Wildlife Fund and the Nature Conservancy have conducted major debt-for-nature swaps in recent years. Even more significantly, in July 1998 President Clinton signed the Tropical Forest Conservation Act, which allows the United States to write off debts owed by other nations in exchange for initiatives that will protect tropical forests.

Untapped Resources

Rain forests cover just seven percent of the Earth's land area but are home to 70 percent of its vascular plant species, 30 percent of its bird species, and no less than 90 percent of its invertebrate species. Furthermore, biologists suspect that tropical rain forests harbor millions of un-documented plant and animal species. By razing this rich habitat, we risk decimating an enormous proportion of the planet's biological wealth.

We may never know the value of the species we're destroying. Worldwide, scientists estimate that one out of every 10 plant species may have anticancer properties; yet only about one percent of tropical plant species have been scientifically tested for their medicinal properties. There may also be thousands of rain-forest food species that could help in the fight against hunger. For example, it is thought that wild relatives of commonly used food species like corn grow in the rain forest and may contain disease- or pest-resistant genes. Transferring these genes to domestic species could significantly increase

Farmland (top) girdles a protected expanse of rain forest in Uganda. Some countries agree to set aside wilderness in exchange for debt relief.

A Brazilian poacher (left) shows off a cache of skins; the illegal trade remains active despite crackdowns.

production. The winged bean of New Guinea is just one of many rain-forest plants that could provide huge economic benefits. It produces edible spinachlike leaves and soybeanlike seeds that are richer in protein than potatoes, need almost no fertilizer, and improve soil fertility for other crops. Many believe this species alone could boost the living standards of millions of people in developing countries.

Watershed Protection

The impact of rain-forest destruction spreads far beyond the geographical boundaries of the forests themselves. At a regional level, for example, rain forests exert a major influence on the water cycle. The close-knit canopy acts like a sponge, absorbing huge amounts of rain and water vapor. Some is returned to the atmosphere through evaporation; the rest is slowly released into the soil and nearby rivers. Once the forest is cleared, this recycling process ceases. Heavy rain inundates the ground, resulting in flooding that destroys habitats, displaces communities, and strips away soil by the ton.

At a global level, rain forests help stabilize the climate by absorbing massive amounts of carbon dioxide from the atmosphere. Clearing forests not only diminishes the amount of carbon dioxide being absorbed but increases the amount of carbon dioxide being released back into the air by burned or decaying vegetation. The overall effect is an increased level of this "greenhouse gas," which traps heat near Earth's surface and may be a major cause of global warming.

Conservation Strategies

Increasing awareness of these problems has inspired an ever-widening search for solutions, and environmental groups now use a broad range of tactics in their conservation efforts. For many years, they have used grassroots campaigns to draw international attention to critical threats and to pressure companies and governments to stop their destructive activities. Such campaigns often seek to persuade the public to boycott consumer goods – such as tropical-wood furniture – whose production involves the misuse of forest resources. A more direct approach is to purchase land and turn it into a privately managed preserve. The Nature Conservancy used this strategy to establish the 4,200-acre (1,700-hectare) Salto Morato reserve in the Brazilian state of Paraná. Now managed by a local foundation, the reserve protects biologically rich Atlantic rain forest from critical threats such as urban sprawl and ranching.

More recently, many environmental groups have sought to address the socioeconomic evils that spur deforestation by meeting the needs of people living in or near rain forests. This approach is based on simple economics: if people have economically viable alternatives to cutting down trees, the rain forests will be left standing. Conservationists are working with local communities to develop forest-friendly enterprises ranging from ecotourism to harvesting crops like cacao and certain kinds of coffee. For instance, Conservation International has helped farmers who grow environmentally friendly "shade coffee" (which grows in the shade of forests instead of in cleared areas) to improve their production methods and find overseas markets.

Another recently developed approach involves presenting governments with detailed reports that describe the long-term consequences of deforestation. When international logging companies put pressure on Suriname to sell logging rights to a quarter of the nation, environmental groups countered with an economic analysis showing that the deal would offer limited revenue. Not only did the government of the small South American nation reject the logging companies, it created, in 1998, the Central Suriname Nature Reserve, a pristine expanse of rain forest the size of New Jersey.

Biological field studies that identify the richest and most fragile habitats can also be instrumental in persuading governments to protect them. Conservationists have successfully used such information to convince policy makers to cancel logging, mining, and other development projects –

and even set aside parks. In 1995, the Bolivian government dedicated the huge Madidi National Park partly in response to scientists who had recorded the region's phenomenal biological diversity.

Rain-forest conservation is now at a crossroads. Environmental organizations have proven that innovative strategies can work, but tropical and temperate forests are still disappearing at an alarming rate. It will take a worldwide effort to halt the destruction and save what remains, but the benefits will be incalculable. Not only will we preserve innumerable life-forms, priceless resources, and Earth's climatic stability, we may also create a society that cherishes rather than ravages our planet's natural wonders.

A researcher (opposite, top) scans for birds atop a 115-foot (35-m) tower in Amazonian Ecuador. A wildlife survey is one of the first steps in determining the health of an ecosystem.

A colonist (opposite, bottom) slashes forest along a new road in Ecuador.

An orphaned orangutan (right), saved from loggers in Borneo, awaits transport to a rescue center.

chapter 5

I t's 8 A.M. on the first day of your five-day trek through a tropical rain forest. Your guide has outlined the day's itinerary: an uphill walk alongside a small stream to the summit of a nearby peak, where you'll set up camp for the night. You set off in high spirits. Tree roots and vines crisscross the trail, which is moist underfoot. The earthy smell of composting vegetation mingles with the delicate fragrance of flowers. Barely 30 minutes into the trek, you catch a fleeting glimpse of a gibbon as it swings gracefully through the forest canopy. ◆ Several hours later, you're still climbing, breathless and sweating in the close heat, swatting at the mosquitoes and brushing off leeches before they get a hold on your flesh. Your clothes are spattered with mud and your boots soaked from fording streams. The other four members of the group are relishing the trying conditions, but you're starting to wonder if a trek is really your gig. You begin to long for a cold beer, and, for the first time, a vagrant thought slips into your mind: "Maybe that lodge-based trip would've been a better choice after all." ◆ Redolent of adventure and teeming with exotic life-forms, rain forests have long held a fascination for armchair travelers and intrepid explorers alike. To travel to a rain forest is to embark on an adventure to another world, a place full of wild beauty and thrills, but it is also to flirt with danger and the unknown – which may include your ability to handle the challenges.

Careful planning and thorough preparation will ensure that you can both cope with and enjoy the world's rain forests.

A hiker pauses at a waterfall in a Costa Rican jungle. Rain forests are extraordinarily beautiful but can be challenging to explore. A little preparation goes a long way.

Be Prepared

The trick to enjoying a rain-forest odyssey is to know what to expect and to prepare accordingly. Rain forests are generally in remote locations; and the more remote the location, the fewer and, for the most part, the more primitive the facilities. Some knowledge of the area you wish to visit – especially its climate and geography – is essential. Research your destination in advance. Visit libraries, bookstores, and natural history museums, search the Internet for information – anecdotes posted on travel websites can provide a useful and "unfiltered" window into travelers' experiences – and contact national parks, tourism boards, tour operators, and travel agents.

Timing is crucial. There is no doubt that a tropical downpour is a sight to behold. The question is, do you want to be trekking in it? Probably not. The precise timing of the wet season varies from country to country and even within countries, and

cyclones can add a wild and unpredictable element. Some regions become inaccessible during these periods, and tours and facilities shut down; in other places, it's business as usual. Check ahead before making any definite plans. Be aware, too, of the peak tourist season for your intended destination; you may need to book up to one year in advance for accommodations, transportation, and tours at such times.

Make sure you are physically and mentally prepared. In tropical rain forests, particularly, expect it to take longer than usual to do things. Even moderately ambitious travel plans will have a tendency to wilt in extreme heat and humidity. Consider your fitness level – honestly. Are you up to the more strenuous forms of rain-forest exploration such as trekking, kayaking, and

Eco-travelers (top) boat a "blackwater" river in Tanjung Puting National Park, Borneo.

The buttress roots (left) of a ceiba tree rise above a visitor in Costa Rica's Cano Negro forest.

rafting, or would you be better suited to day walks that start and finish at a well-appointed jungle lodge?

When pondering that question, consider how you feel about insect life in all its many, varied, and often gargantuan forms. While out on the trail, you may marvel at the transparent beauty of a lacewing butterfly or watch with amazement the aggressive defense postures of the aptly named dead-leaf mantis. But what about late at night, when the lights are out and you hear, from the fastness of your mosquito-netted tent, a rustling in the dark? Visions of South America's giant tarantula, with its 10-inch (25-cm) leg span, may arise in your imagination. If thoughts like that are going to lead to sleepless nights, maybe camping isn't for you.

In fact, most of the largest bugs, such as stick and leaf insects, are completely harmless. It's their diminutive cousins, like the ubiquitous (and sometimes malarial) mosquitoes, as well as scrub mites and ticks, which constitute the most

commonly encountered insect pests. That's why repellent – and some knowledge of the insect-related hazards at your destination – are a must. Second only to mosquitoes as persistent and irritating rain-forest companions are leeches. Their blood-sucking habits are unpleasant but relatively harmless; applying salt or heat from a match will usually dislodge them.

Clothing is your first line of defense against blood-sucking creatures and the rigors of climate. Check climatic conditions for your destination and make sure you bring the right gear. Wear loose, lightweight clothing made from fabrics that don't trap moisture. Cotton used to be the fabric of choice – and is still a good option – but the current range of synthetic travel clothing has the

A suspension bridge (right) gives visitors a bird's-eye view of the forest canopy at Los Cedros Biological Reserve in Ecuador.

Boaters (bottom) view Angel Falls, Canaima National Park, Venezuela.

advantage of drying faster in humid conditions. Even in tropical rain forests, nights at higher altitudes (particularly in cloud forests) can be chilly, so it's a good idea to pack a fleece sweater. For temperate rain forests, you will want to add gloves, a hat, and thermal wear.

Getting There

Having researched your intended destination, you need to decide how to get there. To join a tour, or not to join a tour: that is the question. The answer depends on where you're going, what you want to do once you get there, and your level of "jungle experience."

First and foremost, taking an organized tour means you'll never have to worry about getting lost. And given the tangled density, lack of signage, and remoteness of many rain forests, that's a

reassuring thought. It will also save valuable time, as a reliable operator will ensure that, excepting *force majeure* or natural disasters, your trip runs with the precision of a Swiss clock. Of course, this can also be a disadvantage, given that the group's schedule may dictate that you go whitewater rafting on Tuesday,

something you'd really rather do on Wednesday – *after* you've indulged your new-found passion for photographing every angle of the extraordinary rafflesia, the world's largest flower. Only independent travelers have the prerogative to alter their itineraries en route.

Organized tours are ideal for activity-based and special-interest travel, such as rafting, birding, or conservation-oriented tours, as they usually provide customized equipment and expert guides. Perhaps the greatest advantage of organized tours generally is the 24-hour access you'll have to a guide who can provide informed commentary, not only on ecological and cultural matters but also natural hazards. Blessed be the guide who stops you from brushing against the

stinging tree, or gympie-gympie, an Australian rain-forest plant whose heart-shaped leaves are covered with fine, poisonous hairs that can inflict an excruciatingly painful sting.

When considering travel options, don't count on public transportation as a means of getting deep into rain forests. Wide-ranging and easy-to-negotiate road and rail networks are virtually nonexistent within such areas. Local buses and trains (often an experience in themselves in developing countries) are most useful as a link between gateway towns, where they may connect with other modes of transport such as boats or park vehicles.

Those planning to rent a vehicle in the tropics – in many cases a four-wheel drive will be mandatory – must be prepared to negotiate rugged, narrow, unpaved roads that in the wet season may be washed away by torrential rains, making travel grindingly slow and uncomfortable and river crossings impossible or dangerous. Cost is also a consideration. Gas and vehicle hire are often expensive in remote regions, particularly in countries like Costa Rica, which imports all its fuel and vehicles. Be aware, too, that roads do not generally provide the best access to ecological riches. Forests near roads are more likely to have been affected by human activities, especially in countries where logging is permitted.

Taxi floatplanes or charter planes can sometimes provide an efficient and speedy means of reaching more remote realms, but by far the best ways to explore such wilderness are by boat and on foot. Both modes of travel will provide a close-up experience of the jungle flora and fauna, and in some areas a chance to meet those fast-disappearing denizens of the rain forest – indigenous people.

On the Trail

There are numerous options for getting out on the trail, ranging from day walks on maintained footpaths to multiday camping treks. Whatever you choose, be prepared to get muddy and moist. Avoid trekking in tropical rain forests during the peak of the wet season: trails become slippery, legions of mosquitoes will hunger for your blood, and armies of leeches can make life hell. It should be a holiday, not an endurance test.

For determinedly independent travelers, going it alone can be both rewarding and risky. It's advisable (and sometimes mandatory) to check with a park ranger or local authority about conditions, permits, and essential provisions. Some kind of water-purification system, for example, will almost certainly be necessary, even in seemingly pristine areas. At many destinations, however, variable weather, unmarked trails, and hazardous flora and fauna mean that it's simply foolhardy to undertake treks alone – hence the requirement by some parks that visitors hire a guide.

Waterways often provide the most accessible (and sometimes only) route into

Children (opposite, top) pepper a naturalist with questions in Costa Rica.

A kayaker (opposite, bottom) meets a Quichua boy on the Anzu River, Ecuador.

Flies (right) and other insects often bedevil travelers, but it's the organisms you can't see – such as parasites – that may pose the greatest health risk.

Health Matters

The term "exotic" looms large in perceptions of rain forests – exotic plants, animals, and diseases. However, a combination of preparation and common sense will see you emerge unscathed from whichever wilderness you have chosen to venture into. Keep the following general guidelines in mind:

● Check with the Centers for Disease Control (www.cdc.gov/travel/) for information on vaccinations and other medical issues. Malaria is one of the most prevalent diseases in tropical regions, and antimalarial drugs are advised for high-risk areas.

● Pack a medical kit appropriate for your destination.

● Take time to acclimatize to high temperatures and humidity; avoid dehydration by drinking plenty of fluids.

● Be wary of contaminated water supplies in undeveloped areas. Drink only bottled or boiled water. If you can't boil water, treat it chemically (iodine tablets are particularly effective) or with a filter.

● Treat cuts and scratches immediately, as they can easily become infected in warm, humid climates. Fungus thrives in such conditions; if you contract a fungal infection, keep the area as dry as possible and apply antifungal powder.

● Do not swim in waterways unless you're sure it's safe to do so. Crocodiles have been known to make a meal of hapless travelers, and parasites such as schistosomiasis (or bilharzia) are common in many areas.

Choosing a Guide

Your choice of operator can make your ecotour an experience you'll forever wax lyrical about, a ho-hum affair, or a vacation from hell. There are several things you can do to increase the chances of your journey falling into the lyrical category.

Consider the experience and reputation of the operator by asking detailed questions and requesting referrals. In particular, ask what guidelines the company follows and how it contributes to preserving the environments it visits. Check if the operator is endorsed by conservation or ecotourism organizations, and try to find travelers' testimonials on websites. Travel agents should also be able to steer you toward quality companies.

Find out if the operator's guides are well versed in the ecology, culture, and conditions of your chosen destination. It may not be possible to find a guide who is simultaneously a biologist, an orchid fanatic, a whitewater-rafting expert, and a gourmet cook, but you should make sure his or her field of expertise matches your specific interest, be it birding, trekking, natural history, or indigenous cultures.

For activity-based trips such as rafting, the most important consideration is the operator's experience and safety record. You don't want to be stuck up a remote tributary of the Amazon without a paddle – and a guide ill-equipped to handle the situation.

A mule (above) hauls gear to an Andean cloud forest. Most operators provide transportation and expertise.

A zip line (opposite, top) gives tourists a treetop view of Braulio Carrillo National Park, Costa Rica.

An ecotourism camp (opposite, bottom) in Ecuador offers simple but comfortable lodging.

rain forests, and can be the best way to see wildlife at close range. All animals must drink, and visibility is greatest from the water where the view is not blocked by over-hanging vines and dense foliage. Modes of water transport are many and varied. Some parks and reserves operate regular and cheap ferry services; others hire out canoes and kayaks, which offer wider scope for exploring narrow rivers and tributaries. Many tour companies have their own boats, ranging from simple tubs to luxurious vessels with dining, living, and sleeping areas, bathrooms, gourmet fare, and on-deck showers. As a rule of thumb, the smaller the craft, the smaller the luggage limit.

Adventurous travelers will revel in the high-adrenaline excitement of whitewater rafting, although you may need to prove that you have whitewater experience to travel rivers graded above a certain level (usually Class IV or higher). You should also consider whether you are prepared to negotiate arduous portages and endure cold, wet, and strenuous conditions for days on end. Find out what you're in for and don't contemplate a voyage of discovery on remote waterways unless you're fit, independent, and well equipped – or in the hands of an experienced operator.

At some destinations, it is possible to travel by more traditional methods – beasts of burden. Horseback riding, for example, offers a novel and exciting way to explore the cloud forests of Peru.

Wildlife Watching

Observing wildlife in rain forests presents specific challenges. Like a circus trapeze act, much of the action takes place in the canopy. That not only leads to stiff necks and aching backs, it makes it difficult to see even the most resplendent birds – particularly in the forest's play of light and shadow, the sheer exuberance of its leafy greenness. One way to get around this problem is to venture into the canopy itself, and this is entirely possible in parks and reserves laced with zip lines, cable cars, or suspended walkways. Failing such elevated means of access, try to find a track leading to a ridge or peak, from which you can look down on the canopy.

The majority of rain-forest mammals are nocturnal, and you must be too in order to see them. Night hikes, during which guides locate animals with flashlights, are a great way to see these species. If you're trying this yourself, remember not to shine a bright flashlight into eyes adapted to seeing in the dark. It hurts. Use a maximum 30-watt bulb with a red filter. Pocket flashlights are useful by day for peering into rotting logs or other dark cavities.

As in most other habitats, plan your daytime excursions for early morning or late afternoon, when diurnal species are most active. Seek out untrammeled areas away from visitor centers and lodges, and investigate habitat edges – clearings and riverbanks will be particularly rewarding. Fruiting trees are also a sure bet for sightings: stop when you find one and, within a short time, wildlife of one kind or another will wander, fly, or scuttle in for a feed.

Binoculars are essential, and a tripod-mounted spotting scope (with a magnification of 20x to 30x) is desirable. These devices are particularly useful for viewing dangerous

or elusive animals without imperiling the viewer or scaring off the subject.

Rain forests are often compared to cathedrals. It's a good idea to treat them as such and maintain a similar type of respectful silence. This will not only increase your chances of spotting wildlife but enable you to hear what you can't see – perhaps a violet saber-wing humming-bird, whose distinctive wing shape produces a sound that has been likened to an airborne Harley Davidson. Remember, too, that many rain-forest creatures are masters of disguise. Never presume a leaf is just a leaf or a vine just a vine. Closer inspection may reveal a leaf-mimicking moth, a rolled-leaf caterpillar, a leaf katydid, or a bright-green vine snake. Maintain a skeptical attitude toward vegetation generally, and move slowly to maximize your chances of detecting such animals.

Of course, some wildlife

is just too small to be seen. Barely one-fiftieth of an inch long, the Costa Rican hum-mingbird flower mite, for instance, makes its way from flower to flower by riding inside the nostrils of hummingbirds.

◆

Rain Forest Destinations

◆

From the jungles of the Amazon Basin and the cloud forests of Borneo to the glacier-carved fjords of Alaska, the world's tropical and temperate rain forests sustain a greater density and variety of terrestrial life than any other places on Earth.

Tongass
National Forest
Alaska

CHAPTER **6**

Viewed from the narrow beach on the eastern side of **Tracy Arm**, the walls of the fjord seem to rise almost vertically toward thin, scudding clouds. On the highest reaches, tiny white specks slowly traverse bare rock faces – mountain goats nimbly negotiating the precipitous slopes – and waterfalls dangle like silver threads. Great hunks of ice drift on the aqua-blue inlet, while on the opposite shore, a brown bear and its cub lumber along the sand. Apart from the small tour boat and its passengers, there are no other signs of human presence. This is a world apart. ◆ Behind the beach, a pristine forest of hemlock and spruce cloaks the lower slopes. There are no trails, but here and there slender openings permit short forays into the tangle of wood and foliage. Little light penetrates the canopy and the forest floor is covered with thick, spongy sphagnum moss; hiking here is like walking on a mattress. Devil's club, skunk cabbage, and wild berry plants sprout from the moss. Rain falls intermittently and tendrils of fog waft through the trees. ◆ Ahead, barely visible in the gloom, a Sitka black-tailed deer looks up from browsing. A hiker's footstep cracks a fallen branch, creating a noise like a whipcrack, and suddenly a willow grouse rockets upward from behind a moss-shrouded log. Fast-beating wings take it farther into the forest as the deer, too, dashes for cover, rustling low branches as it weaves between trees. Soon both creatures have vanished, deep into their hidden world, and silence rules once more.

Huge Alaskan brown bears rule a temperate rain forest hemmed in by icy seaways, towering mountains, and immense glaciers.

A bald eagle perches on the moss-draped limbs of an evergreen tree in Alaska's coastal rain forest.

Preceding pages: The Sarapiqui River cascades over Sarapiqui Falls in the montane rain forest of northeastern Costa Rica.

The Biggest Forest

The fjord known as Tracy Arm is only one of hundreds of narrow inlets that penetrate the coastline of the Alaskan panhandle, and just one small corner of the largest national forest in the United States, **Tongass National Forest**. Covering 17 million acres (6.7 million hectares) and 80 percent of southeastern Alaska, Tongass is as large as New Jersey. But that's where the comparison stops; for Tongass is almost entirely wilderness, dominated by towering mountains, deep fjords, great glaciers, wide bays, more than 2,000 islands, and the largest contiguous expanse of temperate rain forest on Earth.

Drenched by up to 220 inches (560cm) of rain a year, Tongass consists mainly of thickets of western hemlock and Sitka spruce, with smatterings of red and Alaska cedar, black cottonwood, subalpine fir, lodgepole pine, and Pacific silver fir. Despite extensive logging in the early days of European settlement, many of the old-growth trees here are between 200 and 700 years old.

The forests and surrounding waterways are home to no fewer than 400 species of terrestrial and marine wildlife. Brown and black bears, Sitka black-tailed deer, and wolverines forage among the trees and along waterways. Mountain goats patrol peaks and bald eagles nest in treetops. Harbor seals and Steller's sea lions bask on ice floes and rocks, and orcas, minke whales, and Dall porpoises swim in deep inlets and open ocean. Tongass is also home to a wide range of bird species, including the tufted puffin, gyrfalcon, peregrine falcon, and marbled murrelet, an endangered species that nests in the tops of old-growth trees and whose presence is a reliable indicator of forest health.

Carved by Ice

Tongass's spectacular landforms are the result of many thousands of years of volcanic activity, glaciation, erosion, and weathering. During the ice ages, the ebb

Black bears (top) are agile tree climbers.

Glacial runoff (left) spills into Tracy Arm.

A veil of mist (right) cloaks old-growth forest on the southeast coast.

and flow of glaciers carved out hundreds of deep, U-shaped valleys. As the ice retreated and sea levels rose, the valleys were flooded, forming fjords. Ice still covers large areas of Tongass, stretching from higher elevations to sea level in some places. The **Malaspina Glacier** complex north of **Yakuta**, for example, swathes nearly 2,000 square miles (5,200 sq km).

Evidence of human habitation dates back 10,000 years. Alaskan natives such as the Tlingit, Haida, and Tsimshian prospered on the abundance of game and seafood and gradually developed a rich cultural heritage. Elaborate totems, clan houses, and art can be seen throughout the region, and visitors to remote areas may still come across stone tools, rock art, the remnants of long-abandoned villages, grave sites, and decayed totems – all of which are protected and should not be disturbed. Some groups of native people still live a traditional lifestyle, hunting, fishing, and gathering, and keeping alive ancient languages and ceremonies.

The Tongass is one of only two U.S. national forests not accessible by highway, and one-third of it, in 16 different units, is classified as wilderness. It also incorporates two national monuments, Admiralty Island and Misty Fiords. The U.S. Forest Service manages all these areas on a multiple-use basis, fostering recreational activities as well as resource extraction such as logging and mining. About 22 percent of the forest is open to commercial logging, but under current plans less than 750,000 acres (304,000 hectares) will be "harvested" over the next century.

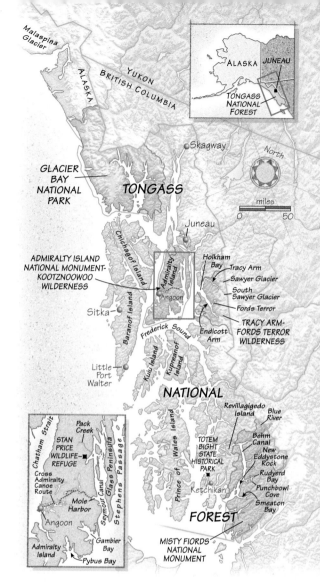

Fortress of Bears

Juneau, the state capital, is situated in the heart of Tongass and makes a good base for exploring the region. Just 13 miles (21km) out of town, and often visible as you fly into Juneau, is the **Mendenhall Glacier**. While this may not be the most dramatic glacier in southeast Alaska, it is easily the most accessible and provides an excellent introduction to the region's landscapes. The informative visitor center offers wonderful views of the glacier, and hiking trails wind up either side of the ice.

Just 15 miles (24km) west of the city lies

Admiralty Island, home of **Admiralty Island National Monument**, which incorporates the **Kootznoowoo Wilderness**. Named in 1794 by British explorer Captain James Vancouver, Admiralty is cloaked in dense rain forests of spruce and hemlock, and has 678 miles (1,091km) of wild coastline and 67 salmon streams. The island is a haven for wildlife, with bears far outnumbering humans, and a recreational paradise for travelers.

There are few forest trails, however, and dense thickets of alder and spiny devil's club, downed timbers, and wet, mossy ground make hiking difficult. Furthermore, there's a good chance of stumbling across a bear as you struggle along. So the best way to view the rain forest is on beach walks or from the water.

A range of watercraft is available for hire at the Tlingit village of **Angoon** on the west coast. Sea kayakers can explore numerous sheltered bays,

and yachters can sail along windy **Chatham Strait** or **Stephens Passage**. Orcas and humpback whales are often seen offshore, with **Frederick Sound** at the south end of the island being a particularly productive area.

Inland, canoeists will revel in the 32-mile-long (52-km) **Cross Admiralty Canoe Route**, which runs between Mitchell Bay near Angoon and **Mole Harbor** off **Seymour Canal** on the eastern side of the island, passing through eight lakes connected by portages. This journey offers excellent opportunities for viewing wildlife, including deer, otters, and bald eagles. Admiralty supports one of the highest concentrations of nesting bald eagles in the world, with approximately 890 nesting sites, just under half of which are occupied each year.

But Admiralty's best-known inhabitants are its bears; indeed, the name *Kootznoowoo* is a Tlingit

word meaning "Fortress of the Bears." All 1,700 bears on the island – more than one per square mile – are Alaskan brown bears, which are grizzlies grown to immense size (up to 1,000 pounds/450kg) on bountiful salmon. The best place in the monument for bear viewing is the **Stan Price State Wildlife Sanctuary** at **Pack Creek**, off Seymour Canal. Hunting was banned here as far back as 1930, and the area later became a 60,000-acre (24,000-hectare) sanctuary. It was named for Stan Price, who retired to Pack Creek in 1950 and spent the next 39 years living peacefully among the bears, many of which he came to regard as pets. Today, up to 25 brown bears frequent the sanctuary to feed on the creek's abundant salmon, with numbers reaching a peak in July. Visitors can observe the animals, which are remarkably tolerant of humans, from two viewing areas, one situated on a sand spit and another located upstream on a raised platform. Access to the refuge requires a permit, available from the Forest Service in Juneau.

A humpback whale (opposite, top) breaches in Frederick Sound.

A canoeist (left) portages through the forest on Admiralty Island.

Forest giants (top) are nourished by more than 200 inches (500cm) of precipitation a year.

The legendary glacier bear (right) is actually a black bear whose coat is flecked with silver.

Fearful Fjords

To explore the spectacular inlets that reach deep into the mainland, take a charter boat from Juneau to the 653,179-acre (264,332-hectare) **Tracy Arm–Fords Terror Wilderness**, 50 miles (80km) to the southwest. This wilderness area surrounds **Holkham Bay** and Tracy and **Endicott Arms** – deep, beautiful fjords that penetrate 30 miles (48km) into the nearby mountains. Here, glaciers and forested slopes drop steeply to the sea and tree-canopied islands seem to float on the tide.

Fords Terror is a narrow waterway flanked by precipitous rock walls, which opens into a secluded fjord. At the entrance to this slender chasm, the changing tides often create rapids, whirlpools, and hazardous surges, so that it often looks more like a whitewater rapid than a seaway. Occasionally, the channel is even blocked by jumbles of surging ice. The Terror was named in

Glacier Bear

Alaska is home to about 35,000 bears, and visitors can see both brown bears and black bears in southeastern rain forests. But sharp-eyed wildlife watchers exploring Tongass may also, if they are lucky, spot one of the state's most mysterious animals – the glacier, or blue, bear.

This seldom-seen, silver-coated bruin is as ephemeral as the mists that swirl through the old-growth forest, and some legends describe it as a forest spirit or sprite. But it's no myth. The glacier bear is in fact a black bear, and its silver-blue hue is simply one of the color variations that occur within the species. These include black, brown, cinnamon, rarely white, and, even more rarely, blue. The variations correlate with habitat and climate, and somehow southeast Alaska's unique conditions have given rise to this rare color phase.

Contrary to popular belief, the glacier bear does not live on tidewater glaciers and ice fields as there is nothing for it to eat there. Though it can live near glaciers, it is most often seen wandering through the forest or grazing quietly in flower-filled meadows.

Totem poles and a longhouse
(right) stand at a reconstructed
Tlingit village at Totem Bight
State Historical Park.

Granite walls (bottom) rise from
the waters of Punchbowl Cove.

1889 by H. L. Ford, a sailor
who had rowed into the
narrow opening and been
caught in the tidal chaos for
more than six hours. To this
day, only small vessels
operated by experienced
skippers dare venture through the opening
at high tide. Once inside, visitors find themselves in a dramatic fjord that looks more
like a lake than an arm of the sea. Spruce-
hemlock rain forest cloaks the lower slopes.
Black and brown bears roam along the tidal
flats and narrow beaches, and mountain

goats peer down from high cliffs.

Wildlife also abounds in nearby Tracy
Arm: look for eagles flying along the forest
edges, harbor seals basking on chunks of
ice, and, in summer, humpback whales sur-
facing in the placid waters. Boat trips usually
put passengers ashore for a short time so
that they can walk along the beach and
examine the rain forest at close quarters,
and visit **Sawyer Glacier**, halfway up Tracy
Arm, where floating ice often threatens to
block passage. At the end of the fjord looms
South Sawyer Glacier. This massive tidewater glacier constantly sheds enormous
slabs of ice into the lapping salt water – a
process known as "calving." When a towering wall of ice topples into the sea, it strikes
with such force that it sends up a huge
splash and generates a mini tidal wave strong
enough to rock nearby sightseeing boats.

Misty and Mystic

From Juneau, visitors can also hop on the
Alaska State Ferry and head south to
Ketchikan. Near this colorful waterfront
town is **Totem Bight State Historical Park**,
a fascinating reconstruction of a Tlingit village, featuring beautifully carved totem
poles and a spectacular clan house. But the
prime destination here for nature lovers is
Misty Fiords National Monument. Drawing
its name from the area's almost constant
precipitation, this spectacular preserve,
located 22 miles (35km) east of the city,
occupies nearly 2.3 million acres (931,000

A **forest trail** (left) leads a hiker through the dense understory of Misty Fiords National Monument.

A **kayaker** (bottom) paddles the iceberg-strewn waters of Tracy Arm near the snout of Sawyer Glacier.

of the forces that helped shape the region. On reaching **Rudyerd Bay**, planes then head south over the mountains to **Smeaton Bay** and the aptly named **Punchbowl Cove**, where sheer rock walls rise 3,000 feet (900m) from sea level.

As the plane traverses the extraordinary landscape of the interior, you'll peer down on sparkling azure lakes and pristine, emerald forests cut by rushing rivers and coruscating waterfalls. Look closely and you'll spot mountain goats on peaks and bald eagles soaring effortlessly on updrafts. With views like these to savor, it's no wonder that many visitors mistakenly refer to the monument as "Mystic Fiords."

hectares), with all but seven percent designated as wilderness. At the heart of the monument, impossibly steep mountains beribboned with waterfalls loom over glaciers, dense moss-draped forests, and breathtaking fjords. No roads lead into this almost impregnable wildlife stronghold, and there are only three short, primitive trails. Although charter boats offer tours of its fjords and more intrepid travelers can explore backwaters in kayaks and canoes, the best way to gain a sense of the monument's majesty is by taking a flightseeing trip from Ketchikan.

A typical flight path takes you across 117-mile-long (188-km) **Behm Canal** and over **New Eddystone Rock**, a 20-story-tall volcanic plug that is a visible remnant

DETAILS

How to Get There

Visitors fly into Juneau International Airport. From Juneau, air taxis fly to towns near Tongass or to wilderness destinations in the national forest.

When to Go

Since Tongass spans nearly the entire Alaskan panhandle, climate in the national forest varies. Annual rainfall ranges from 26 to 220 inches (66–559cm). In general, summer is cool and wet, with temperatures in the 50s and 60s°F (12–18°C); winter is mild and wet, with temperatures in the 20s and 30s°F (-4–2°C). Visitors should note the dramatic seasonal variations in daylight, with as many as 19 hours in summer and as few as six hours in the heart of winter.

Getting Around

Because Tongass is not accessible by highway, most visitors make their way around the region by air taxis and boats – and many rely on tour operators. Alaska Airlines offers transport throughout southeast Alaska. Travelers who rent cars can use ferries on the Alaska Marine Highway System to take their vehicles to all major communities in the region. Call the U.S. Forest Service Information Center, 907-586-8751, for details about transportation.

INFORMATION

Admiralty Island National Monument

8461 Old Dairy Road, Juneau, AK 99801; tel: 800-586-8790.

Alaska Marine Highway System

P.O. Box 25535, Juneau, AK 99802; tel: 800-642-0066; www.dot.state.ak.us/external/amhs/ This system runs the state ferries.

Misty Fiords National Monument

Tongass National Forest, 3031 Tongass Avenue, Ketchikan, AK 99901; tel: 907-225-2148.

Southeast Alaska Tourism Council

P.O. Box 20710, Juneau, AK 99802-0710; tel: 800-423-0568.

Tongass National Forest

U.S. Forest Service, Visitor Center, 50 Main Street, Ketchikan, AK, 99901; tel: 907-228-6214; www.fs.fed.us/r10/tongass

U.S. Forest Service

Tracy Arm–Fords Terror Wilderness and Admiralty Island National Monument, Tongass National Forest, 101 Egan Drive, Juneau, AK 99801; tel: 907-586-8751.

CAMPING

Tongass National Forest

U.S. Forest Service, Visitor Center, 50 Main Street, Ketchikan, AK, 99901; tel: 907-228-6214; www.fs.fed.us/r10/tongass

Tongass has 10 campgrounds, and backcountry camping is unrestricted in most areas. There are also 150 public recreation cabins that are not accessible by road.

LODGING

PRICE GUIDE – double occupancy

$ = up to $49 $$ = $50–$99
$$$ = $100–$149 $$$$ = $150+

Admiralty Island Wilderness Homestead

4 Crab Cove, Funter Bay, AK 99850; tel: 907-586-6243 (winter) or 907-789-4786 (summer).

Open May through September, this homestead on Admiralty Island customizes nature adventures for guests, including rainforest hikes, cruises, beachcombing, and more. There are two guest rooms with private baths and a carriage house. $$$$

Blueberry Hill Bed-and-Breakfast

500 Front Street, Ketchikan, AK 99901; tel: 907-247-2583.

The four rooms in this house in Ketchikan's historic district have queen-size beds and private baths, some with views of the Tongass Narrows or Deer Mountain. $$–$$$

Pearson's Pond Luxury Inn

4541 Sawa Circle, Juneau, AK 99801-8723; tel: 888-658-6328 or 907-789-3772.

This resort, near Mendenhall Glacier, hosts activities ranging from mountain biking to hiking on glacial trails. Guest rooms have queen-size beds and private baths. $$$–$$$$

Pybus Point Lodge

1873 Shell Simmons Road, Juneau, AK 99801; tel: 907-790-4866 or 800-947-9287.

This lodge on Admiralty Island has two-bedroom cabins with harbor and mountain views and private bathrooms. Adventure packages include transportation to and from Juneau, fishing gear, and activities such as fishing and wildlife tours. $$$$

Thayer Lake Wilderness Lodge

P.O. Box 8897, Ketchikan, AK 99901; tel: 907-247-8897 or 907-225-3343; fax: 907-247-7053.

Nestled in the heart of Admiralty Island, Thayer offers fly-fishing, bear watching, and customized trips that include meals, round-trip transportation from Juneau, and private lodging in lakeside cabins. $$$$

TOURS AND OUTFITTERS

Alaska Cruises

P.O. Box 7814, Ketchikan, AK 99901; tel: 800-228-1905.

Passengers see waterfalls, pristine lakes, and majestic cliffs aboard yacht cruises to Misty Fiords National Monument.

Alaska Discovery

5310 Glacier Highway, Juneau, AK 99801; tel: 800-586-1911; fax: 907-780-4220.

Guided adventures include camping, hiking, rafting, canoeing, and sea kayaking. Trips vary in length and activity level.

Alaska Great Escapes

91110 Mendenhall Mall Road, Juneau, AK 99801; tel: 800-478-9188.

This operator customizes packages for fishing, whale watching, flightseeing, and other air, land, and sea adventures.

Orca Enterprises

P.O. Box 35431, Juneau, AK 99803; tel: 907-789-6801 or 888-733-6722.

Passengers on Orca's three-hour whale-watching boat excursions to Admiralty Island see the region's humpback whales, Alaskan brown bears, bald eagles, sea lions, harbor seals, and orcas. Guided bear-watching hikes and helicopter flightseeing trips are also available.

Southeast Sea Kayaks

1430 Millar Street, Ketchikan, AK 99901; tel/fax: 800-287-1607 or 907-225-1258.

Guided sea kayak tours include longer trips to Misty Fiords National Monument. Kayak rentals are available.

Wilderness Swift Charters

6205 North Douglas Road, Juneau, AK 99802; tel: 907-463-4942.

This boat charter company offers one- to five-day wildlife-watching trips to Tracy Arm, Admiralty Island, Pack Creek, and elsewhere in southeast Alaska.

Wings of Alaska

8421 Livingston Way, Juneau, AK 99801; tel: 907-789-0790; fax: 907-789-2021.

Flightseeing adventures visit Tracy Arm, Admiralty Island, Glacier Bay National Park, and other wilderness areas. Charter flights to remote regions of southeast Alaska focus on camping, fishing, photography, or visits to Forest Service cabins.

Excursions

Glacier Bay National Park and Preserve

Park Headquarters, 1 Park Road, P.O. Box 140, Gustavus, AK 99826; tel: 907-697-2230; fax: 907-697-2654; www.nps.gov/glba

Famed naturalist John Muir described Glacier Bay as "a picture of icy wildness unspeakably pure and sublime." Its glaciers, fjords, forests, and views of the St. Elias Mountains awe even the most jaded travelers. Indeed, this 3,328,000-acre (1,346,800-hectare) park has been voted number one in the U.S. National Park System. Visitors can kayak, board tour boats, hike through a rain forest, or camp near tidewater glaciers and cascading waterfalls.

Prince William Sound

Alaska Public Lands Information Center, 605 West 4th Avenue #105, Anchorage, AK 99501; tel: 907-271-2737; www.nps.gov/aplic/center

At the northern edge of Alaska's temperate rain forests, inlets, islands, and channels create a maze of waterways inhabited by abundant marine life clawing its way back after the ravages wrought by the *Exxon Valdez* oil spill. Departing from Valdez, Seward, Whittier, and Cordova on flightseeing trips, boat tours, and kayaking explorations, visitors can expect to see orcas, sea otters, seals, and sea lions, and, along the 3,000 miles (4,800km) of shoreline, Sitka black-tailed deer, and brown and black bears as well as abundant bird life.

Wrangell–St. Elias National Park and Preserve

Headquarters, Old Richardson Highway, P.O. Box 439, Copper Center, AK 99573; tel: 907-822-5234; www.nps.gov/wrst/

Located immediately north of Tongass but accessible by road only from the Alaska and Old Richardson Highways in the north, this awe-inspiring, World-Heritage-listed preserve is the largest national park in the United States. It encompasses the biggest group of glaciers in North America as well as the continent's second-highest peak, 18,008-foot (5,488-m) Mount St. Elias. Hikers must blaze their own trails in this extreme, pathless wilderness, but will be rewarded with astonishing scenery and sightings of Dall sheep, grizzlies, caribou, moose, lynx, and a wide range of birds, including ptarmigan and trumpeter swans.

Olympic
National Park
Washington

CHAPTER **7**

The first storm of the rainy season – the 10-month rainy season – is blowing in, but the folks in **Forks**, a small town on Washington's **Olympic Peninsula**, are greeting it in good cheer. "I love storms, I love the rain, I love the lushness, the green, the moss," enthuses bookstore owner Cheri Fleck. "Besides, it's great for the book business." Artist Susan Gansert Shaw wraps herself in Gore-Tex and continues her daily inspirational walks. "It's nice to be the only person out there on the beach," she says. Fleck and Shaw do hope this won't quite be a reprise of 1998, when Forks gurgled under 135 inches (343cm) of rain, 18 inches (46cm) more than normal. "That was the first time in 23 years here that it affected me negatively," sighs Shaw. "I mean, pul-eeeze!" ◆ As the only settlement on the peninsula's Pacific side large enough to sport a stoplight – just one – Forks is, by default, and perhaps a little reluctantly, the gateway to the rain forests of **Olympic National Park**. It's an honest, rough-hewn logging town that has only lately warmed to tourism because timber harvests are waning. But its 3,450 residents give good advice for appreciating the relentless rain. Newcomers face an emotional trial period of two to five years, they say, but those who survive and learn to embrace the rain also fall in love with the natural extravagance it brings. ◆ Look at a map of the Olympic Peninsula, and the profile of an upturned bear's head springs to mind. Where the neck and shoulders would be, a craggy profusion of mountains scratches 7,965 feet (2,428m) into the sky. More like a sprawling château with an impossible confusion of turrets than a typical spinelike mountain range, the Olympics are the product of two million years of

Silence mantles a cathedral of ancient trees in the temperate rain forests of the Olympic Peninsula.

A hiker strolls through the aptly named Hall of Mosses. Moss will grow anywhere it receives adequate water and nutrients, and may become dormant during temporary dry spells.

of nightmares, the dark haunt of both real and mythical creatures that represented terrible danger. The sea, even with its canoe-eating storms, currents, tide rips, and whirlpools, seemed a friendlier neighborhood. And for several generations after Europeans had a foothold in the Northwest, the Olympics remained *terra incognita*, one of the last unexplored regions of the United States. Not until 1889 did an expedition traverse the mountains, and those pioneers – sponsored by the *Seattle Press* as a publicity stunt – did not find it an enlightening experience. "There is something much like exploring a dark rat hole in this," grumbled Captain Charles Adams Barnes. "One can see only a few yards in any direction near the ground, and overhead the foliage shuts out even the sky."

glacial gouging and rasping. These peaks reach up and snag the bear's share of moisture borne on the storms that continually rumble in from the Pacific, creating dramatically different climates on the east and west sides of the mountains: Forks, 117 inches (297cm) of rain in an average year; Seattle, 38 inches (97cm).

People turned their backs on the somber, overgrown forests of these mountains for at least the first 3,000 years of human habitation in the Pacific Northwest. The peninsula Indians lived on the coast and faced the sea; their ancient stories and traditions make it clear that the forest was their land

But then came World War I and a sudden demand for a critical resource – Sitka spruce, essential for the aircraft frames of the time. Roads and rails penetrated the ancient forests for logging, which quickly

boomed. If President Franklin D. Roosevelt hadn't come for a personal tour, the entire 6,500-square-mile (16,835-sq-km) peninsula might today be shorn like a Marine recruit's skull. In 1937, staring through a car window at the desolation of clear-cut mountainsides, FDR fumed, "I hope the son-of-a-bitch who logged that is roasting in hell!" The next year he signed the bill creating Olympic National Park.

Off the Scale

Loggers still lap at its skirts, but the 1,400-square-mile (3,630-sq-km) park is one of the most extravagantly endowed and yet pristine jewels in the National Park System. "The trees alone are enough to bring humility to man," wrote William O. Douglas, who divided his life between the U.S. Supreme Court and his beloved cathedrals of Sitka spruce, Douglas fir, and red cedar 200 to 300 feet (60–90m) high. But the trees aren't alone. The park encompasses 266 glaciers; half a dozen sparkling rivers that radiate like spokes off the glacial drip; uncounted

alpine meadows grazed by deer, elk, whistling marmot, and black bear; and the longest strip of wild ocean coast left in the continental United States. Thanks to the extremes of weather and topography, visitors can traverse environments of incredible variety. It's a hike of a few minutes from watching gray whales commuting past the beaches to pondering banana slugs scooting (at a top speed of six inches per minute) across the forest.

But it's the rain forests in the valleys of the **Hoh, Queets,** and **Quinault Rivers** that win the most attention of all the park's ecosystems. This is largely due to their accessibility – many hikes are on level, if soggy, ground – but also to their utterly strange and awesome nature. No everyday coniferous forest prepares you for a first encounter with these Olympian trees; like the Grand Canyon, they are off

A black bear (opposite, top) snoozes in the afternoon sun; they tend to be shy but are occasionally spotted by visitors.

Olympic marmots (above) are found in alpine meadows above the rain forest.

Dense undergrowth (left) makes backcountry hiking extremely difficult.

The Owl's Forest

Consider, for a moment, the old-growth forest from the perspective of a northern spotted owl. The taller trees are widely spaced, leaving room to make silent, swooping dives for prey. Dead snags, 50 to 100 feet (15–30m) high, make ideal nests because they offer views unimpeded by foliage. And the dense forest canopy overhead serves as a barrier to great horned owls, which enjoy dining on spotted owls.

These are some of the things wildlife ecologists have learned since this small, reclusive bird became the focus of a sweeping struggle to limit clear-cutting and save what's left of the Northwest's old-growth forests. The owl landed on the endangered list in 1973, the same year Congress passed the Endangered Species Act. Debate over the owl's future polarized tree-huggers and tree-cutters, and the bird became a symbol for the conflict over wilderness preservation. "Some were calling the owl the billion-dollar bird," wrote William Dietrich in *The Final Forest*, a tag that was to prove to be a woeful underestimate. In 1992 a U.S. District Court halted logging of spotted owl habitat, and despite a lot of grumbling – and economic hardship – more enlightened forestry management has begun to replace clear-cutting.

There is more at stake here than the aesthetic loss to humans who like to wander the forest trails. Second-growth forest and "managed" timberland lack the astonishing fecundity and diversity of old growth. Missing, for example, are "nurse" logs, fallen trunks encrusted with moss, ferns, and seedlings of future skyscraper conifers. The rotting logs provide a haven for carpenter ants and bark beetles, which in turn nourish woodpeckers. Sever one link of a complex ecosystem, and the ripples resonate throughout the entire web – sometimes forever.

"In wildness is the preservation of the world," wrote Henry David Thoreau. But on the uncrowded continent of 1862, that was both easier to say and less important to do than it is today.

Retiring by nature, northern spotted owls (left) are more likely to be heard than seen.

Banana slugs (bottom) are hermaphrodites; each animal has both male and female reproductive organs.

Marymere Falls (opposite, top), fed by snowmelt, glacier runoff, and Pacific storms, spills over a basalt ledge.

Sea stacks (opposite, bottom) bristling with evergreens are silhouetted by the setting sun along the park's 60-mile-long (96-km) coastal strip.

fungus, or scrap of bark – is glistening and willing to reflect whatever light there is, so the entire forest seems polished. And what appears at first to be a numbing monochromaticism, a tyranny of chlorophyll, turns out to be a richly endowed spectrum of greens: the deep emerald of the licorice fern, the wan olive of hanging clubmoss, the pale turquoise of Sitka needles. Where foreign colors break out – the wedding-dress white of an angel wing fungus or the Belgian chocolate of an exposed cedar root – they create a dramatic counterpoint. In October, vine maples add the ornamental grace notes of yellow and red.

the scale of conventional human experience. On a drippy, overcast day, which is to say normal, these forests are dark indeed, but they are not necessarily the gloomy labyrinths that pioneers like Barnes described. Every surface – every leaf, twig,

Human eyes never quite adjust to the scale of the botany, however. The country's largest western hemlock lives here, 241 feet (74m) tall and more than 22 feet (6.7m) around. There's a Sitka spruce that reaches 191 feet (58m), a grand fir of 251 feet (77m), and a Douglas fir of 298 feet (91m). They've seen a heap of history; a Douglas fir can live 750 years and a western red cedar more than a millennium. In fact, they seem almost more archaeological than botanical, a collection of oversized Roman columns propping up the dome of the sky. Some even feature flying buttresses, huge roots that stayed above ground because the tree started on a biodegrading nurse log, and the roots had to grow around it to find the floor. Even the hanging clubmoss, signature drapery of the Olympic rain forests, grows big here: a ton or more can sag from a single tree.

On a windless day these rain forests are places of deep and melancholy silence, an ironic quality in an environment so obviously teeming with life. They absorb sound like catacombs lined with wet sponges. "It is seven months," laments one pioneer's journal, "since I recall a songbird." But persistent visitors eventually will hear, and see, wildlife. Herds of Roosevelt elk, scaled as extravagantly as the trees (bulls weigh up to 1,000 pounds/454kg), live year-round in the Hoh River valley or migrate down in winter from snowbound meadows. Cougars, predators of the young elk and smaller black-tailed deer, are always around but so furtive that a ranger says she's sighted only one in her 16 years in the park. The forest floor is alive with restless shrews (they never sleep) and Douglas squirrels (they never hibernate). The promiscuous cigar-sized banana slug can often be spied in a daylong mating orgy, which it is happy to do with either gender (conveniently, each slug produces both sperm and egg).

House of Rain

On a stormy day, these rain forests are places to avoid; as dramatic as it might be

Roosevelt elk (right) browse in the underbrush. About 5,000 elk reside in the park, the largest population in the Pacific Northwest.

Sol Duc Falls (below) gushes through a canyon on the flank of the Olympic Mountains.

Fog (opposite) enshrouds a stand of old-growth giants. The dominant species are Sitka spruce, western hemlock, Douglas fir, and red cedar, some more than 250 feet (76m) tall.

to see 250-foot (76-m) Douglas firs swaying in the wind, that wind can be more than their match. Somewhere on the peninsula every winter there are hurricane-strength winds. And after months of winter rain, winds of only 55 to 60 miles per hour (90-100 km/hour) will topple big trees.

A calm and rainy day is the right time to hike in the rain forest, the time when its world seems most precisely in tune. The rainy season lasts from September through

June. In the Hoh River valley, most of the annual 135 inches (343cm) falls during these months; July and August bring just three inches (8cm) each. During this "dry" season, coastal fog lumbers up the river valleys and evergreen needles comb it into "fog drip" – which is just what the rain forest needs, another 30 inches (76cm) of precipitation.

The Olympic rain forests generally rise astride the three major rivers that squiggle southwestward from the glaciers to the sea. The **Hoh Rain Forest** is the most accessible, thanks to its proximity to Forks and the good paved road to the visitor center. Three easy but spectacular loop trails here provide an awe-inspiring sampler of rain-forest biology. The three-quarter-mile (1.2-km) **Hall of Mosses Trail** is best. More ambitious hikers can continue up the **Hoh River Trail** – way up, if prepared for technical glacier climbing, to the summit of **Mount Olympus**.

The road penetrating 12 miles (19km) into the **Queets** is unpaved, so its rain forest is much lonelier – a fact that takes on special significance when one spots a plop of fresh bear scat on three-mile (5-km) **Sam's Loop Trail**, which starts at the end of the road. The uncanny stillness of this forest is both unnerving and powerful; the complete absence of wind, machinery, and even running water actually becomes a presence, a palpable emotional force.

The **Quinault** offers several well-maintained trails that start within a half mile of the rustic **Lake Quinault Lodge**, built in 1926. Best is the **Quinault Loop**, a three-mile (5-km) trek that wanders through a truly spectacular stand of 500-year-old Douglas firs.

Crest and Coast

"The rain forests are so radiant with soft green light," wrote William O. Douglas, "so filled with endless wonders that I hate to leave them. Yet when I reach the high ridges and meadows of the Olympics I hate to leave them also." This is the eternal quandary of the Olympic Peninsula – where to spend anything less than a lifetime.

Hurricane Ridge is one of the park's prime attractions, in part because of its infamous weather. From atop the 5,242-foot (1,598-m) ridge, clouds seem to snooze in the defiles like ghosts lounging in hammocks; fog and drizzle alternate with what Northwesterners cheerfully call "sun breaks." It's a lovely and easy 17-mile (27-km) drive from **Port Angeles** in summer, but the ridge bears an average of 10 feet (3m) of snow all winter.

Waterfalls crash spectacularly into dark basalt canyons throughout the mountains. Two of the most scenic are **Sol Duc Falls**, which pours three parallel gushes over a moss-encrusted precipice, and **Marymere Falls**, a 100-foot (31-m) silver noodle that splashes into a natural amphitheater – a waterfall in a display case.

The park has also annexed a narrow 62-mile (100-km) strip of the peninsula's western coast, the most primitive shoreline left in the lower 48 states. But the most complete seascape is **Cape Flattery**, the bear's nose of the peninsula and homeland of the Makah people for at least 500 years. A short hike, part of it "paved" with a cedar boardwalk, ends at a cliff where raucous choirs of sea lions trumpet their love songs inside sea caves, while half a mile offshore, fog curls eerily around the historic **Tatoosh Island** lighthouse.

It's the rainy season – the 10-month rainy season – and another storm is rolling in.

TRAVEL TIPS

DETAILS

How to Get There

The major airport closest to Olympic National Park is Seattle-Tacoma International Airport, a three-hour drive from the park's Port Angeles headquarters and a five-hour drive from the Hoh Rain Forest Visitor Center. Greyhound Bus Lines (800-231-2222) and Olympic Bus Lines (360-452-3858) operate between Seattle and Port Angeles.

When to Go

Visitors should be prepared for rain year-round in Olympic's rain forests. Average annual rainfall in the Hoh Rain Forest is 135 inches (343cm). July and August are the driest months, while November, December, and January have the heaviest rains. Summer high temperatures range from 65°F to 75°F (18–24°C), lows from 45°F to 55°F (7–13°C). Winter is mild, with temperatures in the 30s and 40s°F (1–7°C).

Getting Around

Car rentals are available at Seattle-Tacoma International Airport. The park has several scenic roads, though none penetrates the interior. There are, however, 600 miles (966km) of hiking trails. Backpacker shuttle service to trailheads is provided by Olympic Tours and Charters (360-452-3858).

Backcountry Permits

A wilderness use permit is required for all backcountry camping; reservations are recommended. Although permits can be purchased at staffed ranger stations, it is best to call the Wilderness Information Center (360-452-0330) in advance to register.

INFORMATION

Hoh Rain Forest Visitor Center

18113 Upper Hoh Road, Forks, WA 98331; tel: 360-374-6925.

North Olympic Peninsula Visitor and Convention Bureau

P.O. Box 670, Port Angeles, WA 98362; tel: 800-942-4042; www.olympicpeninsula.org/

Olympic National Park

600 East Park Avenue, Port Angeles, WA 98362; tel: 360-452-4501; www.nps.gov/olym/home.htm

Washington State Tourism

P.O. Box 42500, Olympia, WA 98504-2500; tel: 800-544-1800 or 360-586-2088; www.tourism.wa.gov/

CAMPING

Olympic National Park

600 East Park Avenue, Port Angeles, WA 98362; tel: 360-452-0330; www.nps.gov/olym/home.htm

There are four campgrounds in the Hoh, Quinault, and Queets Rain Forests, which range from primitive to developed. Campsites are available on a first-come, first-served basis. The Hoh Rain Forest is the most easily accessible by car, while the Queets is reached only by a dirt road.

LODGING

PRICE GUIDE – double occupancy

$ = up to $49 $$ = $50–$99

$$$ = $100–$149 $$$$ = $150+

Eagle Point Inn

384 Stormin Norman Lane, Beaver, WA 98305; tel: 360-327-3236.

Set on the Hoh River 10 miles (16km) north of Forks, this bed-and-breakfast has three rooms in a luxurious log house. $$

Huckleberry Lodge

1171 Big Pine Way, Forks, WA 98331; tel: 360-374-6008 or 888-822-6008; fax: 360-385-6623.

This bed-and-breakfast, on five acres (2 hectares) next to the Calawah River and minutes from the Hoh Rain Forest, has three guest rooms and three detached cabins. $$–$$$

Kalaloch Lodge

157151 Highway 101, Forks, WA 98331; tel: 360-962-2271.

Perched on a seaside bluff within Olympic Coast National Marine Sanctuary, this rustic lodge has a restaurant, coffee shop, gift shop, and 58 units, including 18 ocean-view cabins and a secluded 10-room motel. The cabins have kitchenettes and fireplaces and can sleep four to nine people. $$–$$$

Lake Crescent Lodge

416 Lake Crescent Road, Port Angeles, WA 98363; tel: 360-928-3211.

This lodge sits at the foot of Mount Storm King, steps away from Lake Crescent. Thirty comfortable motel rooms and 17 modern cabins have private baths. All cabins have decks; four have fireplaces. Amenities include a lakeside restaurant and rowboat rentals. $$–$$$

Lake Quinault Lodge

P.O. Box 7, Quinault, WA 98575-0007; tel: 800-562-6672.

Built in 1926 next to Lake Quinault, this resort has 92 rooms with private baths, some with fireplaces. A restaurant, an indoor heated pool, and boat rentals are also on the premises. $$–$$$$

Sol Duc Hot Springs

P.O. Box 2169, Port Angeles, WA 98362-0283; tel: 360-327-3583.

This secluded hot-springs resort is nestled in the northern section of the park and includes 32 cabins, each with a full bath and two double beds; some have kitchens. Amenities include a poolside restaurant, deli, and grocery store. $$

TOURS AND OUTFITTERS

Kayak Port Townsend

435 Water Street, Port Townsend, WA 98368; tel: 360-385-6240.

Guides lead half-day, full-day, and overnight sea kayak tours in the bays of Puget Sound for people with all levels of experience. Sea kayak rentals and instruction are also available.

Olympak Llamas

1614 Dan Kelly Road, Port Angeles, WA 98363; tel: 360-452-5867.

Operated by the former trail foreman of Olympic National Park, this outfitter provides llama pack trips of any length in the park. Travelers can opt to meet the guide at the trailhead.

Olympic Raft and Kayak

123 Lake Aldwell Road, Port Angeles, WA 98363; tel: 360-452-1443 or 888-452-1443.

Guided half-day, family-oriented raft trips for beginners and intermediates explore the Elwha and Hoh Rivers. There are also opportunities for sea and lake kayaking. Canoe and kayak rentals are available.

Olympic Wilderness Tours

5196 Lars Hansen Road Southeast, Port Orchard, WA 98367; tel: 360-871-9087.

Customizing day hikes, backpacking, and technical mountain-climbing trips, this outfitter works with small groups at all levels of experience anywhere within the park.

Puget Sound Express

431 Water Street, Port Townsend, WA 98368; tel: 360-385-5288.

All-day whale-watching tours of the San Juan Islands and Strait of Juan de Fuca offer frequent sightings of killer whales, gray whales, minke whales, Dall porpoises, eagles, and other wildlife.

Quinault Packing

42 Liscumm Road, Quinault, WA 98575; tel: 360-288-2240.

Custom-designed donkey-pack trips vary in length.

Excursions

Mount Rainier National Park

Star Route, Tahoma Woods, Ashford, WA 98304-9751; tel: 360-569-2211; www.nps.gov/mora/

Old-growth forests, lush subalpine meadows, and cold, rushing rivers sustain a wide variety of plants and animals in this park south of Seattle. The tallest peak in the volcanic Cascade Range, Mount Rainier is encased in more than 35 square miles of snow and ice, and receives 75 to 126 inches (190–320cm) of precipitation a year. Surrounding the mountain are 1,000-year-old stands of western hemlock and Douglas fir that support 54 species of mammals, 126 species of birds, and 17 species of amphibians and reptiles, including black bears, cougars, mountain goats, red-tailed hawks, hummingbirds, and northern spotted owls. In July and August, the park's subalpine meadows are a rainbow of colors, as more than 30 flower species come into bloom.

Pacific Rim National Park

P.O. Box 280, 2185 Ocean Terrace Road, Ucluelet, BC V0R 3A0, Canada; tel: 250-726-7721; parkscan.harbour.com/pacrim/

As its name reflects, this Canadian park is arrayed along the western coast of British Columbia's Vancouver Island, where old-growth rain forest meets

the Pacific Ocean. Paddlers ply canoes and kayaks along the beaches and rocky shoreline and among the park's island clusters. Backpackers can experience the park on trails, including the West Coast Trail, a 45-mile (72-km) route that makes a rewarding week-long trek through old-growth cedar, spruce, and fir.

San Juan Islands

San Juan Islands Visitor Information Service, P.O. Box 65, Lopez Island, WA 98261; tel: 360-468-3663; www.guidetosanjuans.com/

The islands in this archipelago number either 172 or 743 or some figure in between, depending on one's definition of "island." The two largest, San Juan and Orcas, are served by ferries from Anacortes and are the best-equipped visitor destinations. San Juan's Friday Harbor is a lovely seaport village, and Orcas's 4,800-acre (2,000-hectare) Moran State Park offers a bracing hike (or drive) to the 2,400-foot (730-m) summit of Mount Constitution, with views from Mount Rainier to Vancouver Island. The ferry trips are like scenic cruises, but visitors should expect long waits in summer.

Kauai
Hawaii

CHAPTER 8

little fluffy black bird with fierce yellow eyes once sang in the rain forest on the Hawaiian island of Kauai. He sang and sang, and his lovely, intricate song drifted through the scarlet ohia lehua blossoms, through the ferns and mosses. He built a nest every spring, he preened himself, and he called for a mate. But there was no answering song. There never would be. He was the last of his kind. ◆ The bird was the Kauai ʻoʻo, and he broke the hearts of conservationists as they listened to his calls in the late 1980s. He hasn't been heard since. Barbara Maxfield of the U.S. Fish and Wildlife Service says, "We suspect the species no longer exists. He was such a beautiful little bird." ◆ The Kauai ʻoʻo was typical of Hawaiian wildlife in that it lived only on this remote archipelago. Hawaii, indeed, has the highest rate of endemism in the world, with 96 percent of its species found nowhere else on Earth. Sadly, it also has one of the highest rates of extinction. Since the arrival of humans, half of its 140 native species have disappeared. Fifty percent of those remaining are endangered. ◆ Fortunately, various conservation bodies are working hard to preserve natural habitats and protect remaining species, and numerous parks and reserves have been established. One of the best places to view Hawaii's unique and extraordinary wildlife is on the oldest and, many would say, most spectacular island in the chain, **Kauai**. In particular, two contiguous preserves on the western side of this small, mountainous island – **Kokee State Park** and **Alakai Wilderness Preserve** – offer an enthralling introduction to one of the world's most unusual rain-forest environments. ◆ The centerpiece of Kauai's

Atop a heavily eroded caldera, a remarkable array of rare endemic species inhabits a rain-soaked, primeval landscape.

Waimea Canyon, about a mile (1.6km) wide and 3,600 feet (1,100m) deep, runs like a green gash through Kauai's mountainous northwest coast. It was eroded out of a geologic fault created by an earthquake.

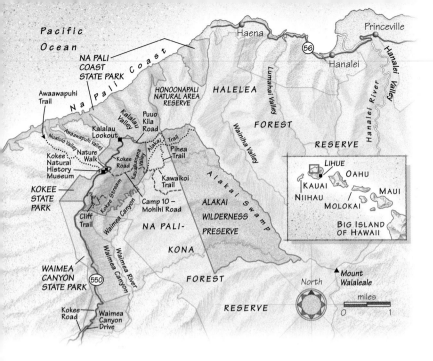

by endemic plant species such as the ohia lehua, koa, milo, kukui, and iliahi (sandalwood).

Windows onto a Distant Past

The departure point for Kokee State Park and Alakai Wilderness Preserve is the coastal town of **Waimea**, site of British Captain James Cook's first landfall in the islands in 1778. From here, **Waimea Canyon Drive** (Highway 550) climbs steeply, following the edge of **Waimea Canyon**. As you ascend, gaps in the trees offer tantalizing windows onto the deepening chasm. About halfway up, take the right-hand turnoff to **Waimea Canyon Lookout**. Here, the glory of the buttes, gorges, and cliffs unfolds in a magnificent panorama, rendered in layered colors of rose, ocher, amber, umber, and rosy red. Mark Twain took one look at this view and pronounced that Waimea was the "Grand Canyon of the Pacific." Waimea is, of course, smaller than its mainland cousin, a mere 12 miles (19km) long and one mile (1.6km) wide, but it fills the eye as far as you can see.

rain-forest wilderness is **Waialeale**, an extinct volcano in the middle of the island. Rising 5,000 feet (1,520m) above the Pacific Ocean, the mountain is shrouded in mystery – parts of it have never been explored – and dense, moisture-bearing clouds. In fact, this is the wettest spot on Earth, with an astounding 40 feet (12m) of rain a year. This torrent of water drains into the volcano's huge caldera – 13 miles (21km) in diameter and 4,000 feet (1,220m) above sea level – where it has formed an enormous wetland called the **Alakai Swamp**. It also fuels the growth of rain forest across much of the center of the island. Thick with epiphytes and ferns, these forests are dominated

Geologists can read the story of Kauai's fiery formation, its earthquakes and eruptions, in the layers of rock that plunge 3,600 feet (1,100m) deep into the heart of the island. The Hawaiian Islands are the peaks of a range of mid-ocean mountains formed by volcanic activity. Over millions of years, as a tectonic plate slid slowly across a hot spot – a column of magma that penetrates the crust like a blowtorch – magma bubbled out onto the seafloor, mounding and pillowing, and, in places, rising above the water to form a chain of islands. Kauai was the first to appear, more than six million years ago, and is therefore the island on which nature has had the longest time to work.

Kalalau Lookout (opposite) offers spectacular views of the Na Pali cliffs.

Backpackers (below) explore a lush, coastal valley, with the turquoise waters of the Pacific in the distance.

Anoles (right) are one of many exotic species that have made a home in the Hawaiian Islands, often to the detriment of native plants and animals.

Erosion and weathering have carved precipitous peaks and razor-sharp ridges, fluted sea cliffs, and deep river valleys.

Waimea Canyon began to form after a fierce earthquake created a massive fault in the western side of the landmass. Several rivers flowed into the fault and the action of their waters deepened and widened the fracture, shaping the spectacular sight you see today.

It's another six miles (10km) to the entrance of Kokee State Park and its 4,640 acres (1,877 hectares) of cool upland wilderness. The park visitor center lies just inside the entrance, but for an impressive overview of this landscape push on another two miles (3.2km) to the **Kalalau Lookout**. Here, the views sweep over the top of the island to the ocean, stretching from the sculpted turrets of the mountains, across the broad, emerald lap of the Kalalau Valley to the natural fortress of the 2,700-foot (820-m) Na Pali cliffs, which tower over the dark turquoise sea and thunderous

cries that are the bleating of mountain goats echoing in the palisades. They lean on the railing, reluctant to move or speak, and they become absorbed in beauty, peace, tranquility. They spend a long time watching the hundreds of graceful koae keas – white-tailed tropic birds – swooping and gliding in the canyon drafts. Enchanted, and as if they are alone, they do private things – kiss, pray, or just stand in companionable silence.

Once you've taken in this must-see view, head back toward the park entrance and stop off at **Kokee Natural History Museum**, adjacent to the rustic Kokee Lodge. The fowl squabbling and strutting on the lawn outside the museum appear, at first glance, to be common barnyard chickens, but they are in fact moas – rare red jungle fowl – the surviving descendants of the poultry brought by the first Polynesian settlers. Their presence serves as a prologue to the fascinating story of evolution that is chronicled in this small museum's big exhibits.

Isolated in the middle of the vast Pacific, thousands of miles from the nearest landmass, the Hawaiian archipelago was colonized slowly. Plants, blown by the winds, carried by ocean currents, and deposited by migrating birds,

surf. Rainbows regularly saturate the sky with color, and drifting clouds usually add an extra element of drama. It is an awesome spectacle.

Arriving here, people get out of their cars, creaky from the twisting ride along the rim of the canyon, and approach the railing at the edge of the overlook with a "this better be good" attitude. And then something happens. They go quiet. They listen to the wind, the faint roar of the surf assaulting the shore far below, and they hear eerie

arrived at the rate of one new species every 70,000 years. Colonizing biota then adapted so specifically to local habitats that not only did unique species evolve, but some species found on one island may not be found on another, or even in one valley and not in its neighbor. Indeed, scientists consider Hawaii to be the most remarkable illustration of the theory of evolution.

The museum's other natural history exhibits include a stuffed boar head – a cautionary trophy from Kokee's rain forest. The boar is the enemy of the native forest. As it browses, it uproots and tramples plants, creating wallows in pristine areas. The ravaged earth then becomes an incubator for more aggressive alien plant species. These pests may be beautiful – the lovely pink banana poka, the colorful, prolific lantana, and the handsome, bouffant hydrangea, for instance – or even delicious – in season you can reach out and pick blackberries and plums along the hiking trails – but all pose a major threat to the survival of native species.

Forest Treasures

Behind the museum is the easiest of the park's trails, the **Nature Walk**, which makes a short loop through the rain forest.

With interpretive signs labeling the principal plant species, it's a great introduction to Hawaiian rain forests. One of its highlights is a stand of koa trees. Known as the king of the Hawaiian forest, the koa looks similar to mahogany. It often grows to 75 feet

Hawaii's Honeycreepers

About seven million years ago, a few small birds, possibly Eurasian rosefinches or North American house finches, were caught in strong winds, carried thousands of miles across open ocean, and deposited, exhausted, on the Hawaiian Islands. In complete isolation, this single colonizing species, adapting to a variety of conditions, evolved into at least 54 new species, known collectively as the Hawaiian honeycreepers. This remarkable example of adaptive radiation eclipses the evolution of 14 Galapagos finch species that, famously, so astonished Charles Darwin.

In Hawaii, nectar-feeding honeycreepers developed long curved bills to extract nectar from the lobelia, ohia lehua, and other flowers. Insect-feeding honeycreepers acquired thin, warbler-like bills for picking insects from foliage, while seed-eaters produced strong, wide beaks for cracking husks. Specializing even further, a few honeycreepers developed hardy, hooked bills for extracting wood-boring insects from trees.

The only environmental factor the honeycreepers did not prepare for was the arrival of humans. As early as A.D. 300, Polynesians reached the islands along with their dogs and pigs, and some stowaway rats. While the early Hawaiians set to clearing lowland forests, these animals soon wiped out ground-nesting birds. Europeans had an even greater impact, introducing yet more species that competed with native wildlife, including noxious weeds and insect pests that degraded honeycreeper habitat.

Today, only about 23 honeycreeper species remain and some are perilously close to extinction. Whether they will survive in their island strongholds depends mainly on the efforts of conservation groups such as the Nature Conservancy, the Peregrine Fund, and the Hawaii Department of Land and Natural Resources, all of which are cooperating in preserving habitat and managing captive breeding programs. – *Sara Hare*

Waterfalls (opposite) at Kokee State Park stream down sheer canyon walls cloaked in vegetation.

Hiking through mud (above) is unavoidable in the "wettest place on Earth." Come prepared with sturdy boots.

The iiwi (below) uses its curved bill to reach the nectar of flowering plants. Its call, resembling a door on rusty hinges, is unmistakable.

(23m), and one specimen was recorded at 140 feet (43m).

In the old days, the Polynesians used the koa to make their great voyaging canoes. To find the perfect tree to log, they would carefully select and fell a koa, then camp out and observe the elepaio. This timid little gray bird with a white necklace and a long black tail was believed to be an incarnation of Lea, goddess of canoes. If the elepaio ran the length of the log and then flew away, the timber was pronounced perfect. If it remained on one part of the trunk, this was taken as a sign of a flaw and the log would be rejected. Today, if you stand quietly amid the koa trees, you may hear the rapid series of abrupt notes that make up the elepaio's rushed song, but you are unlikely to see this shy creature.

The most common native forest bird at Kokee is the iiwi, a small, bright red bird with black wings and tail, orange legs, and a pale orange beak. If you hear an approxi-

mation of *please*, *please*, *please*, it's almost certainly the iiwi. And if you stand a while longer, the bird will probably add a little toot and some small flute notes to its repertoire, all the while performing an acrobatic routine as it extracts nectar from flowers.

Similar is the apapane, another scarlet bird with black wings and tail and a curved black bill. The easiest way to spot one of these scarlet songsters is to stake out a blossom fairly high in one of the many tall, silver-leaved ohia lehua trees that can be seen along trails and even around the museum. The flower is as red as the bird and looks like a spiky powder puff. The apapane's curved beak developed expressly for the purpose of obtaining nectar from this flower.

Both the apapane and the iiwi were once prized for their brilliant red feathers, which were made into lustrous capes worn by Hawaiian nobles. Bird catchers would trap the birds, pluck the choice feathers, then release the creatures back into the wild.

To view some of Hawaii's rarer plants and birds, and explore some of the wildest parts of the island, head for the three-and-a-half-mile (5.6-km) **Alakai Swamp Trail**, accessed via the Camp 10–Mohihi Road or from the Pihea Trail. The 10-square-mile (26-sq-km) swamp has become a refuge for species under threat elsewhere on Kauai. No road crosses it, and the deep mud has kept cattle and other alien species like wild boar at bay. It's also too wet here for agriculture, too high for mosquitoes, and devoid of other commercially valuable resources.

In 1998, a boardwalk was laid down across the muddiest parts of the bog, but you can still count on getting wet. It's important to stay on the trail, not only to protect the wayside plants but to keep from becoming lost. The Alakai has no distinguishing landmarks and thick clouds can roll in at any time.

The first part of the track is relatively easy, but once you cross the Pihea Trail you face a steep descent to a small stream followed by an equally steep ascent on the other side. Keep an eye out here for small native honeycreepers such as the greenish-yellow anianiau and amakihi. That anise smell you'll notice is the mokihana tree, a small, shrublike plant found only on Kauai. Its green berries are used to make leis, the garlands traditionally worn by Hawaiian people. In fact, the mokihana is the official lei of Kauai. Another plant favored by lei makers, the maile, also perfumes the trail with its clean, mossy scent. A vine with shiny, dark leaves, the maile was traditionally used to adorn altars of Laka, the goddess of the hula.

After climbing and descending a few more fern-fringed gulches, you'll reach **Kawaikoi Stream**, a good spot for a picnic, then come to the flat core of the swamp, where things start to get really wet. The mist can be so thick here that it fogs up camera lenses and eye glasses, and drenches clothing. Visibility drops to five feet (1.5m), companions becoming ghostly spectres. You feel you are tiptoeing through a scene from Earth's distant primeval past – lush, silent, and haunted by clouds.

The trail ends at **Kilohana Lookout**, where the hardships of the hike evaporate before an astonishing vista encompassing

An isolated crescent of sand (opposite) punctuates the rocky headlands of the Na Pali Coast.

Wildflowers (left) compete for pollinators with color and scent. Blossoms are most abundant in late spring and early summer.

A helicopter (below) buzzes into a remote corner of Waimea Canyon, giving tourists views of places they may not be able to reach on foot.

the emerald depths of **Wainiha Valley**, broad **Hanalei Bay**, and a lei of exquisite beaches. It's scenes like these that help you understand why early Hawaiians, always attentive to the beauty of the places in which they lived, referred to Kokee as *Wao Akua* – "the mountains of the gods."

DETAILS

How to Get There

To reach Kauai, most travelers first arrive at Honolulu International Airport on the island of Oahu. Airplanes are the easiest mode of transportation among the islands, and there are frequent flights from Honolulu to Lihue, the county seat of Kauai.

When to Go

While it can rain at any time of year, winter (November to February) is generally the rainiest, most overcast season. However, some birds, especially nectar feeders, are easier to spot during this period. Temperatures range between the 60s and 80s°F (16–27°C) year-round, and are typically five to ten degrees cooler at higher altitudes and in winter. Most flowering occurs in late spring and early summer.

Getting Around

Kauai's public buses serve the island's major communities but don't travel to most trailheads. Renting a car, easily done at Lihue Airport, is the best way to reach Kauai's parks. Cars, however, can get visitors only so far; most of the island is inaccessible by road, making backpacking the best option in many regions.

INFORMATION

Hawaii Division of State Parks

3060 Eiwa Street, Room 306, Lihue, Kauai, HI 96766; tel: 808-274-3444; www.hawaii.gov/dlnr/dsp/

Hawaii Ecotourism Association

P.O. Box 61435, Honolulu, HI 96839; tel: 808-956-2866; www.planet-hawaii.com/hea

Kauai Visitors Bureau

4334 Rice Street, Suite 101, Lihue, Kauai, HI 96766; tel: 808-245-3971 or 800-262-1400; www.kauaivisitorsbureau.org

Kokee Natural History Museum

P.O. Box 100, Kekaha, Kauai, HI 96752; tel: 808-335-9975; www.aloha.net/~kokee

CAMPING

Hawaii Division of State Parks

3060 Eiwa Street, #306, Lihue, Kauai, HI 96766; tel: 808-274-3444; www.hawaii.gov/dlnr/dsp

There is camping in Kokee State Park, and backcountry camping in Waimea Canyon. Visitors must apply for permits by writing to the Division of State Parks at least six weeks in advance.

LODGING

Nearly all accommodations on Kauai are in Poipu Beach, Lihue, Wailua, and Princeville. There are only a few places to stay west of Poipu, making this town a common overnight destination for those visiting Kokee State Park and Waimea Canyon.

PRICE GUIDE – double occupancy	
$ = up to $49	$$ = $50–$99
$$$ = $100–$149	$$$$ = $150+

Gloria's Spouting Horn Bed-and-Breakfast

4464 Lawai Beach Road, Poipu, HI 96756; tel: 808-742-6995.

This bed-and-breakfast, on a secluded beach at Spouting Horn, has three guest rooms with private bathrooms and lanais just 30 feet (9m) from the surf. $$$$

Kokee Lodge

P.O. Box 819, Waimea, Kauai, HI 96796; tel: 808-335-6061.

Twelve state-run, self-contained cabins are set at an elevation of 4,000 feet (1,220m) in Kokee State Park, with views of Waimea Canyon. The cabins have stoves, refrigerators, and hot showers, and include one- and two-bedroom units. Reservations should be made four to six months in advance. $

Koloa Landing Cottages

Rural Route 1, Box 70, Koloa, HI 96756; tel: 808-742-1470 or 808-742-6436.

Up to five people can stay in these two-bedroom, two-bath units with full kitchens, in a quiet residential area near Poipu. $–$$

Poipu Kai Resort

1941 Poipu Road, Poipu-Koloa, HI 96756; tel: 808-742-6464 or 800-367-8020.

Beachfront condos and villas have queen-size beds, private bathrooms, washers and dryers, and kitchens. The resort's activity center can arrange excursions, including helicopter tours of the island. $$$–$$$$

Waimea Plantation Cottages

9400 Kaumualii Highway, #367, Waimea, Kauai, HI 96796; tel: 808-338-1625 or 800-922-7866.

Nestled in a 27-acre (11-hectare) coconut grove near Waimea Canyon, this complex has furnished cottages and a two-story, five-bedroom house that was formerly part of a sugar plantation. All units have full kitchens and bathrooms. $$$–$$$$

TOURS AND OUTFITTERS

Crane Tours

22351 Mission Circle, Chatsworth, CA 91311; tel: 818-773-4601 or 800-653-2545.

Kayaking, backpacking, and other eco-adventure tours explore the Hawaiian Islands; destinations include Waimea Canyon and the Na Pali Coast.

Hawaii Audubon Society

850 Richard Street, Suite 505, Honolulu, HI 96813; tel: 808-528-1432.

This advocacy and education group leads hiking and birding trips throughout the Hawaiian Islands.

Kauai Mountain Tours

P.O. Box 3069, Lihue, HI 96766; tel: 808-245-7224 or 800-452-1113.

Local guides take travelers to normally inaccessible backcountry areas using four-wheel-drive vans. This is the only operator licensed to run tours in Kokee State Park and the Na Pali-Kona Forest Reserve. Excursions focus on natural history, wildlife, and Hawaiian history and culture.

Na Pali Eco Adventures

P.O. Box 1017, Hanalei, Kauai, HI 96714; tel: 808-826-1913 or 808-826-6804.

This tour boat company offers excursions along the Na Pali Coast and other regions. Activities include snorkeling, whale watching, and explorations of Hawaiian history, folklore, and ecology.

Outfitters Kauai

2827A Poipu Road, Poipu Plaza, P.O. Box 1149, Poipu Beach, Kauai, HI 96756; tel: 808-742-9667 or 888-742-9887.

Visitors have the opportunity to learn about natural history, native legends, and folklore on guided kayak, hiking, and mountain-bike tours. Bicycle and kayak rentals are available.

Sierra Club Trips

Sierra Club Outing Department, 85 Second Street, Second Floor, San Francisco, CA 94105; tel: 415-775-5500.

Sierra Club trips to Kauai, led by experienced guides, include sea kayaking along the Na Pali Coast and camping in Kokee State Park.

TEOK Investigations

1770 Pe'e Road, P.O. Box 549, Poipu, Kauai, HI 96756; tel: 808-742-8305 or 888-233-8365.

TEOK offers programs throughout Kauai, including nature tours and weeklong educational trips focusing on ecology, geology, and other subjects.

Excursions

Hanalei National Wildlife Refuge

c/o Kilauea Point National Wildlife Refuge, P.O. Box 1128, Kilauea, Kauai, HI 96754-1128; tel: 808-828-1413; www.r1.fws.gov/pacific/wnwr/khanaleinwr.html

This 917-acre (371-hectare) refuge is part of a unique arrangement between the U.S. Fish and Wildlife Service and taro farmers that allows farming to coexist with wildlife habitat protection. The result is a sanctuary for nearly 50 different species of birds, including endangered Hawaiian stilts, ducks, golden plovers, tattlers, coots, and gallinules.

Na Pali Coast

Kauai Visitors Bureau, 4334 Rice Street, Suite 101, Lihue, Kauai, HI 96766; tel: 808-245-3971 or 800-262-1400; www.kauaivisitorsbureau.org

The best way to view this spectacular coastline and its sheer 2,000-foot (600-m) peaks close up is to hike the 11-mile (18-km) Kalalau Trail. Arduous climbs, dizzying drops, and crumbling footpaths mean this isn't an outing for the faint of heart, and the return trip will take at least two days. But the rewards include astonishing views along the coast and into the Hanakapiai, Hanakoa, and Kalalau Valleys, detours to enchanting, rain-forest-shrouded waterfalls, and idyllic (though perilous) beaches.

Wailua River State Park

Hawaii Division of State Parks, 3060 Eiwa Street, Room 306, Lihue, Kauai, HI 96766; tel: 808-274-3444; www.hawaii.gov/dlnr/dsp/

A fine silver thread in a dense weave of green, the Wailua is Kauai's best rafting river. Departing from just off the Kuhio Highway, kayakers can paddle and drift for hours along its tranquil waters, past lowland tropical forest, fern-fringed caves, and historic petroglyphs and *heiaus* – shrines built from piles of volcanic rock by native Hawaiians. Several walking trails are accessible from the river, including a short hike to enchanting Wailua Falls, where the river tumbles 80 feet (24m) down a sheer cliff face.

El Yunque
Puerto Rico

CHAPTER **9**

Puerto Rico's **Sierra de Luquillo** rises from the island's east end like the prow of a ship coursing through the Caribbean. And like a ship's prow, it gets a lot of moisture. Its 3,000-foot-high (900-m) ridges and peaks are drenched with as much as 200 inches (500cm) of precipitation a year, and rain falls much of the time. Even when it's not raining, the tangles of *Clusia* trees, sierra palms, bamboos, and tree ferns that overhang the trails are soaked by the mists that shroud the mountains. It might be a gloomy environment if it weren't such a lively one. Cicadas, katydids, and tiny frogs called coquis sing, spindly anolis lizards hop about, and the trees are full of birds that are clearly not put off by intermittent downpours. ◆ The Sierra de Luquillo, called **El Yunque** after a central peak, contains the last remnant of the forest **An island forest spared** that covered much of Puerto Rico when **the axe by rugged terrain and** Christopher Columbus arrived in 1493 **dense vegetation is a haven** during his second voyage to the New World. **for rare Caribbean wildlife.** A refuge for native Taino people during the colonial period, El Yunque escaped destruction because of its mountainous terrain until the Spanish government formally designated 12,000 acres (4,850 hectares) as a forest reserve in 1876. President Theodore Roosevelt included the area in the U.S. forest reserve system in 1902, and Congress established the 28,000-acre (11,330-hectare) **Caribbean National Forest** in 1935. Since then, the U.S. Forest Service has managed El Yunque mainly for recreation and watershed protection, although in the 1980s it proposed to log 5,000 acres (2,000 hectares) on the lower slopes. Opposition from conservationists prevented the logging, and the forest continues to be preserved for its ecological,

The coqui, a type of tree frog, is endemic to Puerto Rico. Thirteen species inhabit El Yunque, and one species, the burrow coqui, is found only in its cloud forest.

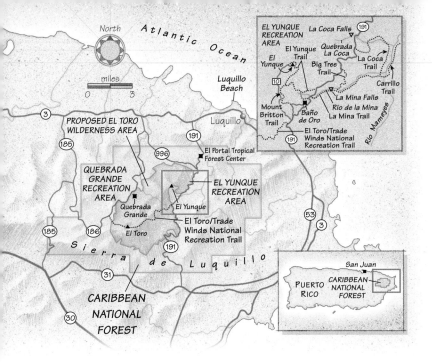

resembles Central American lowland rain forest and is named for its predominant tree, *Dacryodes excelsa*, also known as tabonuco or candlewood, a species common throughout the neotropics. Palo colorado forest occurs above 2,000 feet (600m) and is named for *Cyrilla racemiflora*, which also grows in the southeastern United States. Above 2,500 feet (760m), the sierra palm forms pure stands on unstable, shallow soils, while a gnarled elfin forest of *Clusia* and other hardy trees grows on acidic, poorly drained soils.

scientific, and recreational value. More than a million visitors a year come to walk its trails or to swim and picnic at its many breathtaking waterfalls.

Diversity and Endemism

As one of the few primary forests in the Caribbean under government protection, El Yunque is precious, and, in 1976, was among the first areas to be declared a UNESCO World Biosphere Reserve. El Yunque alone has 32 known reptile and amphibian species and 68 bird species, one of which – the elfin woods warbler – was not discovered until 1972. Many of these animals are endemic, occurring only on the island, and others are limited to the Caribbean.

Plant diversity and endemism are even greater. El Yunque has some 253 native tree species, 23 of which live nowhere else. These are found in four distinct forest types. Below 2,000 feet (600m) grows tabonuco forest, which

El Yunque's wildlife has its limits: don't expect to see monkeys or even squirrels. Generally speaking, island forests have fewer species than those on the mainland because it is difficult for land organisms to reach them, and because habitat is limited. When Columbus arrived, Puerto Rico had no native mammals except bats, although paleontologists have since found fossils of ground sloths and large rodents. (How these mammals died out is unknown. Indians may have exterminated them, although humans have inhabited the island for only a few thousand years.) Eleven bat species now inhabit El Yunque. One of them, the red fruit bat, was first identified from a museum specimen in Paris in 1813 but was thought to be extinct until biologists captured live animals in a mist net in 1965.

Although El Yunque has more than a dozen lizard species, it has only five snakes, all rare, and none poisonous to people. Even mosquitoes and other biting insects are not very abundant, although tarantulas, wasps, and scorpions are present. Aquatic life also is sparse. Only four fish species are native to El Yunque, and only two of these, American eels and gobies, are common.

A biologist (opposite, bottom) feeds an orphaned Puerto Rican parrot chick.

An elevated walkway (right) at El Portal Tropical Center introduces visitors to the forest; guided tours are also available.

La Mina Falls (below) cascades 35 feet (11m) into a plunge pool – a favorite spot for hikers to cool off.

lation to 23. Breeding picked up after the hurricane. Six pairs nested in the wild throughout the 1990s, and almost a dozen chicks were hatched each year.

You're more likely to hear the raucous calls of a Puerto Rican parrot at El Yunque than actually see one, although other endemic birds are often spotted. In fact, with the exception of the winter months, when migratory birds arrive from the north, most birds at El Yunque live only on Puerto Rico and other Caribbean islands. One of the most common endemics is the Puerto Rican tanager,

More diverse are freshwater shrimps, of which there are 10 native species.

The uniqueness of El Yunque's wildlife compensates for the lack of diversity. A number of rare, endemic species are found here, including two endangered hawk sub-species and the Puerto Rican boa, the island's largest snake. The boa can measure up to 10 feet (3m) long, but the species is shy and seldom seen. Three of the forest's 13 species of coqui frogs are classified as "sensitive."

Plain and Fancy

El Yunque's best-known rarity is the Puerto Rican parrot, a bright green bird with bluish wingtips and a red forehead. As many as one million of these parrots shared the island with endemic macaws and parakeets in 1493, but the parrot is Puerto Rico's last native member of the group, and it is on the U.S. Endangered Species list. Restricted to the Sierra de Luquillo by the 1960s, its wild population fell to 14 in 1975. Although Sierra palm and tabonuco fruits are its preferred foods, El Yunque's rain forest is not an optimum habitat for the species. Heavy rains tend to wash the parrots out of their tree-hole nests. Strenuous protection raised the wild population to about 47 in 1989, but that summer Hurricane Hugo blew down much of the forest and reduced the popu-

which sometimes approaches closely to scold intruders. It's not a particularly attractive bird. In fact, its brown plumage and white breast are rather drab compared to the gorgeous colors of many other tanagers. Another common but dull-colored endemic is the Puerto Rican bullfinch, which is black with a rufous throat and scalp.

The rare elfin woods warbler is equally drab compared to some of its relatives, with a black back and white, black-streaked breast. Even El Yunque's endemic hummingbirds – the green mango and Puerto Rican emerald – aren't showy by tropical standards. Both are mostly green, with blackish or purplish coloring on the tail. This plainness may reflect the island's relatively low level of biodiversity. Since the birds have less trouble finding mates of their own species than in the more diverse tropical mainland, bright breeding plumage isn't necessary.

There are several endemic birds that are as gaudy as any tropical species. The Puerto Rican woodpecker, for example, has a bright red breast and throat, a white rump and forehead, and a glossy black back. The Puerto Rican tody is a four-inch (10-cm) ball of feathers with a green back and head, a red throat, a white breast, and a yellow belly.

An ancient group related to kingfishers, todies occur only on Caribbean islands. Like kingfishers, they nest in burrows, usually in steep stream banks or road cuts. They feed on insects and small lizards, darting out to catch them from exposed perches.

Into the Woods

Although El Yunque has been studied intensively over the years, the difficulty of penetrating its rugged terrain and dense vegetation has left much of it shrouded in mystery. The first road across El Yunque wasn't built until the 1930s and became impass-

The Amazing Coqui

In 1979, two students working at El Yunque in the wee hours of the morning suddenly found themselves pelted by tiny frogs falling from the sky. It took researchers several years to discover what the frogs, known as coquis, were up to, but they eventually figured out what was behind the unexpected shower. Apparently, coquis climb into the forest canopy at dusk in order to feed on insects. Just before dawn, they "parachute" back to earth, where they hide in the moist leaf litter on the forest floor.

The 13 species of coquis (named for the distinctive call of certain species) found at El Yunque are unusual in another regard. Unlike most frogs, they lay their eggs on land, and their offspring skip the vulnerable tadpole stage, hatching as fully formed, though minuscule, versions of their parents. In fact, one Puerto Rican species doesn't lay eggs at all but bears live young instead. This trait may have allowed ancestral coquis to reproduce on floating mats of vegetation while they sailed from the mainland to the Caribbean islands. If so, it explains why, with one exception, coquis are the only kind of frog native to Puerto Rico.

Coquis (left) are named for the distinctive call – *ko-kee, ko-kee* – of certain species.

A ranger (opposite, top) leads a group of students on a tour of the forest.

Forest topography (opposite, bottom) ranges from gentle slopes at lower elevations to the jagged rock face of 3,533-foot (1,077-m) El Toro Peak.

The fallen blossoms of an African tulip tree (below) are strewn across a streamside boulder.

able in the 1970s because of landslides. Parts of the Forest Service's 10,000-acre (4,047-hectare) proposed **El Toro Wilderness Area** remain virtually unexplored, and this *terra incognita* has engendered tales of giant trees, lost hikers, bottomless caves, and UFOs.

Fortunately, casual visitors will have few problems seeing El Yunque. Less than an hour on good roads from San Juan, the forest has about 25 miles (40km) of well-maintained hiking trails, many of them paved as a protection against erosion.

Most trailheads are located in **El Yunque Recreation Area** on Route 191 in the center of the forest. A good choice for first-time visitors is **La Mina Trail**, where hikers can cool off under a 35-foot (11-m) waterfall at the end of a moderate one-mile (1.6-km) climb. An easy one-mile (1.6-km) loop on the **Baño de Oro** and lower **El Yunque Trails** is a pleasant introduction to the palo colorado forest and gives you the option of taking a steep, two-mile (3-km) spur to the stunted cloud forest at the 3,412-foot (1,040-m) summit of El Yunque. A far more demanding hike on **El Toro/Trade Winds National Recreation Trail** labors along ridge tops through the wild southwest

part of the forest and passes through the four main vegetation types.

El Portal Tropical Forest Center near the main entrance has a nature trail, trail maps, interpretive trail guides, interactive exhibits, and other information in English and Spanish. At the forest's west side on Route 186 is the **Quebrada Grande Recreation Area**, with a small picnic area and pleasant pools and rapids on **Quebrada Grande**.

DETAILS

How to Get There

Most visitors to Puerto Rico arrive at San Juan's Aeropuerto Internacional de Luis Muñoz Marin. Occasional flights from the United States arrive at Ponce's Aeropuerto de Mercedita on the south coast, and Aguadilla's Aeropuerto Rafael Hernández.

When to Go

El Yunque is the rainiest part of Puerto Rico, soaked by as much as 200 inches (508cm) of rain per year. The hottest and wettest months, July through October, are also hurricane season. Travelers visiting at this time are advised to check local weather broadcasts in Puerto Rico (tel: 787-253-0840); up-to-date information on Caribbean weather is also posted at www.huracan.net. Daily temperatures average 73°F (23°C) along the coast during the coolest months – January and February. The hottest months see temperatures around 80°F (27°C). Nighttime temperatures in the mountains can dip below 50°F (10°C). Park visitation is lowest from mid-April through mid-June and September to October.

Getting Around

Public transportation is not available to El Yunque; most travelers come to the reserve with a tour from San Juan. Another convenient option is renting a car in San Juan and driving 25 miles (40km) to El Yunque, an easy day trip. Cars can be rented in most major cities and resort towns along the coast.

INFORMATION

Caribbean National Forest

El Portal Tropical Forest Center, Highway 191, Kilometer 11.6, P.O. Box 490, Palmer, PR 00721; tel: 787-888-1810 or 787-888-1880; fax: 787-888-5622; www.r8web.com/caribbean

Puerto Rico Tourism Company

Paseo de la Princesa No. 2, La Princesa Building, Old San Juan, San Juan, PR 00901; tel: 787-791-2551; web: www.prtourism.com

This company is the commonwealth's official tourism bureau.

CAMPING

Only backcountry camping is allowed in the forest, and permits are required. For information, call 787-888-1880. There is also camping in the nearby beach town of Luquillo (tel: 787-721-2800).

LODGING

PRICE GUIDE – double occupancy

$ = up to $49 $$ = $50–$99

$$$ = $100–$149 $$$$ = $150+

Casa Cubuy Eco Lodge

P.O. Box 721, Río Blanco, PR 00744; tel: 787-874-6221 or 787-874-4316; e-mail: cubuy@east-net.com

This bed-and-breakfast a short walk from the national forest has 10 rooms, several with private balconies overlooking waterfalls and mountains. A special three-night package includes a guided hike and kayak excursion in nearby mangroves. $$–$$$

Casa Flamboyant

P.O. Box 175, Naguabo, PR 00718-0175; tel: 787-874-6074; e-mail: casaflam@east-net.net

This mountaintop retreat on the edge of El Yunque has a one-bedroom house and a three-bedroom house, and views from the ocean to the waterfalls. $$–$$$$

Gran Hotel El Convento

100 Calle Cristo, P.O. Box 1048, San Juan, PR 00902; tel: 787-723-9020 or 800-468-2779; fax: 787-721-2877.

Set amid the restaurant scene in Old San Juan, this restored 17th-century convent is now a luxury hotel with more than 100 rooms. $$$$

La Caleta

P.O. Box 9021747, Old San Juan Station, San Juan, PR 00902-1747; tel: 787-725-5347.

This guest house is a three-story apartment building on a quiet street in Old San Juan, with balconies overlooking La Fortaleza. The owner rents apartments to travelers planning to stay for at least a week. $$–$$$$

Numero Uno

1 Santa Ana Street, Ocean Park, San Juan, PR 00911; tel: 787-726-5010; fax: 787-727-5482; e-mail: roman@caribe.net

This guest house just east of Condado beach in Ocean Park has air-conditioned rooms with private baths, and a restaurant. $$–$$$$

Parador Martorell

6A Ocean Drive, P.O. Box 384, Luquillo, PR 00773; tel: 787-889-2710; fax: 787-889-4520.

This 11-unit inn a block from the beach has air-conditioned double rooms, some with private baths. $$

Phillips Forest Cabins

HC1, Box 4449, Naguabo, PR 00718; tel: 787-874-2138; e-mail: phillips@east-net.com

This exotic fruit farm on the south side of El Yunque, on Highway 191 above Naguabo, offers economy cabins and campsites with views of the ocean and Vieques Island. Cabins have a full-sized bed, cots, and a shared bathroom. $

TOURS AND OUTFITTERS

Aventura Tierra Adentro

272B Avenida Pinero, University Gardens, Río Piedras, PR 00927; tel: 787-766-0470; fax: 787-754-7543.

Expert guides lead natural excursions and adventures throughout Puerto Rico.

Caribbean National Forest

El Portal Tropical Forest Center,

P.O. Box 490, Palmer, PR 00721; tel: 787-888-1880; www.r8web.com/caribbean

As part of the forest's Rent-A-Ranger program, rangers take visitors on two-hour guided tours and discuss history, wildlife, and forest management.

Copladet Nature and Adventure Tours

528 Soller Street, San Juan, PR 00923; tel: 787-765-8595; e-mail: copladet@coqui.net

Group tours, custom packages, and tours for individuals include island-wide day or multiday nature and adventure trips focusing on birding, caving, hiking, horseback riding, kayaking, and rain-forest and mangrove-forest excursions.

Encantos Ecotours

P.O. Box 619, Guaynabo, PR 00970-0619; tel: 787-272-0005; fax: 787-789-1730; e-mail: ecotours@caribe.net

Encantos's nature-oriented group tours and biking, rafting, and kayaking excursions cover the entire island. Equipment rentals are available.

Northwestern Land Tours

P.O. Box 215, Angeles, PR 00611; tel: 787-374-0783 or 787-894-7804.

Day trips visit Parque Ceremonial Indigena, Guanica Forest, El Yunque, Ponce, Río Camuy Caves, and other locations.

Tropix Wellness Tours

P.O. Box 13294, Santurce, PR 00908; tel: 787-268-2173; fax: 787-268-1722; e-mail: tropix@msn.com

Tropix specializes in tailor-made daylong or multiday adventure tours to places such as El Yunque, Culebra, Vieques, and Guanica Forest. Activities include caving, birding, biking, hiking, kayaking, rafting, and sailing.

Victor Emanuel Nature Tours

P.O. Box 33008, Austin, TX 78764; tel: 800-328-8368; fax: 512-328-2919.

Bird-watching tours are a specialty, and naturalists lead trips to many Caribbean destinations.

Excursions

Cabezas de San Juan Nature Reserve

Fideicomiso de Conservation de Puerto Rico, P.O. Box 9023554, San Juan, PR 00902; tel: 787-722-5882 or 787-860-2560.

This 316-acre (128-hectare) reserve on the island's northeast tip encompasses mangroves, coral reefs, lagoons, savannas, and a dry deciduous forest. Reservations are required to visit the reserve, where a trolley provides guided tours. A visitor center, housed in a 19th-century lighthouse, has exhibits, aquariums, and an observation deck. Piñones Forest Reserve, just east of San Juan, has marshes, lagoons, and Puerto Rico's largest mangrove forest, but no visitor facilities.

Río Camuy Cave Park

Puerto Rico Tourism Company, Paseo de la Princesa No. 2, La Princesa Building, Old San Juan, San Juan, PR, 00901; tel: 787-791-2551; www.prtourism.com

One of the world's most extensive cave networks is found at Río Camuy Cave Park, a 268-acre (109-hectare) reserve a few miles northwest of Caguana. Much of western Puerto Rico is a karst landscape where surface water escapes into highly soluble limestone bedrock, forming sinkholes, underground rivers, and some 220 caves. Explorers found a new species of blind fish in the Río Camuy Cave in the 1950s. The subterranean river here is among the world's largest. The park operates guided cave tours.

Virgin Islands National Park

P.O. Box 710, St. Thomas, VI 00831; tel: 340-776-6201; www.nps.gov/viis/

Tropical forest caps 1,277-foot (389-m) Bordeaux Mountain on St. John, a volcanic island ringed by white beaches and coral reefs. Nourished by about 50 inches (125 cm) of rain a year, the forest canopy can exceed a height of 75 feet (23m), with such trees as kapok, mango, sandbox, strangler fig, and genip. Shade-tolerant wild coffee, teyer palm, and lime trees fill in the subcanopy. Hiking trails and picturesque beaches are plentiful, and since more than a third of the park is underwater, visitors find abundant opportunities for scuba diving and snorkeling.

Cockscomb Basin Wildlife Sanctuary

Belize

CHAPTER **10**

ew things send chills up the spine like the sight of jaguar prints pressed into the mud along a jungle trail. Not only is the jaguar – known locally as *el tigre*, or the tiger – the largest cat of the Americas, it is one of the most endangered. Only a few hundred remain in Central America, and nowhere is the population denser than in the **Cockscomb Basin Wildlife Sanctuary** of southern Belize. ◆ The name jaguar comes from an Indian word, *yaguara*, which means "he who kills with one leap." It's not the leaping that proves fatal, however, so much as the stout canine teeth that pierce the skull or snap the neck of its prey. Fortunately, these stealthy hunters aren't known to fancy humans, though it's not recommended that visitors wander around the sanctuary dressed as armadillos, one of the cats' favorite foods. They also prey on peccaries, deer, and tapirs but will eat just about anything they can catch, including an occasional fish, which they snatch from the water with surprising skill. ◆ The sanctuary is set in the **Cockscomb Range** of the **Maya Mountains** and encompasses **Victoria Peak**, which, at 3,675 feet (1,120m), was recently dethroned as Belize's tallest summit when a nearby crest was found to be a few meters higher. The mountains surround a geological bowl, or basin, created when soft volcanic deposits eroded away, exposing the harder rock below. The result is a craterlike depression filled with steamy jungle foliage hemmed in on three sides by thickly forested sawtooth peaks. ◆ In all likelihood, the first humans to see Cockscomb Basin were the Maya. They knew the jaguar as *balam*, a lord of the underworld linked to the night and

The New World's largest cat slips undetected through the night in a remote mountain sanctuary rich with tropical wildlife.

Jaguars are solitary creatures; males and females are found together only during the breeding season. Cubs stay with their mothers for about two years before establishing their own territory.

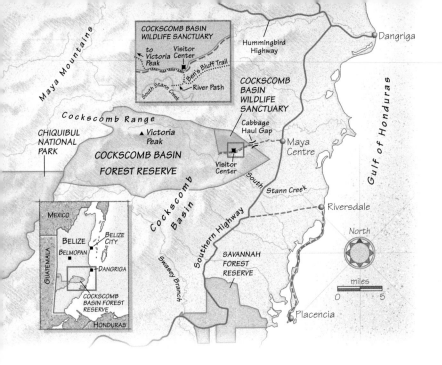

and now encompasses more than 100,000 acres (40,500 hectares).

A First Look

Belize has few roads and Cockscomb Basin is easy to find along the Southern Highway, a one- to two-hour drive from the funky beach town of **Placencia**, depending on the season. A seven-mile (11-km) dirt road cuts through the forest from the village of **Maya Centre** and leads into the sanctuary. A four-wheel-drive vehicle is highly recommended, especially during the rainy season (June to January), when southern Belize is doused with 100 to 180 inches (250–460cm) of rain. The downpours are torrential but rarely last for more than a few hours.

The road crosses two streams and labors up **Cabbage Haul Gap**. Animals use the track more often than people, and it's a great place to start watching for wildlife. It's not unusual to spot keel-billed toucans (Belize's national bird) steering a zigzag course from one patch of jungle to another. Back on earth, lizards dart away from vehicles into the safety of the ground cover. Iguanas, long part of the local diet (they're referred to as "bamboo chickens"), and basilisk lizards are frequently spotted here. The basilisk's ability to rear up on its hind legs and run across the surface of water has led to a colorful nickname: the Jesus Christ lizard.

The visitor center is built on the site of an abandoned logging camp and offers a campground and small museum. The trail system here, maintained by the Belize Audubon Society, is the best in the country. A dozen trails begin at the center and con-nect with other paths that lead through the sanctuary's varied habitats. Hikes range from an easy one-hour jaunt to a strenuous three-day trek to Victoria Peak. The head-

hunting. The Maya built several ceremonial sites in the basin, now overgrown and as much a part of the jungle as their sacred cats.

Next to trek into the basin were loggers greedy for the stands of cedar and mahogany. They cut trees and floated them down the same rivers where modern ecotourists spy otters and Baird's tapirs, the largest terrestrial animal in Latin America, often weighing more than 600 pounds (270kg). Along with loggers came hunters. The jaguar's golden coat, patterned with the dark rosettes that provide such effective camouflage in the sun-dappled forest, was highly coveted by fur fanciers.

A groundbreaking study of the big cats led to the declaration of a no-hunting zone in the basin in 1984, followed by the creation of the world's first jaguar refuge in 1986. The sanctuary was expanded several years later

waters of two major water-ways, **South Stann Creek** and the **Swasey Branch**, rise in the basin, and streams are unavoidable. Cool, clear waterfalls and swimming holes are a welcome relief after slogging through the shirt-soaking humidity of the lowland forest or getting fried under the tropical sun on exposed hillsides.

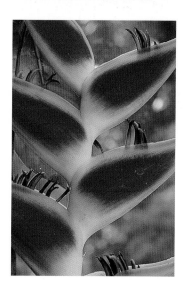

The Baird's tapir (opposite, bottom) resembles a pig but is more closely related to horses and rhinos.

Heliconia (left) adds a dash of vivid color to the relentless green of the understory.

The keel-billed toucan (below) feeds mostly on fruit but will sometimes eat insects, snakes, or lizards.

Ben's Bluff is the best trail for visitors to get an overall impression of the basin. It climbs up a forested ridge to an overlook used by scientists to track radio-tagged jaguars. The sanctuary sprawls magnificently below. Much of the lush broadleaf forest presents a solid, verdant wall of green broken only by splashes of living color – the bright orange and yellow of heliconia, the iridescent blue of butterflies, the delicate palette of a hundred species of orchid.

The canopy ranges from a height of more than 100 feet (30m) in stands of old-growth forest to less than 50 feet (15m) in patches of secondary growth left in the wake of loggers and tropical storms. Tree ferns lend a Jurassic feel to the hillsides, while the giants of the forest, gray-barked ceiba, known to the Maya as the "tree of the gods," tower over the basin floor.

The reintroduction of black howler monkeys to Cockscomb is a great success story and a prize for wildlife viewers … and listeners. The basin's original monkey troops were lost to hurricanes and disease, so several animals were transplanted from the Community Baboon Sanctuary (howlers were traditionally misnamed baboons) outside Belize City.

Bird-watching at Cockscomb (left) is superb; 290 species have been recorded in the sanctuary.

Black howler monkeys (bottom) are more often heard than seen; their piercing calls are used for communication and to establish territory.

Kinkajous (right) reside in the canopy and are active at night.

Howlers move through the jungle canopy and prefer to stay near water. The best chance to see them is when they stop to feed on wild fruits in the trees along the **River Path Trail**. If it rains, the monkeys begin to howl – a deep-throated roar that can be heard as far away as two miles (3km).

Nighttime is the Right Time

The most productive times to view wildlife are dawn, late afternoon, and, considering the number of nocturnal species, at night. It's virtually impossible to have a full experience of Cockscomb without spending at least one night under mosquito netting.

Morning begins with a "dawn chorus" of monkey howls and flights of brilliant tropical birds. Scarlet macaws are being spotted with increased frequency in the basin. These brilliant red-and-blue birds can be seen over clearings as they fly from their nighttime roosts into the forest to feed on fruit.

At dusk, bats drop from

the trees and join the nocturnal hunt, and tree frogs sing a persistent chorus. Follow their peeps into the jungle and you'll find these red-eyed amphibians clinging to leaves in the underbrush, where they call for mates and hunt for insects. To see just how varied their menu is, illuminate a white towel with a lantern or flashlight. It will soon be crawling with all manner of alien-looking bugs.

Night is also a good time to see mammals. Petite, rabbit-faced rodents called agoutis tiptoe around the forest litter, ever alert for predators like ocelot and margay, both small spotted cats. Shine a flashlight into the trees and you may see a kinkajou – a relative of the raccoon – hanging from its prehensile tail, or a weasel-like tayra patrolling for rodents, birds, fruit, or honey.

And the jaguars? Chances are that paw prints and claw marks are all that you'll see of "he who kills with one leap." But the big cats know you're there. You may sense their presence, prowling nearby in the jungle, safe from hunters and those that would destroy their habitat. And that is good enough.

TRAVEL TIPS

DETAILS

How to Get There

Travelers to Belize fly to Phillip Goldson International Airport in Belize City, where many tour operators provide flights or shuttle service to hotels and jungle lodges. Cockscomb Basin is in the Stann Creek District, accessible by road from the Southern Highway at Maya Centre, 25 miles (40 km) south of Dangriga, or from Placencia.

When to Go

The dry season extends from February to May. Rainfall in the wet season, June through January, ranges from 100 to 180 inches (250–460cm). Hurricanes are a possibility between June and November. December and January are the coolest months, though the temperature rarely falls below 55°F (13°C) at night. Coastal temperatures usually reach 96°F (36°C), and it can be much hotter inland.

Getting Around

Travelers have several transportation options, including plentiful buses and domestic planes. For instance, a Cockscomb-bound traveler can take a 20-minute plane ride from Belize City to Dangriga, and then a bus from Dangriga to the preserve (about an hour). Renting a car is possible in Belize City but difficult elsewhere. This is also an expensive option, and many of the roads in Belize are unpaved, creating problems in the rainy season.

INFORMATION

Belize Audubon Society

P.O. Box 1001, 12 Fort Street, Belize City, Belize; tel: 501-2-35004; fax: 501-2-34985; e-mail: base@btl.net; www.belizeaudubon.org

Belize Tourism Board

New Central Bank Building, Level 2, Gabourel Lane, P.O. Box 325, Belize City, Belize; tel: 501-2-31913 or 800-624-0686; fax: 501-2-31943; e-mail: info@travel-belize.org; www.travelbelize.org

CAMPING

Cockscomb Basin

Belize Audubon Society, P.O. Box 1001, 12 Fort Street, Belize City, Belize; tel: 501-2-35004; fax: 501-2-34985; e-mail: base@btl.net; www.belizeaudubon.org

There is a campground in the preserve; overnight visitors can also stay in cabins.

LODGING

PRICE GUIDE – double occupancy

$ = up to $49 $$ = $50–$99

$$$ = $100–$149 $$$$ = $150+

Belize Audubon Society

P.O. Box 1001, 12 Fort Street, Belize City, Belize; tel: 501-2-35004; fax: 501-2-34985; e-mail: base@btl.net; www.belizeaudubon.org

Most people who stay at the reserve sleep in dorms or a guest house (used mostly by groups) run by the Belize Audubon Society. Each dormitory room has three bunk beds. There's no food service, but visitors can prepare meals in the house's communal kitchen. Reservations are advisable. $

Bluefields Hotel

15 Mahogany Street, P.O. Box 21, Dangriga, Belize; tel. 800-798-1558 or 501-5-22165; fax: 501-5-22296.

This hotel has 10 rooms with private baths and hot water, a restaurant, and a staff that can arrange a variety of tours in the area, including visits to Cockscomb Basin. $–$$

Jaguar Reef Lodge

3512 Plymouth Road, Victoria, BC V8P 4X4, Canada; tel: 501-2-12041 or 800-289-5756; e-mail: jaguarreef@btl.net

Situated on the coast near Hopkins between the barrier reef and Cockscomb Basin, this secluded resort has 14 rooms in seven cottages, offers use of sea kayaks and mountain bikes, and organizes Cockscomb excursions, river and reef trips, and hiking at Antelope or Hummingbird Falls. $$$–$$$$

Nu'uk Che'il Cottages

P.O. Box 126, Dangriga, Belize; tel/fax: 501-5-12021.

Maya Indians run cottages and a restaurant in the village of Maya Centre, the closest town to the reserve. Transport to and tours of the reserve can be arranged for individuals and groups. One of the owners served as the sanctuary's director for many years and knows the flora and fauna well. $

Pelican Beach Resort

P.O. Box 14, Dangriga, Belize; tel: 501-5-22044; fax: 501-5-22570; e-mail: pelicanbeach@alt.net

This seafront resort has 20 rooms with bathtubs and hot water. The staff offers boat trips, arranges day tours of Cockscomb, and can set guests up with a driver to take them to the sanctuary. Stays at a nearby reef can be arranged. $$–$$$$

Ransom's Seaside Garden Cabanas

P.O. Box 114, Dangriga, Belize; tel: 501-5-22889; fax: 501-5-22038; e-mail: cabanabelize@hotmail.com

This resort in the village of Hopkins offers two-room units with libraries, full kitchens, bathrooms, and the use of bicycles and kayaks. $

TOURS AND OUTFITTERS

In addition to the following companies, guides in Maya Centre, a village just outside the reserve, can be hired by travelers going to Cockscomb.

Discovery Expeditions

126 Freetown Road, P.O Box 1217, Belize City, Belize; tel: 501-2-30748, 501-2-30749, or 501-2-31063; fax: 501-2-30750 or 501-2-30263; e-mail: info@discoverybelize.com

Tours of the rain forest, reef, and other natural areas throughout Belize are available in half-day to multiday adventures, including an eight-day natural history tour of the country.

Dolphin Bay Travel

P.O. Box 8, Front Street, Caye Caulker, Belize; tel/fax: 501-2-22214; e-mail: dolphinbay@btl.net

Dolphin Bay offers travel services for individuals and operates group tours and packages throughout Belize that include scuba diving and rain-forest excursions.

International Expeditions

One Environs Park, Helena, AL 35080; tel: 800-633-4734; e-mail: nature@ietravel.com

Trips emphasizing wildlife watching and natural history include eight- to 14-day "Rain Forests, Reefs, and Ruins" adventures in Belize and visits to Tikal.

Island Expeditions

368-916 West Broadway, Vancouver, BC V5Z 1K7, Canada; tel: 800-667-1630 or 604-452-3212; fax: 604-452-3433; e-mail: info@islandexpeditions.com

Travelers can choose from a range of adventure and natural history tours that feature small groups, involve local communities, and generate funds that support conservation organizations.

Magnum Belize

P.O. Box 1560, Detroit Lakes, MN 56502; tel: 800-447-2931 or 218-847-3012; fax: 218-847-0334; e-mail: information@magnumbelize.com

Diving, fishing, and excursions to the rain forest and to Mayan ruins are offered by this specialist.

Excursions

Altun Ha

Belize Tourism Board, New Central Bank Building, Level 2, Gabourel Lane, P.O. Box 325, Belize City, Belize; tel: 501-2-31913 or 800-624-0686; fax: 501-2-31943; e-mail: info@travelbelize.org; www.travelbelize.org

About 31 miles (50km) north of Belize City lie the ruins of Altun Ha, once a highly developed Maya ceremonial center devoted to worshiping the Sun God. The name "Altun Ha" means "stone water" – a reference to the nearby reservoir dammed for irrigation. One of the most remarkable treasures found in the Maya world – a huge jade replica of the Sun God's head – was discovered in a tomb here. Altun Ha's temples are clustered around two main plazas. The site is also a good place to spot colorful birds such as green Aztec parakeets.

Ambergris Caye

Belize Tourism Board, New Central Bank Building, Level 2, Gabourel Lane, P.O. Box 325, Belize City, Belize; tel: 501-2-31913 or 800-624-0686; fax: 501-2-31943; e-mail: info@travelbelize.org; www.travelbelize.org

A southern extension of Mexico's limestone Yucatán coast, Ambergris Caye is a leading destination for Belize-bound travelers seeking a beachfront idyll. The diving here is legendary, and dive instruction can be quite affordable. Snorkeling is even less expensive, and given the shallow waters around much of the caye, it can be just as exciting. Most visitors arrive in San Pedro, an old fishing village, by boat or plane. It's a quick hop from Belize City – about 15 minutes by air or as little as an hour by boat.

Guanacaste National Park

Belize Tourism Board, New Central Bank Building, Level 2, Gabourel Lane, P.O. Box 325, Belize City, Belize; tel: 501-2-31913 or 800-624-0686; fax: 501-2-31943; e-mail: info@travelbelize.org; www.travelbelize.org

There's only one mature guanacaste tree in central Belize's Guanacaste National Park, but it's quite a sight. Towering 131 feet (40m) above the jungle floor, the tree supports about three dozen plant species – including orchids, bromeliads, and strangler figs – that cling to its trunk and branches. Not many mature guanacaste trees remain, because they've been felled en masse for their water-resistant bark, which is ideal for building dugout canoes. The park's solitary guanacaste managed to avoid the ax because its trunk is split near the base, and thus not very suitable for lumber. Also in this accessible 52-acre (21-hectare) park: young mahogany trees, cohune palms with hanging clusters of red fruit, and more than 50 species of birds.

Monteverde
Cloud Forest
Biological Reserve
Costa Rica

CHAPTER 11

T here is an enchanted quality to **Monteverde**, with its pastures and chaletlike houses tucked away in one of the world's richest cloud forests. Although only a two-hour drive from the Inter-American Highway, it seems a world apart, veiled in mists and gentle showers. Walking its trails is like entering a not-quite-real world of brightly colored birds and butterflies. The slopes are cloaked in a thousand shades of green; the air resounds with strange cries. ◆ **Monteverde Cloud Forest Biological Reserve** straddles the **Cordillera de Tilarán**, the mountainous spine of Costa Rica, with the rain forests of the Caribbean slope to the east and the savannas and dry forests of the Pacific plain to the west. Elevation in the reserve ranges from more than 6,000 feet (1,828m) on the peaks to less than 3,000 feet (900m) in the **Peñas Blancas Valley**. Moist Caribbean trade winds unburden themselves as they climb the ridge, dousing the reserve with about 96 inches (244cm) of precipitation a year. Most falls during the May to October rainy season, but mist and showers keep the forest dripping year-round and foster an extraordinary profusion of plant life, including more than 500 kinds of trees, 300 types of orchids, and 200 kinds of ferns. ◆ The Cordillera de Tilarán was virtually uninhabited in the early 1950s when Quakers from the United States moved into the area and established dairy farms. They set aside the slopes above their farms as *bosque eterno*, eternal forest, to protect the watershed. In the 1970s, the Tropical Science Center in San José, Costa Rica's capital, began acquiring the land that would become the reserve. A local organization, the Monteverde Conservation League, joined the effort

> **Swirling mists shroud a mountain forest inhabited by a profusion of living things, including a stellar checklist of tropical birds.**

A clear day, a rarity at mist-shrouded Monteverde, affords magnificent views of the cloud forest from a ridgeline trail. The reserve sits astride the Continental Divide.

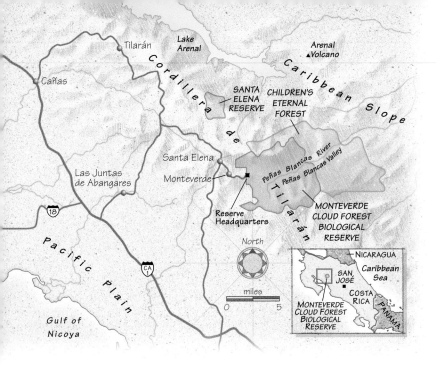

uplifted tails as they file through the undergrowth. The piglike tapir – actually a distant relative of the horse and rhinoceros – is occasionally seen browsing on foliage around dusk, and its big, three-toed tracks are often found around pools and streams. Sloths can be seen hanging upside-down in the treetops, though their shaggy, greenish coat (the color is caused by algae that grows on their fur) and slow-motion lifestyle make them hard to spot. Consider yourself lucky if you encounter one on the ground; they come down only about once a week to urinate and defecate at the base of trees. Five species of cats – jaguars, pumas, margays, ocelots, and jaguarundis – are also present but seldom seen.

Bizarre and Beautiful

The mammal population is dwarfed by the number and diversity of birds. Nearly 400 species have been recorded in the reserve,

in the 1980s when deforestation threatened the Peñas Blancas Valley. With the help of numerous other groups and individuals, the two organizations assembled the roughly 46 square miles (119 sq km) of protected land in the reserve today. A parcel of about the same size on the east side, the Children's Eternal Forest, was purchased with donations from schoolchildren all over the world.

The range of elevation encompassed by the reserve sustains a wide variety of animals, many of which move up and down the mountain slopes on seasonal migrations. Among the larger mammals are three types of monkeys – white-faced capuchin, spider, and howler – which inhabit both the lowlands and the much cooler Tilarán crest. Bands of coati – cousins of the raccoon – are common, though you're likely to spot only their

The bright colors of an orchid (top) and climbing lily (bottom) attract animals that the plants depend on for pollination and seed dispersal.

but none is more sought after than the resplendent quetzal. Considered sacred by the ancient Maya, male quetzals have an iridescent green body, a bright crimson breast, a helmetlike crest, and extravagant plumes that grow as much as 18 inches (46cm) past their tail feathers. Quetzals feed on fruits and insects, and nest in cavities that both males and females peck into decaying tree trunks. They usually stay in the canopy, so observers hear their cackling and cooing more often than they see them, although groups of birds are sometimes spotted in summer feeding in fruit trees on the edge of pastures. Another good time to see them is the March to June breeding season, when they nest in the upper parts of the refuge. Many disperse to lower elevations at other times of the year.

Another species on every birder's wish list is the three-wattled bellbird, a crow-sized member of the cotinga family with a brilliant white head, a dark rufous body, and three black, wormlike wattles hanging from its beak. Males occupy perches above the forest canopy during the spring breeding season and repeat a loud, ringing call – *QUANG! treeeee, QUANG! treeeee.*

Monteverde also sustains some 30 hummingbird species, many of which frequent feeders at the information center. The birds range in size from the six-inch-long (15-cm) violet sabrewing to the two-and-a-half-inch (6.4-cm) snowcap, and vary in coloration from the multihued fiery-throated hummingbird to the grayish-brown long-tailed hermit. All feed on flower nectar and tiny insects, but their methods of feeding are as distinct as their plumage. Drab species such as hermits live under the forest canopy, moving about nomadically and feeding on scattered

The curved claws of a three-toed sloth (opposite, right) are used to hang upside down from branches.

The resplendent quetzal (left), a member of the trogon family, is prized for its iridescent colors and luxuriant green plumes.

A purple-throated mountain gem (bottom) feeds on the nectar of an epiphytic orchid.

flowers. Brightly colored birds live above the canopy or in other open spaces and feed on masses of sunlit flowers, often guarding their territory with surprising vigor.

Hummingbird bills are adapted to the flowers on which the birds feed. The curved bill of the white-tipped sicklebill is suited for the hanging flowers of understory heliconias, while the long, straight bill of the plain-capped starthroat is designed to reach into the tubular corollas of flowers in the canopy. Whatever their habits, all hummingbirds are incessant eaters, consuming nearly their own weight in food every day.

Another small active bird is the chickadee-sized long-tailed manakin, known locally as *el toledo*. Males of the species have red crests, light blue backs, and two thin tail feathers that are longer than their bodies. During the April to July breeding season, they can be observed performing

elaborate dances in duos or trios and whistling their signature call – *to-le-do* – in unison. When one of the drab greenish females appears, the male with the finest plumage goes away to mate with her,

An eyelash viper (left) waits patiently for a meal; its yellow scales lure prey attracted to bright colors.

A stream (bottom) tumbles through the forest. Waterways are good places to spot wildlife.

then rejoins his dancing partners, leaving the female to nest by herself. *Toledos* are common west of the Tilarán crest and are relatively easy to find and observe. Most are too absorbed in their own behavior to notice a reasonably quiet audience.

With a little luck and perseverance, visitors will catch a glimpse of rarer birds in the forests of the Caribbean slope. The bare-necked umbrellabird is a large, glossy black cotinga named for the umbrella-shaped crest atop its head. The male erects its crest and inflates a bright red throat sac during its mating display. It also sings a rather bizarre song that sounds something like a heavy mallet striking an oil drum. Umbrellabirds prefer to perch in foliage and, given their peculiar vocal talents, are more often heard than seen.

Somewhat more visible is the sunbittern,

a heron-sized waterbird that forages on the banks of the **Peñas Blancas River**. Its brownish plumage seems unremarkable until it opens its wings to display vivid sunburst markings of orange, yellow, and black. This unusual behavior is thought to be a show of aggression designed to startle predators and rivals.

Hit the Trail

The reserve's trail system is extensive, and it would take days to walk it all. Most visitors stay on the trails near reserve headquarters in an area known as the **Triangle**. These include self-guiding nature trails interpreting plants, geology, and other natural features. The trails pass through cloud forest dense with tree ferns and a great variety of epiphytes as well as through the dwarf

The Mystery of the Golden Toad

While conducting research at Monteverde in 1967, herpetologist Jay M. Savage documented a spectacular new amphibian species, the golden toad, males of which were such a brilliant orange-gold that they looked as if "someone had dipped the examples in enamel paint." The toads were endemic to a small part of the reserve, where they spent most of their lives underground, emerging to breed for only a few weeks in March. The species, *Bufo periglenes*, quickly became a symbol of Monteverde, and as late as 1987 hundreds appeared "like jewels on the forest floor" during their brief but frenetic breeding season.

Then, as suddenly as they were discovered, they disappeared. Despite much searching, only 10 golden toads were observed in 1988, and only one the following year. Not a single toad has been seen since, and scientists are at a loss to explain why.

One theory is that a reduction of moisture caused by an increase in El Niño events (which, in turn, may be related to global warming) stressed the toads beyond their ability to adapt. The exact reason for their disappearance remains elusive, however, although it's clear that the golden toad is just a small part of a worldwide decline of amphibian species that some scientists believe is an early warning of global climate change.

Golden toads (below), now thought to be extinct, emerged from their underground burrows for only a few weeks to mate.

A giant silkmoth (bottom), *Rothschildia orizaba*, is one of more than 500 butterfly and moth species that have been found at the reserve.

vegetation of elfin forest growing in the thin soil of exposed ridge tops.

Farther east, trails drop toward the warmer lowland forests of the Peñas Blancas Valley. The area was partly deforested by squatters but has been recovering since the 1970s. Trails are less clearly marked away from headquarters, so hikers should exercise caution. Getting lost is easy in the steep, heavily overgrown terrain, and poisonous snakes like the fer-de-lance (a large pit viper, known as *el terciopelo*) are found at lower elevations. First-time visitors are advised to hire a private guide or join one of the morning or evening tours. No more than 100 visitors are admitted to the park each day, so plan on getting an early start, particularly during the peak season, February through May.

Interpretation is limited within the reserve, but several attractions around the nearby village of Santa Elena will help put the area's natural history into perspective. Visit the **Serpentario Monteverde** (506-645-5238) for a closer look at the amphibians and reptiles – including

about 20 species of snakes – that inhabit the forest. **El Jardin de las Mariposas** (506-645-5512), or the **Butterfly Garden**, offers tours of greenhouses and a netted garden where about 40 of the area's more than 500 butterfly species are raised and studied. Travelers with a head for heights can hike half a mile (800m) of suspension bridges at the **Sky Walk** (506-645-5238) in **Santa Elena Reserve** or glide through the treetops on zip wires on a **Canopy Tour** (506-645-5243). The latter is designed more for thrills than serious wildlife watching but will certainly give you a new perspective on life in the canopy.

TRAVEL TIPS

DETAILS

How to Get There

About 20 airlines have regular flights to Costa Rica, most of which land at Juan Santamaría International Airport in San José. The Daniel Oduber International Airport in Guanacaste is a good entry point for travelers going to the northwest provinces.

When to Go

Temperatures in the cloud forest range between 55°F and 75°F (13–24°C). Rainfall averages 97 inches (246cm) a year, and most of it falls between June and November. December to April is drier, but mist is common and rain is always possible. Crowds are much thinner during the wet season, making it a good time for those seeking solitude – especially considering that the reserve limits entry to 100 people a day. The best times to see birds are early morning and late afternoon.

Getting Around

Public buses run from San José to Monteverde. Rental cars are available in San José, but many of the roads along the route to Monteverde (and elsewhere) are unpaved. Four-wheel-drive vehicles are highly recommended, especially in the wet season when flooding can turn dirt roads into a quagmire. Most lodges and hotels in Santa Elena, 3.7 miles (6km) from Monteverde, can arrange transportation to the reserve.

INFORMATION

Costa Rica National Tourist Bureau

P.O. Box 12766-1000, San José, Costa Rica; tel: 800-343-6332; www.costarica.com

Monteverde Cloud Forest Biological Reserve

Apartado 55-5655, Monteverde, Puntarenas, Costa Rica; tel: 506-645-5122; fax: 506- 645-5034.

Monteverde Cloud Forest Ecological Center Foundation

Apartado 75, Santa Elena 5655, Monteverde, Costa Rica; tel: 506-645-5390; fax: 506-645-5014.

Monteverde Conservation League

Apartado 10165, San José 1000, Monteverde, Costa Rica; tel: 506-645-2953; fax: 506-645-1104.

CAMPING

Travelers can camp on the grounds of several hotels in nearby Santa Elena, including Albergue Arco Iris (tel: 506-645-5067) and Hotel Fonda Vela (tel: 506-257-1413). Hikers can also stay at any of the three shelters in Monteverde but should make reservations in advance by calling 506-645-5212.

LODGING

It is advisable to book accommodations in advance during the dry season (December to April), the reserve's busiest period.

PRICE GUIDE – double occupancy

$ = up to $49	$$ = $50–$99
$$$ = $100–$149	$$$$ = $150+

Albergue Arco Iris

Apartado 003-5655, Santa Elena de Monteverde, Costa Rica; tel: 506-645-5067; fax: 506-645-5022.

This hillside property has seven hotel rooms and six cabins with private bathrooms. Guests can rent horses. $–$$

Cloud Forest Lodge

Apartado 531-1000, San José, Costa Rica; tel: 506-645-5058; fax: 506-645-5168; e-mail: cloudforest@catours.co.cr

Secluded on a 25-acre (10-hectare) private cloud forest reserve near Santa Elena, this lodge has 18 cabins with bathrooms, forest trails, and a canopy tour. $$

Hotel Belmar

Apartado 17-5655, Monteverde, Costa Rica; tel: 506-645-5201; fax: 506-645-5135; e-mail: belmar@sol.racsa.co.cr

This Swiss-style hotel in the mountains adjacent to the reserve has great views over the valley. Thirty-four rooms have private baths and hot water. Guided tours of the reserve are available as part of a special package. $$–$$$

Hotel El Establo

Apartado 549, San Pedro 20501, Costa Rica; tel: 506-645-5033 or 506-645-5110; fax: 506-645-5041.

Situated on a private 120-acre (49-hectare) farm, El Establo has 20 rooms, each with a double and single bed, a bathroom with hot water, and wraparound windows. There is also a stable where guests can rent horses. $$

Monteverde Cloud Forest Biological Reserve Field Station

Apartado 55-5655, Monteverde, Puntarenas, Costa Rica; tel: 506-645-5276.

The field station can accommodate up to 30 people in a basic dormitory-style lodging with kitchens. $

Monteverde Lodge

Apartado 6941, San José 1000, Costa Rica; tel: 506-257-0766; fax: 506-257-1665.

This lodge is a favorite of birders and nature groups, as it offers three-day packages with personal guides and transfers from San José. Rooms have two double beds and private bathrooms. $$–$$$$

Sapo Dorado

Apartado 9-5655, Monteverde, Costa Rica; tel: 506-645-5010; fax: 506-645-5180; e-mail: elsapo@sol.racsa.co.cr

Ten duplex cabins spread out on a hill have private bathrooms, two queen beds, private balconies, and great views. The restaurant is acclaimed for its vegetarian meals. $$

TOURS AND OUTFITTERS

Adventure Center

1311 63rd Street, Emeryville, CA 94608; tel: 510-654-1879; fax: 510-654-4200; e-mail: crh@adventure-center.com

A 16-day tour visits Monteverde and several other parks, and offers whitewater rafting, hiking, bird-watching, and more.

Costa Rica Expeditions

Apartado 6941-1000, San José, Costa Rica; tel: 506-257-0766; fax: 506-257-1665; e-mail: crexped@sol.racsa.co.cr

The operators of Monteverde Lodge arrange rafting, natural history trips, and other tours.

Costa Rica Experts

3166 North Lincoln Avenue, Suite 424, Chicago, IL 60657; tel: 800-827-9046 or 773-935-1009; fax: 773-935-9252; e-mail: crexpert@ris.net

This Costa Rica specialist offers extensive special-interest packages, including a three-day "Monteverde Cloud Forest Odyssey" and an eight-day trip to a variety of natural areas.

International Expeditions

One Environs Park, Helena, AL 35080; tel: 800-633-4734; e-mail: nature@ietravel.com

The eight-day "Volcanoes, Rivers, and Rain Forests" tour is a sampler of Costa Rica's natural wonders, including two nights at Monteverde.

Wilderness Travel

1102 Ninth Street; Berkeley, CA 94710; tel: 510-558-2488; fax: 510-558-2489; e-mail: info@wildernesstravel.com

A 14-day "Costa Rica Wildlife" package visits Monteverde, Corcovado National Park, and Tortuguero National Park. In Monteverde, visitors stay at Monteverde Lodge and hike in search of wildlife.

Excursions

Corcovado National Park

Servicio de Parques Nacionales, Calle 25 between Avenidas 8 and 10, San José, Costa Rica; tel: 506-257-0922 or 506-259-8635.

At this 133,530-acre (54,035-hectare) national park on the Osa Peninsula, you can bathe in warm ocean waters where sea turtles glide over coral reefs, while watching the country's largest colony of scarlet macaws feed in adjacent almond trees, then hike through mangroves and holillo (palm) forest to cloud forest of oaks and ferns. These varied habitats harbor 500 tree species, 140 types of mammals, 117 reptile species, and 367 species of birds ranging from scarlet tanagers to tovi parakeets and the majestic harpy eagle.

La Selva Biological Station

Organization for Tropical Studies, Apartado 676-5050, San Pedro, Costa Rica; tel: 506-240-6696 (in San José), 506-710-1515 or 506-716-6987 (on site).

Set on the Atlantic coastal plain about 50 miles (80km) from Monteverde, this area has been recognized by the U.S. National Academy of Sciences as one of the world's premier sites for tropical rain-forest research. Dozens of miles of well-maintained trails lead through the 3,800-acre (1,538-hectare) reserve and adjacent 110,000-acre (44,515-hectare) Braulio Carrillo National Park, making it an incomparable place to experience rain-forest wildlife.

Rincon de la Vieja National Park

Servicio de Parques Nacionales, Calle 25 between Avenidas 8 and 10, San José, Costa Rica; tel: 506-257-0922 or 506-259-8635.

This beautiful 35,000-acre (14,000-hectare) park is a few hours north of Monteverde in Guanacaste province. It harbors an intermittently active volcano covered with dense cloud forest. Trails lead to volcanic features such as fumaroles in the dry deciduous forest at lower elevations and through cloud forest to the bare peak of the volcano. Primitive campsites are available.

Manu Biosphere
Reserve
Peru

CHAPTER **12**

Even before the rising sun has begun to gild the leaves of the vast canopy, the haunting, double-note calls of the great tinamou, a secretive chickenlike bird, reverberate through the rain forest surrounding **Manu Lodge**. As bleary but eager travelers rise for early-morning hikes, red howler monkeys herald the dawn with the loud, roaring calls that earned them their name. Gradually increasing in frequency and number, the overlapping "howls" build to an ululating cacophony that resembles nothing so much as water boiling in an enormous teakettle. Soon, this wall of sound is pierced by other notes: the plaintive three-note whistle of the great potoo, the chirruping of crickets, and the raucous shrieks of a pair of blue-and-yellow macaws. ◆ The welling chorus heightens the anticipation of the hikers, who have now **No habitat on Earth sustains** assembled outside the lodge and stand peering **more species of plants and** into the rapidly shrinking shadows of **animals than the tropical rain** the forest. White-fronted capuchin monkeys, **forest of the Amazon Basin.** already on the hunt for palm fruits, return their stares from high branches. Iridescent, blue morpho butterflies, their wingspans as wide as a human hand, flash in shafts of sunlight. Overhead, a mixed flock of tanagers streams through a gap in the canopy: a veritable rainbow of species – paradise, opal-crowned, masked-crimson, green-and-gold. ◆ A sudden rustling at the base of the trees announces the entrance of a collared peccary. Emerging from the gloomy understory, the shortsighted mammal rushes across the grassy clearing, entirely oblivious to the astonished onlookers who nudge one another and grin with delight. Mere minutes into the morning and barely a few footsteps from the lodge, the adventure has already begun.

A sharp-backed monkey frog finds protective cover in the underbrush. Its skin secretions are used by some indigenous people to induce altered states of consciousness.

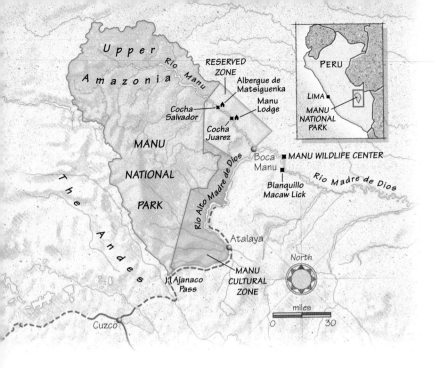

km) **Río Manu**, in the lowland rain forest of Upper Amazonia, in southeastern Peru. Covering some 7,300 square miles (19,000 sq km) and almost as large as Massachusetts, it is the largest tract of protected rain forest in the world. Home to seven groups of indigenous people, it also harbors more species of plants and animals than any other place on Earth – a mind-boggling 1,000 species of birds, 200 species of mammals, and 15,000 species of plants.

A scene like this unfolds every morning in **Manu Biosphere Reserve**. Yet, in reality, no two days here are ever alike. For this Amazonian reserve's inhabitants are so numerous and diverse and its plant life so exuberant that the permutations are endless, the picture ever-changing.

Manu Biosphere Reserve encompasses the entire watershed of the 200-mile (320-

The region was first set aside as a reserve in 1968 and five years later became a national park. In 1977 it was declared a UNESCO Biosphere Reserve, and in 1987 the national park became a World Heritage Site. The biosphere reserve is now divided into three areas: the national park, which is set aside for flora and fauna and groups of Matsiguenka Indians who continue to hunt there; the Manu Cultural Zone, where local people are permitted to settle; and the Reserved Zone, which is set aside for research and tourism.

The High Road

Getting to Manu is an adventure in itself. The gateway to the region is **Cuzco**, situated 11,200 feet (3,400m) up in the Andes and once the capital of the Incan Empire. From here, the easiest and quickest way into the reserve is to take one of the twice-weekly charter flights to the dirt airstrip at **Boca Manu**, near the muddy mouth of the Río Manu, where a motorized dugout canoe will transfer you to a jungle lodge. Those with more time and a taste for adventure can opt for the overland route, which entails two days of road travel by van, with optional stages on mountain bikes, and an overnight stay at a lodge in

Tent-making bats (opposite) huddle under a banana leaf.

A butterfly (right) alights on the snout of a side-necked turtle.

The whitetoe tarantula (bottom) is a retiring tree spider that prefers to hide when not hunting.

the cloud forest. Though it's more taxing and time-consuming, this alternative offers a great opportunity to experience the full range of Manu's habitats.

The road from Cuzco to **Atalaya**, at the edge of Amazonia, skirts the southern edge of the reserve and traverses one of the most species-rich regions in the world – no fewer than 700 kinds of birds have been recorded along this route. Initially, the road zigzags over several high ridges. As you cross the **Ajanaco Pass**, you'll have a spectacular view of adjacent orchid-clad forests and the distant Amazonian jungle. Descending through *paramo* (a high-altitude treeless habitat), elfin, and temperate mixed forests, past countless waterfalls, you enter the cloud forest at around 8,000 feet (2,400m).

An overnight stay here provides an opportunity to explore one of the most beautiful of all habitats. The trees are regularly bathed by a thick mist – known locally as *neblina* – which rises from the moist tropical zones far below. As a result, the branches are decorated with delightful epiphytes such as bromeliads, orchids, ferns, and mosses. The forest's inhabitants are equally enchanting. Colorful tanagers swoop low through the trees, jewel-like hummingbirds flit from flower to flower, and magnificent quetzals perch on high branches. You might even catch a glimpse of a woolly monkey or a

spectacled bear, South America's only bear, feeding in the canopy. But perhaps the most intriguing resident is another bird, the cock-of-the-rock. Attired in brilliant red plumage, the males of this species gather before dawn each day at a site known as a lek to perform a noisy courtship display. As the drabber females look on, the males jump, snap their wings, and emit loud screeches and strange piglike oinks.

Emerging from the cloud forest at around 5,000 feet (1,500m), the road continues downward through pristine upper tropical forest, a habitat mostly intact here

A warm, humid climate and high rainfall allow plant life to thrive continuously. As many as 300 species of trees have been identified in a single acre, and these plants in turn support myriad animal species. A giant emergent ceiba, bearing epiphytes on every branch, may nurture as many as 400 species of wildlife.

Manu is one of only a handful of sites in the world (all of them in Amazonia) with a checklist of more than 500 species of birds. Experts have seen as many as 331 species in one day, and most visitors are able to notch up 100 species during a four-day visit. Riding up the Río Manu to your lodge, you'll see hordes of birds on the river's sandbars, including large-billed terns, pied lapwings, sand-colored nighthawks, Orinoco geese, and horned screamers – a huge aquatic species with an unforgettably loud call. Pairs of squawking Amazonia parrots streak overhead, yellow-spotted side-necked turtles sunbathe on logs, and scores of white caimans (members of the crocodile family) laze on the riverbanks. Up in the trees, there's an almost constant parade of up to 13 monkey species – more primates than can be seen anywhere else in the world. Your guide will be calling out species names in rapid-fire succession, all the while scanning the sandbars for a sunbathing jaguar. Sandbars are among the jaguar's favorite haunts, and sightings are most likely during the dry season when low water levels expose the sand along the river's edge.

One of only two lodges located within the reserve, Manu Lodge is situated on **Cocha Juarez**, an old oxbow lake formed by the Río Manu. It is home to giant river otters, the world's largest otter, which can grow to seven feet (2m) in length. These playful creatures are common only in Manu, having been hunted to near extinction elsewhere. Waterbirds are also abundant here, including striated herons, sungrebes, and wattled jacanas.

A number of trails depart from the lodge and guided walks take place at least twice a day. Along

but heavily cut elsewhere for tea, coca, and coffee plantations. Situated at 2,015 feet (614m), Atalaya is a good base for exploring the foothills of the eastern Andes and lowland Amazonia. Colorful russet-backed oropendolas (large relatives of orioles that build hanging nests in a communal tree) are common in the area, and spotlighting trips after dark may reveal tiny night monkeys – the world's only nocturnal primate – their huge eyes and white facial disks giving them the appearance of large owls.

Departing Atalaya, travelers board a 50-foot (15-m) motorized dugout canoe for a thrilling four-hour whitewater river ride down the clear **Río Alto Madre de Dios** to Boca Manu and the Reserved Zone.

Exploring Amazonia

As soon as you reach the lowland forests, you are struck by the abundance of life – and moisture.

the forest pathways, fruiting fig trees attract large numbers of animals such as blue-throated piping-guans (large, turkey-like birds), Couvier's toucans, squirrel monkeys, and tayras (neotropical weasels). Butterflies of all sorts float through the trees, including birdwings and delicate glasswings. Enormous strangler figs reach groundward from their host trees, and woody vines as thick as your leg spiral upward. Scan the ground and you'll see great processions of leaf-cutter ants marching along their self-made trails.

The **Lake Trail** leads through secondary forest, paralleling the water's edge, where it connects with the **Mirador Trail**. This path branches off inland into *terra firme* (the forest above the flood zone) – where you may spot troops of agile spider monkeys that seem to fly through the treetops – to two lookout points, or *miradors*. From their summits, you'll enjoy awesome views across the jungle to the snow-covered peaks surrounding Cuzco, as well as close encounters with canopy species such as the spangled cotinga, a fruit-eating neotropical bird whose neon-blue plumage will have you reaching for your sunglasses. Occasion-

A high-country waterfall (opposite, top) splashes into a rocky stream.

Mushrooms (opposite, bottom) play a vital role in the decomposition of organic matter.

Pygmy marmosets (left) are the world's smallest monkeys; an adult weighs only four ounces (114g).

A yellow-throated parrot snake (bottom) prowls the leaf litter in search of prey.

ally, visitors to the *miradors* spot a harpy eagle. The largest and rarest eagle in the Western Hemisphere, the harpy swoops down into the canopy to seize howler monkeys in its huge golden talons, a feat that requires considerable agility given the bird's seven-foot (2-m) wingspan.

River Scenes

The main thoroughfares in Amazonia are the rivers, and exploring farther afield requires that you take a boat tour. The type of craft

The Harpy Eagle

You might think that an animal as large as a sloth, wrapped around the end of a branch hundreds of feet above the ground and concealed in dense foliage, would be safe from predators. But should just one chink appear in that fragile armor of vegetation, the slow-witted mammal may suddenly find itself being flown across the forest in the massive talons of a harpy eagle, on its way to a rather unpleasant rendezvous with the rest of the harpy family.

The most fearsome bird of prey in the Amazon, the harpy specializes in swooping down into the canopy to seize sloths, monkeys, and opossums – a feat that requires considerable agility given the bird's seven-foot (2-m) wingspan. A powerful, stocky bird weighing up to 10 pounds (4.5kg), the harpy has a dark gray back, upper chest, and wings, a pale gray head with a prominent crest, and cream-colored underparts. A deep, hooked bill and those fearsome claws, which can grow to five inches (13cm), make short work of tender prey.

Harpies inhabit forests from Mexico to northern Argentina, but require large home territories and are therefore widely scattered. Furthermore, breeding pairs usually produce only one chick every two years. These factors make the species highly vulnerable to threats such as hunting and deforestation, and sadly it is now endangered.

Even a reserve as large as Manu may have only one or two pairs of harpy eagles. However, visitors to treetop miradors may occasionally spot this majestic bird soaring over the forest or – should they be truly fortunate – plummeting into the canopy to pluck another meal from the trees. – *Scott Forbes*

The harpy eagle (left) can reach 50 miles per hour (80kph) in flight and specializes in snatching tree-dwelling mammals from the canopy.

A little hermit humming-bird (bottom) feeds on a heliconia flower.

Katydids (opposite, top) communicate by rubbing their wings together; the "song" is recognized by others of the species.

Blue-headed parrots (opposite, bottom) gather on a collpa, or clay lick.

depends on the waterway: paddle canoes are preferred for maneuvering quietly along narrow, tannin-stained "blackwater" streams; long motorized dugout canoes are used to cover longer distances on wider rivers; and motorized catamaran platforms are sometimes employed on tranquil oxbow lakes.

From Manu Lodge, tours regularly head upriver to **Cocha Salvador**, one of the reserve's largest and richest oxbows and the site of the reserve's second lodge, the **Albergue de Matsiguenka**. Rufescent tiger-herons, green-and-rufous kingfishers, curl-crested aracaris (small toucans), brown capuchin monkeys, and giant otters are just a few of the species you can expect to see at this beautiful spot. Look here too for the capybara, the world's largest rodent, which can measure up to four feet (1.2m) in length and whose webbed feet make it a strong swimmer. You'll also see families of hoatzins, which are endemic to Amazonia. These unusual birds are born with claws on their wings that are used to climb trees, much like the prehistoric "dinosaur" bird, *Archaeopteryx*. Although snakes are usually difficult to find in Manu, this is one place where you might come across an anaconda, the world's largest, entwined in overhanging branches at the water's edge.

At Boca Manu, the Río Manu and the Río Alto Madre de Dios merge, becoming the **Río Madre de Dios**. Located on this

lower river, **Manu Wildlife Center** doubles as a jungle lodge and research facility for visiting biologists. The lodge is surrounded by gardens of flowering heliconias and gingers, which attract somber-colored hummingbirds known as long-tailed hermits. It also boasts a 100-foot-high (30-m) canopy platform, built in a giant ceiba and accessed by a sturdy spiral staircase, where you can watch euphonias (small tanagers), hummingbirds, toucans, and hawks as they feed or rest in the treetops.

A network of trails fans out from the center, leading into *terra firme*, where you may encounter the spectacular Pavonine quetzal or come across an army ant swarm. Army ants emerge from their nests in huge numbers and attack any insects that do not immediately flee. Their swarm is accompanied by antbirds, which feed on the insects stirred up by the ants. As many as half a million ants may sweep through a 25-foot-wide (8-m) swath in a matter of a few minutes, followed by up to 200 antbirds – an astonishing spectacle.

It's a short trip from Manu Wildlife Center along the Río Madre de Dios to one of the most celebrated sites in the whole of Amazonia, the **Blanquillo macaw lick**. Macaws and other parrots rely on minerals to detoxify many of the seeds and leaves that they consume, and they obtain the minerals by eating mud at sites known as clay licks, or *collpas*. Just after dawn, around 300 parrots (mostly blue-headed parrots with smaller numbers of orange-cheeked, yellow-crowned, and mealy parrots) gather noisily in the trees near a 130-foot-high (40-m) section of the riverbank where the mineral-rich clay is exposed. There, they wait their turn to alight on the collpa and scoop up a beakful of mud. When the parrots have finished, up to 30 pairs of red-and-green macaws arrive to take their turn. The sight of hundreds of multihued birds clinging to the almost vertical slope and wheeling over the river is unforgettable and at its best during the dry season on clear mornings.

Mineral licks are also visited by other animals, and at dusk guides from Manu Wildlife Center lead guests into the forest to a blind overlooking a clay lick frequented by Brazilian tapirs. The blind provides a rare opportunity to view this shy, nocturnal creature, which is South America's largest mammal and a relative of the horse.

The return walk is a magical experience. Under clear, star-studded skies, cicadas and treefrogs strike up a loud refrain punctuated by the hoots of the spectacled owl and the bass notes of a gray-winged trumpeter, a seldom-seen nocturnal bird. The rain forest's nighttime soundscape forms a glorious counterpoint to the early-morning chorus, highlighting the rich cycle of life sustained by this extraordinary wilderness.

DETAILS

How to Get There

Direct flights to Lima are available on many airlines and depart daily from the United States via Miami and other major cities. There are frequent flights to Lima from other South American countries. Local flights link Lima to Cuzco, the gateway to Manu.

When to Go

Visitors can travel to Manu year-round but should be prepared for rain at any time, even during the June to October dry season. The rainy season lasts from November to May; travelers should allow extra time for weather-related delays. Daytime temperatures average 81°F to 90°F (27–32°C), and nighttime low temperatures average 69°F to 79°F (21–26°C).

Getting Around

Travelers are permitted to enter the Reserved Zone of Manu Biosphere Reserve only with an accredited guide, so it is essential to purchase a package from a tour outfitter. Packages usually include charter flights and/or overland travel, as well as river transport and accommodations within the reserve. Some tours also visit neighboring parts of Upper Amazonia. Outside of Manu, visitors with more time can explore independently by renting a car in Cuzco and motorized canoes on waterways.

INFORMATION

Embassy of Peru

1700 Massachusetts Avenue, N.W., Washington, DC, 20036; tel: 202-833-9860; fax: 202-659-8124; www.peruemb.org

Peru Tourist Office

Portal Belen 115, Cuzco, Peru; tel: 51-84-237-364.

PromPeru (Commission for Promotion of Peru)

Edificio Mitinci, 14th floor, Calle 1 Oeste #050, Urb. Corpac, San Isidro, Peru; tel: 51-1-224-3113; fax: 51-1-224-3323; e-mail: postmaster@promperu.gob.pe

South American Explorers

126 Indian Creek Road, Ithaca, NY 14850; tel: 607-277-0488.

This organization also has offices in Cuzco and Quito, Ecuador.

CAMPING

Camping expeditions into the rainforest interior can be arranged with some jungle lodges.

LODGING

PRICE GUIDE – double occupancy

$ = up to $49	$$ = $50–$99
$$$ = $100–$149	$$$$ = $150+

Explorer's Inn

Peruvian Safaris, Avenida Garcilasa de la Vega 1334, P.O. Box 10088, Lima 1, Peru; tel: 51-1-431-6330; fax: 51-13-326-676.

Four hours upriver from Puerto Maldonado, this lodge in the Tambopata–Candamo Reserve has ready access to a heavy concentration of bird species. Seven thatched-roof bungalows contain 30 twin-bed rooms with private baths. Easy to moderate trails are nearby. $$–$$$$

Manu Cloud Forest Lodge and Manu Lodge

Manu Nature Tours, Avenida Pardo 1046, Cuzco, Peru; tel: 51-84-252-721; fax: 51-84-234-793; e-mail: mnt@amauta.rcp.net.pe

Perched near a waterfall in prime cloud forest habitat, Manu Cloud Forest Lodge is on the forested slopes of Río Manu's tributaries. A six-hour drive from Cuzco, it provides a base for exploring the mid-Andean elevations. Guests at Manu Lodge in Manu Biosphere Reserve choose among two- to eight-day packages that include transportation to the park, naturalist guides, entrance fees, and meals. The lodge offers private rooms, cold-water showers, a dining room, outhouses, and more than 12 miles (19km) of trails. $$$$

Manu Wildlife Center

Manu Expeditions, P.O. Box 606, Cuzco, Peru; tel: 51-84-226-671; fax: 51-84-236-706; e-mail: adventure@manuexpeditions.com, or InkaNatura Travel, 17957 Southwest 111 Street, Brooker, FL 32633; tel: 888-287-7186; fax: 352-485-1452; e-mail: kit@inkanatura.com

This lodge is situated on the Río Madre de Dios, near the largest known collpa for viewing macaws. It features 20 twin-bed bungalows, private bathrooms with hot-water showers and flush toilets, and a network of maintained trails. Guests usually stay here on package tours booked through Manu Expeditions or InkaNatura. $$$$

TOURS AND OUTFITTERS

Field Guides

9433 Bee Cave Road, Building 1, Suite 150, Austin, TX 78733; tel: 800-728-4953; fax: 512-263-0117; e-mail: fgileader@aol.com

Field Guides offers extensive birding tours of the cloud forests and rain forests of Ecuador and Peru, including a 16-day tour in Manu Biosphere Reserve.

Manu Ecological Adventures

Calle Plateros #356, Cuzco, Peru; tel: 51-84-261-640; fax: 51-84-225-562; e-mail: manuadventures@computextos.com.pe

Seven-day float trips in motorized canoes on the Río Madre de Dios and Río Manu afford excellent opportunites for bird- and wildlife watching. Experienced guides accompany the group at all times.

Manu Expeditions

P.O. Box 606, Cuzco, Peru; tel: 51-84-226-671; fax: 51-84-236-706; e-mail: adventure@ manuexpeditions.com

This operator runs nature tours from Cuzco to Hacienda Amazonia and Manu Wildlife Center, including horse-supported treks and birding trips led by experienced ornithologists.

Manu Nature Tours

Avenida Pardo 1046, Cuzco, Peru; tel: 51-84-252-721; fax: 51-84-234-793; e-mail: mnt@amauta.rcp.net.pe

Tours leave from Cuzco for Manu Cloud Forest Lodge and Manu Lodge, with camping options in Manu Biosphere Reserve.

Mountain Travel-Sobek

6420 Fairmount Avenue, El Cerrito, CA 94530; tel: 888-687-6235; fax: 510-525-7710; e-mail: info@mtsobek.com

Nature and rafting tours explore the rain forests of Ecuador and Peru. Guides also lead trekking adventures to Machu Picchu and year-round small-yacht nature cruises in the Galapagos Islands.

Victor Emanuel Nature Tours

P.O. Box 33008, Austin, TX 78764; tel: 800-328-8368 or 510-328-5221; fax: 512-328-2919; e-mail: ventbird@aol.com

Expert guides lead this operator's birding and natural history tours in Upper Amazonia.

Excursions

Galapagos Islands National Park

Puerto Ayora, Santa Cruz, Galapagos, Ecuador; tel: 593-5-526-511 or 593-5-526-189; fax: 593-4-564-636; e-mail: spng@fcdarwin.org.ec

A visit to the Galapagos is on the top-10 lists of most wildlife enthusiasts. Located 600 miles (970km) west of Ecuador's mainland, these "Enchanted Isles" are home to many species found nowhere else on the planet and have been designated a UNESCO Biosphere Reserve. During the cool season (April to October), mists encircle the higher altitudes of the larger islands, nurturing *Scalesia* cloud forests and verdant moorlands. Many nature cruises include a hike in the highlands of Santa Cruz Island for a view of giant tortoises.

Machu Picchu National Park

PromPeru, Edificio Mitinci, 14th floor, Calle 1 Oeste #050, Urb. Corpac, San Isidro, Peru; tel: 51-1-224-3113 or 51-1-224-3126; fax: 51-1-224-3323; e-mail: postmaster@promperu.gob.pe

Machu Picchu is one of the most spectacular archaeological sites in the world. Situated in an Andean cloud forest at an elevation of 7,500 feet (2,300m), it's a great site for natural history as well. On a clear day, visitors can scan the skies for the spectacular Andean condor, whose wingspan is 10 feet (3m). The endemic Inca wren can be sighted in the bamboo among the ruins. In nearby Aguascalientes, brilliant hummingbirds, tanagers, and the amazing Andean cock-of-the-rock can be found in flowering inga trees.

Tambopata–Candamo Reserve

PromPeru, Edificio Mitinci, 14th floor, Calle 1 Oeste #050, Urb. Corpac, San Isidro, Peru; tel: 51-1-224-3113; fax: 51-1-224-3323; e-mail: postmaster@promperu.gob.pe

Created in 1990 by the Peruvian government in partnership with international conservation organizations, this expansive reserve in southeastern Peru encompasses Andean uplands, rain forest, and almost the entire watershed of the Tavara, Candamo, and Tambopata Rivers. Its staggering biodiversity includes 10,000 plant species, 200 types of mammals, 1,200 butterfly species, and no fewer than 1,300 kinds of birds; a recent survey of six square miles (15.5 sq km) yielded a world record of 560 bird species. Visitors can stay at a lodge run by the indigenous Ese'eja people and visit the world's largest mineral lick, where up to 17 species of parrots and macaws gather daily.

Atlantic Forest
Brazil

CHAPTER 13

The golden lion tamarin looks like it might have been designed by Steven Spielberg. Covered with luxuriant reddish-orange fur, it is a tiny and precocious New World monkey with a doll-like face that absolutely redlines the cuteness meter. ◆ Golden lion tamarins live communally in family groups, foraging through the canopy of wetland forests for fruit, insects, and small vertebrates. They are heard more often than seen, calling shrilly to each other when they are on the move. ◆ There's another reason why these beautiful monkeys are seldom spotted in the wild: not many of them are left. There are only about 400 subsisting in nature, virtually all on a reserve in the Brazilian state of Rio de Janeiro. ◆ Their plight precisely tracks the fate of their historic habitat: the **Mata Atlantica**, or **Atlantic Forest**. In its primeval state, this subtropical and tropical woodland covered 368,000 square miles (953,000 sq km) along the coastal and eastern interior portions of Brazil, Argentina, and Paraguay.

Isolated reserves protect the precious remains of Brazil's Mata Atlantica and the rare creatures who inhabit it.

But its proximity to the sea sealed its unhappy fate. It was the first of Brazil's wild ecosystems subject to exploration and settlement by Europeans. It has been gradually diminished during the past three centuries, with the rate of destruction accelerating greatly since the 1940s. Today, only about 5 percent of the original forest remains, and that only in protected "islands" surrounded by agricultural zones, grasslands, and cities. ◆ Arguably, the Mata is the most endangered forest on the planet. Yet even in its degraded state, it is a treasure of biological diversity. Fifteen primate species (and four subspecies) live here, including six kinds of lion tamarins. Fourteen of these primate species are endemic to the

The golden lion tamarin is a small monkey found only in the rain forests of Brazil. It eats fruit, insects, and other small animals and is extremely dextrous, using its long slender fingers to extract prey from tree bark and other plants.

and numerous state and private parks. Many of these preserves contain sizable portions of rain forest, and different preserves contain different fauna and flora. Seeing a variety of species involves visiting several destinations.

There's only one place to see the golden lion tamarin: the 12,300-acre (5,000-hectare) **Pocos das Antas Biological Preserve** in Rio de Janeiro state. Unfortunately, the experience is apt to be less than satisfying. Entry is tightly controlled, and preserve staffers escort visitors to tamarin groups that are fitted with radio collars and marked with black paint for identification purposes.

A far better place to see a rare primate is the privately owned **Caratinga Biological Station**, 17 miles (27 km) west of the town of **Ipanema** in Minas Gerais state. This is the home of the muriqui, the New World's largest monkey – a remarkable creature with a three-foot-long (1-m) tail and six-foot (2-m) arm span. Muriquis are the only nonviolent primates on the planet. Because they are large animals that live in the upper reaches of the forest canopy, combat over mating privileges, territory, or food would result in a high incidence of fatal falls. Gene dominance is therefore established through testicle size. Male muriquis have been observed placidly lining up to mate with willing females. The male with the biggest testes produces the most sperm, thus improving his chance of successful conception.

Also in Minas Gerais state is **Caraça Natural Park**, a 150,000-acre (60,700-hectare) tract of privately owned forest a few hours east of **Belo Horizonte**, the state capital. Originally a seminary preserve, this is a spectacular venue of steep, lushly forested mountains jigsawed with open grasslands.

Mata, and 13 are endangered. There are five species of wild felines: the jaguar, ocelot, margay, puma, and oncilla. About 160 species of birds are endemic to the forest, and it supports a mind-boggling variety of botanical species. A 1993 survey identified 3,000 species of trees in a one-hectare (2.5-acre) plot of forest in southern Bahia state.

Forest Archipelago

Visiting the Mata involves a trip of many miles, since the forest is fragmented across the Brazilian littoral and interior. Brazil has 42 national parks, an impressive system of federal ecological and biological reserves,

Toucans, guans, and hummingbirds are the star attractions, and four species of primates also live here. Lucky visitors will see maned wolves, the only wolf in South America, and a species endangered for two reasons: habitat destruction and its insatiable appetite for chickens. Priests at a seminary in the park leave out food for the wolves, so nocturnal sightings are almost guaranteed.

The most renowned reserve in the Mata is undoubtedly **Itatiaia National Park**, a 100,000-acre (40,470-hectare) tract of pristine forest off the Rio de Janeiro–Sao Paulo national highway near the town of **Itatiaia**. Established in 1937, Itatiaia is Brazil's oldest national park. It is situated on a slope that reaches an elevation of 9,104 feet (2,775m), and its pronounced change in elevation results in a variety of habitats. At 5,500 feet (1,675m), the flora and fauna shift radically from that found in the lowland forests, and a similar shift occurs at about 7,000 feet (2,150m). Comfortable lodgings, abundant wildlife, and easy access make this park an essential destination for anyone visiting the Mata.

This is a birder's paradise, containing a spectacular array of hummingbirds as well as a tremendous variety of other notable species. Particular stars are the spot-billed and saffron toucanets, the endemic Itatiaia thistletail, the orange-breasted subspecies of the surucua

trogon, and a number of antbirds. Inns are set at the 2,000-foot (600-m) level and are excellent sites for seeing and hearing masked titi monkeys – exuberant primates that announce their presence with extremely loud, hooting calls as they travel through the forest.

Birds in Abundance

In Espirito Santo state are three reserves that offer some of the finest birding in South America. The first, **Novo Lombardia Biological Reserve**, is about six miles (10 km) north of the town of **Santa Teresa**. It isn't easy exploring this rugged 13,000-acre (5,260-hectare) preserve, because a tremendous quantity of bureaucratic red tape is involved. You can drive through it, but you can't get out of your car unless you obtain a permit from the Department of National Parks in Brasilia. It's worth the effort, however, for Novo Lombardia abounds in wondrous birds. Among the most notable is the shrikelike cotinga, an extremely rare bird with a yellow- and black-striped breast. In Santa Teresa, the **Mello Leitão Museum** displays the hummingbird feeders of the late Augusto Ruschi, one of Brazil's pioneering ornithologists. Seventeen species of hummers have been recorded at the feeders within a few hours.

Thirty-one miles (50 km) north of **Linhares** is the 59,000-acre (24,000-hectare) **Sooretama Biological Reserve**. Situated near sea level, this reserve is particularly known for its multispecies flocks, a phenomenon that disproves the adage that birds of a feather flock together. Sooretama's flocks are quasi-permanent aggregations of birds that congregate in coopera-

The maned wolf (top) is categorized as a carnivore, but fruits and other plants make up half of its diet.

The black-and-white hawk eagle (right) has short wings, useful for hunting in the forest.

The prominent bill of the toco toucan (left) is laced with air cavities that make it lightweight.

The Pantanal

There are three ecosystems of global significance in Brazil: Amazonia, the Mata Atlantica, and the Pantanal. Of these, the Pantanal is perhaps the least known. Located in western Brazil near Bolivia and Paraguay, the Pantanal is an alluvial plain of vast scope, encompassing more than 55,000 square miles (142,500 sq km) of evanescent marshes, seasonally flooded grasslands, lakes, lagoons, heavily wooded riverine corridors, and upland forests.

Each year, the rivers of the region overflow, spreading out across an area roughly the size of Colorado and creating one of the largest seasonal wetlands on the planet. Tens of millions of waterfowl breed here, as do a great many other birds, including the rare hyacinth macaw.

The waters of the Pantanal teem with more than 250 species of fish as well as caiman. This is rich habitat for mammals, too, supporting giant otters, capybaras, marsh deer, tapirs, giant anteaters, and a particularly large and robust jaguar population.

The Pantanal is under increasing threat from development and poaching, but efforts have accelerated in recent years to preserve this priceless citadel of biological diversity. The core of the region's protected holdings is 338,000-acre (137,000-hectare) Pantanal National Park; access currently remains problematic at best. During the flood season, the park is virtually cut off from the outside world.

Tourism is growing in the Pantanal, a development that could prove both boon and bane. As long as strict ecotourism precepts are followed, a reasonable number of visitors could provide an economic motive for preserving the region's wild legacy. Too many unregulated tourists, on the other hand, would only exacerbate the problem of environmental degradation.

Giant river otters (left) have suffered from habitat loss and hunting.

Giant anteaters (below) have sharp claws and sticky tongues to dig up and eat ants and termites.

An ocelot (bottom) drags its prey to a safe place.

though there are a great many other birds that are worth seeking out.

Foremost among these is the red-billed curassow, a spectacular turkey-size bird that is

tive hunting forays. Typically, the leader is an eastern slaty antshrike. It flits above the forest floor, calling constantly, directing the progress of the flock. When it spies danger, it trills a different call, and the flock scatters, regrouping later when conditions are safe. During the hunt, ground-foraging species such as antbirds, tinamous, gnateaters, and spinetails kick through the forest litter for insects. The bugs they disturb are consumed by birds that feed higher in the forest. This elegant symbiotic relationship may be unique among avifauna and is reason enough to visit Sooretama,

found at only three places in the Mata. Good as Sooretama is for curassows, there's one place that's even better: the adjacent, 54,000-acre (22,000-hectare) **CVRD Linhares Reserve**. The canopy here is extremely impressive; some of the trees reach a height of 130 feet (40m). Access points are guarded, and the reserve is regularly patrolled, so poaching is kept to a minimum. As a consequence, wildlife is bountiful, and red-billed curassows are positively abundant.

Also common are cotingas, a family that includes some of the New World's most extravagantly plumed birds. Among them are the banded cotinga, a bird with iridescent purplish-blue dorsal feathers, glittering maroon wings and tail, and a rich blue band across the breast; the spangled cotinga, which sports deep blue spots; and the bare-throated bell bird, which has white plumage, a green facial mask, prominent wattles, and an extremely loud, plangent call. The CVRD Linhares Reserve also teems with mammals, including masked titi monkeys and brown capuchins. Black jaguars (a melanistic phase, not a separate species) have been spotted here.

Twin Parks

One of the world's most significant reservoirs of terrestrial biodiversity is **Iguaçu National Park** in Parana state and its sister park in the adjacent region of Argentina. Here, it's possible to get a landscape-size perspective on the forest, and a sense of its historic scope and richness. Iguaçu encompasses 250,000 acres (100,000 hectares) of forestland around the astounding falls that give the parks their names. About a million visitors flock annually to the parks, primarily to see the cataracts – actually 275 separate falls – that drop 225 feet (69m) over a semicircular ledge several kilometers in length.

The two parks harbor many rare mammals, including jaguars, ocelots, margays, jaguarundis, pumas, two species of brocket deer, bush dogs, southern river otters, and tapirs. They also support a remarkable concentration of birds, including five species of toucans. Knowledgeable naturalists look for army ants in the hopes of witnessing a foraging chain reaction. The aggressive phalanxes of ants scare up insects, which lure monkeys and small insectivorous birds. Attracted by the commotion, forest falcons swoop in to prey on the birds.

Theoretically, the parks enjoy full protection from exploitation, but regional politics have undermined their status. Road-building, logging, and hunting have been increasing during the past few years, in direct contravention of Brazilian and Argentine law but with the open connivance of local politicos. The rangers that patrol the parks are dedicated and do the best they can to enforce their mandate, but they are in dire need of assistance.

Brazilian tapirs (left) are usually found near water. Their long, flexible snouts help them feed on leaves, shoots, and aquatic plants.

Vegetation (left) clings to rock ledges at the edge of Iguaçu Falls.

Visiting the Mata is apt to both depress and inspire. True, it is a greatly degraded ecosystem, and the pressures on its remaining fragments are likely to increase rather than diminish. But the Atlantic Forest remains one of the most awe-inspiring places on Earth. And if forces are conspiring to destroy what remains, local, national, and international efforts are gaining momentum to protect and even restore large portions of the Mata. There is genuine reason for hope and even guarded optimism.

TRAVEL TIPS

DETAILS

How to Get There

Rio de Janeiro's Aeroporto Galeão is the most common entry point into Brazil, although international travelers can fly into many other cities. The second most popular gateway is Aeroporto São Paulo/Guarulhos in São Paulo.

When to Go

Daytime temperatures during the dry season, May to October, are typically around 75°F (24°C), while nighttime temperatures are in the 50s and 60s°F (13–18°C), and drop into the 40s°F (6–9°C) at higher altitudes. Some areas, like Itatiaia National Park, occasionally fall below freezing and even have snowfall. The remainder of the year is much wetter, hotter, and more humid: 90s°F (33–36°C) during the day and 70s°F (22–26°C) at night, cooler at higher altitudes. January and February are the wettest months of the year.

Getting Around

Many Atlantic Forest destinations are located in Rio de Janeiro, São Paulo, Espirito Santo, Minas Gerais, and Parana states, making them easily accessible from the cities of Rio de Janeiro and São Paulo. Frequent, inexpensive buses, the most common means of domestic transportation, link all major cities in Brazil. Car rentals, available in most cities, allow for exploration of remote locations.

INFORMATION

Brazilian Environment and Natural Resources Institute

Avenida L4 Norte, Setor Areas Isoladas Norte, DF, 70620, Brazil; tel: 55-61-316-1000 or 55-61-316-1001; www.ibama.gov.br

Embratur/Brazilian Tourist Board

Setor Comercial Norte, Quadra 2, Bloco G, Brasilia, DF, CEP 70710, Brazil; tel: 55-61-224-9100; www.embratur.gov.br

SOS Mata Atlantica

Rua Manoel da Nobrega, 456 São Paulo, SP, CEP 04001-001, Brazil; tel: 55-11-887-1195; fax: 55-11-885-1680; e-mail: smata@ax.apc.org

This is an environmental organization protecting the Atlantic Forest.

CAMPING

There are few organized camping facilities in the Atlantic Forest region, and camping is not recommended except on organized tours, which are increasingly available in Brazil.

LODGING

PRICE GUIDE – double occupancy

$ = up to $49 $$ = $50–$99

$$$ = $100–$149 $$$$ = $150+

Caraça Seminary

Caixa Postal 12, Santa Barbara, MG, Brazil; tel: 55-31-837-2698.

With stunning scenery and multiple hummingbird species in the vicinity, this accommodation is a seminary built in the 1700s and nestled in the mountains of Caraça Natural Park, which is privately owned by the church. $$

Hotel Cataratas

Ruta 12, Km 4, Porto Iguazú, Misiones, Argentina; tel: 54-3757-421100.

This hotel is just outside Iguaçu National Park on the Argentinean side of the border. It offers double rooms with private bathrooms, forested grounds, and a restaurant. $$–$$$

Hotel das Cataratas

Rodovia das Cataratas, Km 28, Iguaçu National Park, PR, Brazil; tel: 55-45-523-2266; fax: 55-45-574-1688.

This historic luxury hotel next to Iguaçu Falls has single and double rooms with private bathrooms. $$$–$$$$

Hotel do Ype

Estrada do Parque Nacional, Km 14, Itatiaia, RJ, Brazil; tel/fax: 55-24-352-1453.

This hotel near Itatiaia National Park offers modern cabins with private bathrooms and fireplaces. $$–$$$

Hotel Simon

Estrada do Parque Nacional, Km 12, Itatiaia, RJ, Brazil; tel: 55-24-352-1122.

Centrally located in Itatiaia National Park, Hotel Simon has single and double rooms with bathrooms, a restaurant, and views of the valley. $$–$$$

San Martin Hotel

Rodovia das Cataratas, Km 17, Foz do Iguaçu, PR, Brazil; tel/fax: 55-45-523-2323.

Just outside Iguaçu National Park, next to the Bird Park aviary, this hotel has forested grounds and a swimming pool. $$

Sheraton International Iguazú Resort

Parque Nacional Iguazú, Misiones, Argentina; tel: 54-3757-420748.

Set within Iguazú National Park in Argentina, this resort has rooms with views of the falls and less expensive accommodations overlooking the forest. $$$$

TOURS AND OUTFITTERS

Cheesemans' Ecology Safaris

20800 Kittredge Road, Saratoga, CA 95070; tel: 408-867-1371 or 800-527-5330; fax: 408-741-0358; e-mail: cheesemans@aol.com

Natural history trips emphasize animal behavior, birding, and photography. Small-group trips explore Brazil and other South American countries.

Field Guides

9433 Bee Cave Road, Building 1, Suite 150, Austin, TX 78733; tel: 800-728-4953 or 512-263-7295; fax: 512-263-0117; e-mail: fgileader@aol.com

A 25-day birding tour visits five states in southeastern Brazil and includes excursions to Itatiaia National Park and the Augusto Ruschi Reserve, famed for its hummingbirds.

Focus Tours

103 Moya Road, Santa Fe, NM 87505; tel: 505-466-4688; fax: 505-466-4689; e-mail: focustours@ aol.com; www. focustours.com

Focus operates tours with a strong conservation perspective to Itatiaia National Park, Iguaçu Falls, Caratinga Biological Station, the Amazon, the Pantanal, and other destinations in Brazil and South America. Tours emphasize bird-watching and wildlife photography. Naturalist guides use special equipment to call out shy fauna from the forest. The company also offers private tours and "on your own" packages for independent travelers.

International Expeditions

1 Environs Park, Helena, AL 35080; tel: 800-633-4734; e-mail: nature@ietravel.com

Local naturalists lead expeditions to the Pantanal, Caraça, and Iguaçu National Park. Group trips focus on environmental awareness, natural history, bird-watching, and wildlife conservation. This outfitter will also make arrangements for independent travelers.

Excursions

Jaguar Ecological Reserve

Focus Tours, 103 Moya Road, Santa Fe, NM 87505; tel: 505-466-4688; fax: 505-466-4689; e-mail: focustours@aol.com

This private reserve deep in the Pantanal encompasses natural open areas where millions of waterbirds roost in the winter months. More than 50 resident hyacinth macaws are accustomed to and curious about visitors. Toucans, trogons, black and gold howler monkeys, brown capuchins, and Brazilian tapirs are also common. The star attractions, however, are the jaguars. Dozens are seen yearly. Weighing up to 400 pounds (180kg), they are the largest cats in tropical America.

Serra da Canastra National Park

Brazilian Environment and Natural Resources Institute, Avenida L4 Norte, Setor Areas Isoladas Norte, DF, 70620, Brazil; tel: 55-61-316-1000 or 55-61-316-1001; www.ibama.gov.br

This park takes its name from its shape. *Canastra* is Portuguese for the long lockbox placed atop a mule to carry precious stones from the mines of Minas Gerais. The upper portion of the park has gently rolling grasslands, gallery forests, and, in places, termite mounds. It's a reliable location for spotting giant anteaters; other animals include the endangered maned wolf, South American fox, giant armadillo, and, occasionally, the rare Brazilian merganser. The lower part of the park encompasses the impressive Casca d'Anta waterfall and a mix of Atlantic Forest and Cerrado bird species.

Serra das Orgãos National Park

Brazilian Environment and Natural Resources Institute, Avenida L4 Norte, Setor Areas Isoladas Norte, DF, 70620, Brazil; tel: 55-61-316-1000 or 55-61-316-1001; www.ibama.gov.br

This mountainous park is cloaked with rain forests and laced with streams and waterfalls. Bird-watchers from around the world come to see toucans, trogons, parrots, antbirds, spinetails, fruitcrows, and bellbirds. Two species of cotingas are found only in the upper areas of the park, rarely seen in their cloud-covered habitat. Mammals include anteaters, endangered sloths, coatis, and agoutis. A memorable sight is the Finger of God rock formation, a narrow, rocky peak that juts 5,522 feet (1,683m) into the heavens. A 26-mile (42-km) trail system leads through the park; experienced guides are available to assist rock climbers.

Lake District
Chile

From the shores of **Reloncaví Fjord**, a narrow, glacier-scoured inlet at the southeastern edge of Chile's Lake District, the Andes rise precipitously. Great granite walls and domes loom over thick forests, and streams brimming with trout tumble through a landscape that rivals the majesty of Yosemite. ◆ At **Cochamó**, a steep-sided valley slices deep into the interior, narrowing to a seemingly impassable cliff face, beneath which the trees crowd closer, rise taller and sturdier. Above the valley floor, there are no roads; only a few long-established horse trails and ox tracks thread through the emerald-clad timbers, toward the oldest, grandest forests on the far rim. Here, stunning cathedral-like groves of alerces – a redwood analogue that is the second-longest-lived tree species on Earth and grows to 150 feet (46m) in height and 13 feet (4m) in diameter – stand like sentinels around an enchanting cascade framed by a rock arch known as El Arco. ◆ Some of these trees are

Geographically isolated, Chile's rain forests support plants and animals found nowhere else on Earth.

thought to have been here for 3,000 years. Older than the Parthenon and the Hanging Gardens of Babylon, they have endured in their mountain fastness through its centuries of occupation by indigenous Tehuelche people, through Spanish colonization and settlement, through the myriad developments that have transformed the Chilean landscape in the modern age. In the late 20th century, however, their time seemed to be running out. Loggers and road builders were beginning to encroach upon this 250,000-acre (100,000-hectare) wilderness, sizing up its rich resources. To halt this advance, a coalition of Chilean and international conservation organizations was formed in the early 1990s. By acquiring sufficient land in the valley, the coalition aims to

Tough bark and spinelike leaves protect araucarias, or monkey-puzzle trees, from grazers. They are among the most prominent trees in the temperate rain forests of southern Chile, though their valuable lumber has made them increasingly scarce.

ensure that the alerce saplings growing in the shade of their giant forebears endure another 3,000 years.

The battle to save Cochamó reflects a wider struggle going on within Chile to protect the country's great temperate rain forests, a battle that should concern nature-lovers the world over. For southern Chile and the Andean fringe of Argentina harbor not just all of South America's temperate rain forests, but no less than one-third of the world's total.

Valdivian Forests

Cut off from the rest of the planet's forested realm by Antarctica to the south, the Andes to the east, the Pacific Ocean to the west, and the sere deserts to the north, the Chilean rain forests constitute a veritable botanical island. As a consequence, they support one of the highest levels of endemism on Earth. Of their 82 woody genera, for example, 28 are endemic. Many have only one or two species, identifying them as relicts from an earlier epoch. Additionally, 23 percent of reptiles, 30 percent of birds, 33 percent of mammals, 50 percent of freshwater fish, and 76 percent of amphibians are found nowhere else.

Botanists divide Chile's rain forests into three categories: Valdivian, North Patagonian, and Magellanic. The most diverse of these, Valdivian, is found mainly in the Lake District, a beautifully scenic region that lies about 370 miles (595km) south of the nation's capital, Santiago. Extending from near the town of **Temuco** in the north to **Puerto Montt** in the south, the Lake District is noted not only for its forests but also its soaring, snow-mantled volcanic peaks, thermal springs, and sparkling sapphire lakes. The traditional homeland of the country's largest indigenous group, the Mapuche, it is today one of Chile's most popular ecotravel destinations.

The growth of the great Valdivian rain forests is fueled by huge Pacific storms that regularly collide with the western face of the Andes. The mountains force the clouds to yield their liquid cargo, drenching the peaks and forests below and charging the region's innumerable lakes and streams. Valdivian forests are home to several unique hardwood species, primarily beeches, but they are best known for their evergreens, most notably the giant alerce and the araucaria, or monkey-puzzle tree, an umbrella-like conifer of ancient lineage; botanists estimate that it has been around for 200 million years.

A rich array of fauna also inhabits Valdivian forest. Mammals include the puma and several endemics such as the pudu deer and the monito del monte, an arbo-

Alerce trees (top), relatives of the sequoia, reach a height of 150 feet (46m) and live up to 3,000 years.

Climbers (left) traverse the icy slopes of Villarrica Volcano.

Great horned owls (right) hunt small mammals, reptiles, and other birds, and can capture prey two or three times larger than themselves.

real possum with exceptionally large, dark eyes. Native birds are exquisitely adapted to the environment. Magellanic woodpeckers, for example, depend on old-growth snags for successful nesting, as do a number of owl species. Other notable and commonly sighted rain-forest birds include fire-crowned hummingbirds, white-crested elaenias, chucaos, thorn-tailed rayaditos, austral thrushes, and Patagonian sierra finches.

The Lake District has numerous national parks, natural monuments, and national reserves. This would suggest that the forests are heavily protected, but, unhappily, this isn't the case. Conservation statutes are not always enforced in Chile and poaching, logging, mining, and road building have infiltrated many supposedly protected areas. Transnational timber companies, in particular, are intent on clearing native trees and replanting them with fast-growing exotics. According to some reports, at the current rate of harvest all of the country's virgin forest will be gone within 35 years.

The Lake District faces an especially dire threat: the Cascada Chile megaproject. A planned joint venture between the U.S. firm of Boise Cascade and the Chilean Maderas Condor corporation, it involves the construction of a woodchip and fiberboard plant in Ilque Bay, to be supplied by local native forests. Over a 20-year period, almost one million acres of rain forest would be denuded. Environmentalists are currently fighting the project in both local and international arenas.

Lakeside Groves

These threats notwithstanding, there are several places in the Lake District where prime Valdivian forest can still be enjoyed. Situated near Temuco is 60,832-acre (24,618-hectare) **Conguillío National Park**, which is dominated by **Llaima Volcano**, an active cone that erupts with some regularity. Its last serious spasm occurred in 1958, when lava destroyed the forest on the volcano's southern flank. The

northern slope, however, still supports lovely, mature stands of araucarias. Visitors can either climb the volcano (a challenging 12-hour scramble) or follow a five-hour circuit trail through the araucaria groves. As you hike here, you may come across pudu deer browsing in the forest or a vizcacha skulking through the understory; other resident but more elusive mammals include gray foxes and pumas. Large flocks of slender-billed and austral parakeets often wheel above the

The Araucaria Tree

In a cluster of ramshackle dwellings in the Andean foothills, an elderly indigenous woman with a deeply lined face, dark leathery skin, and sparkling eyes extends her quavering hand. It is filled with brown-shelled nuts about an inch and a half long. "You see these?" she says, referring to the nuts from the araucaria trees that inhabit the slopes above her home. "We can't live without these." The woman is a Pehuenche (literally, "people of the pine-nut tree"), a highland Mapuche group for whom the nuts are a staple food and an important trading commodity.

Araucarias, called pehuéns by the Mapuches and also known as Chilean pines or monkey-puzzle trees, are conifers that grow from central Chile southward throughout most of the Lake District and are typically found several thousand feet up mountain slopes, often as high as the timberline. They can take up to five centuries to mature, growing as high as 150 feet (46m), and can live for 1,500 years or more. Imposing trees, they have tiered, oddly shaped branches covered with spiky, overlapping emerald leaves and produce male and female cones in order to reproduce. In the 20th century, to the dismay of conservationists and the Pehuenche, araucarias were logged heavily for their prized, yellow-white hardwood. In 1990, however, President Aylwin signed a decree banning further logging of these stately forest guardians. – *Michael Shapiro*

canopy, squawking raucously, while jewel-like endemic songbirds such as the chucao, with its blue head and orange breast, flit from branch to branch. Watch, too, for scavengers such as crested caracaras and Andean condors, as well as a rich variety of waterfowl on and around the lakes.

Situated nine miles (15km) outside the popular tourist center of **Pucón**, the privately owned **Cañi Forest Reserve** is very small – about 1,200 acres (486 hectares) – but choice. Occupying the caldera of an extinct Pleistocene volcano, part of the traditional homeland of the Pehuenche people, it is bordered by rocky outcrops that provide stunning vistas of surrounding forest, four volcanoes, and

Lake Villarrica. The caldera supports mature stands of araucarias and is home to austral wildcats, pumas, and a wide variety of birds. Star avian attractions include the black-necked swan – an elegant fowl that frequents the lakes and marshes – a stunning range of hummingbirds, and condors, which are often seen coasting over crags and cinder cones in search of choice carrion.

Valdivia National Reserve, located near the coast, west of the colonial riverside town of **Valdivia**, is, as yet, little known. That means that its 25,000 acres (10,000 hectares) of dense temperate rain forest remain relatively untouched, but it also means that services are limited and access difficult. The best bet is to contact the forestry commission office in Valdivia to arrange a visit. Wildlife watching is at its best early or late in the day, when you're likely to see scores of avian species disporting in the canopy. In winter, the edge of the reserve is grazed by cattle, which helps keep the underbrush down and, in turn, improves your chances of spotting shy mammals such as austral wildcats and pudu deer.

If alerces pique your interest, **Alerce**

Andino National Park, east of Puerto Montt, is a must. Covering 97,000 acres (39,300 hectares), it extends from sea level to 5,112 feet (1,558m) and includes some of the country's finest extant

stands of alerces in around 50,000 acres (20,200 hectares) of old-growth groves. In many places, the rain-forest canopy is multi-storied, with subsidiary stands of southern beeches – coihue de Chiloé, tineo, manio, and canelo – growing under the alerces.

An excellent network of trails allows visitors to explore these forests as well as the 50 or so pristine mountain lakes and tarns sequestered in the park's lush interior. At dawn or dusk, you may spot pudu and huemel deer in clearings or at forest edges. The region's wild felines, including pumas and austral wildcats, are more retiring, but you may come across their spoor, especially near streambeds. Condors are often seen riding thermals over high peaks, while upland geese, southern ringed kingfishers, and Chile higeons (a kind of duck) frequent the lakes and streams. Other species keenly sought by birders include Magellanic woodpeckers, bat-winged hawks, black- and chestnut-throated huet-huets, and tufted tit-tyrants.

The **Cochamó Valley** lies about 80 miles (130km) east of Puerto Montt. Its magnificent scenery and ancient trees are best viewed on hiking and riding trips organized by local outfitters. In the forests, where more than 300 kinds of plants have been recorded, thick foliage can make it hard to spot mammals. The trees, however, are normally alive with avian species: hummingbirds sip nectar from flowering shrubs, carrion hawks scan for carcasses from prominent snags, and Chilean lapwings and slender-billed parakeets swarm through the canopy.

One of the most popular tours here follows the so-called **Gaucho Trail**, a historic horse route across the Andes originally pioneered by Jesuit missionaries in the 17th century. In the early 20th century, Butch Cassidy and the Sundance Kid rode this trail regularly, bringing cattle to Chilean markets from their ranch on the Argentinian pampas, where they lived a respectable, law-abiding life for five years or so.

Generally, however, facilities and services are limited at Cochamó, and the region has been little developed for tourism. And if local conservationists have their way, that's the way it will stay – it and all the other ancient rain forests of this majestic region.

TRAVEL TIPS

DETAILS

How to Get There

The main gateway to Chile is Santiago's international airport, which has connections to major cities throughout the country.

When to Go

The parks in the region, especially temperate rain forests, can receive 158 to 197 inches (400–500cm) of rain annually. May through August are the coldest, wettest months, with temperatures as low as 50°F (10°C). September to December and March to April are mild with little rain. January and February are warm, with temperatures reaching 84°F (29°C), but can also be rainy. October to December is a good time to see many flowers in bloom. The Lake District is a popular holiday destination for Chileans; January and February, the peak vacation months, can be exceedingly busy.

Getting Around

Travelers can head south from Santiago to the Lake District by rail, bus, or domestic airline. There is bus service from all major cities to Pucón, a good base from which to explore the northern Lake District, and Puerto Montt in the south. However, some of the parks are off public transport routes, so those who wish to cover a lot of ground and access out-of-the-way places should rent a vehicle in Santiago and drive south on the Panamerican Highway.

INFORMATION

Chile Tourism Promotion Corporation

Santa Beatriz 84B, Santiago, Chile; tel: 56-2-235-0105; fax: 56-2-235-3384; www.prochile.cl

Comité Nacional pro Defensa de Flora y Fauna

Bilbao 691, Providencia, Santiago, Chile (casilla 3675); tel: 56-2-251-0262; fax: 56-2-251-8433; www.netup.cl~codeff

This is the local arm of Friends of the Earth.

National Forestry Corporation

Avenida Bulnes 285, Santiago, Chile; tel: 56-2-390-0000 or 56-2-696-6724; Pucón/Villarrica office: O'Higgins 1355, Pucón; tel: 56-45-441-261; www.conaf.cl

Sernatur

Avenida Providencia 1550, Santiago, Chile (casilla 14082); tel: 56-2-236-4054 or 56-2-236-1420; fax: 56-2-251-8469 or 56-2-236-1417.

Sernatur is Chile's national tourism agency.

Travelhouse

San Pedro Number 422, Puerto Varas, Chile; tel/fax: 56-65-232-747; www.travelhouse.cl

A good source of information on the Lake District.

CAMPING

Car and backcountry camping are allowed in many of the parks of the Lake District.

LODGING

PRICE GUIDE – double occupancy

$ = up to $49 $$ = $50–$99

$$$ = $100–$149 $$$$ = $150+

Hosteria ¡École!

General Urrutia 592, IX Region, Pucón, Chile; tel: 56-45-441-675; fax: 56-45-441-660; e-mail: trek@ecole.cl

United States: P.O. Box 2453, Redway, CA 95560; tel: 800-447-1483; fax: 707-923-3001.

Chilean ecotravelers flock to this environmentally sound accommodation, which offers shared and private rooms with either shared or private bathrooms, and has a good vegetarian restaurant. The Hosteria also offers activity packages through ¡Ecole! Adventures International, including hiking, biking, horseback riding, whitewater rafting, kayaking, volcano climbing, volunteer conservation work, and fishing, as well as excursions to nearby hot springs. $–$$

Hotel Antumalal

One kilometer outside Pucón, Chile; tel: 56-45-441-011 or 56-45-441-012; fax: 56-45-441-013; e-mail: antumalal@pucon.com

Situated on a wooded hilltop overlooking Lake Villarrica, this resort has 16 rooms and cottages with fireplaces, floor-to-ceiling windows, and private bathrooms. The management arranges rafting, horseback riding, caving, excursions to hot springs, and other activities. $$$–$$$$

Outsider

San Bernardo 318, Puerto Varas, X Region, Chile; tel/fax: 56-65-232-910; e-mail: outsider@telsur.cl

This lodge, housing rooms with private baths, offers packages focusing on rafting, trekking, geology, sea kayaking, and horseback riding in the rain forest. $

Termas Puyehue

Casilla 36-0, Ruta 215, Km 76, Osorno, X Region de Los Lagos, Chile; tel: 56-2-293-6000 or 56-2-231-3417; fax: 56-2-283-1010 or 56-64-232-881; e-mail: puyehue@ctcreuna.cl

At the foot of Puyehue volcano, Termas Puyehue offers basic rooms, suites, and interconnected family rooms, all with private bathrooms and hot water. Hiking, biking, fishing, skiing, and other activities are available. $$–$$$

TOURS AND OUTFITTERS

ACE Turismo

Avenida Libertador Bernardo O'Higgins 949, Piso 16, Santiago, Chile; tel: 56-2-696-0391 or 56-2-698-1433; fax: 56-2-672-7483.

Chile's oldest adventure tourism

company offers trips throughout the country.

Altué Expediciones

Encomenderos 83, Las Condes, Santiago, Chile; tel: 56-2-32-1103; fax: 56-2-233-6799.

Travelers can choose from a range of hiking, rafting, and sea-kayaking trips throughout the Lake District.

AquaMotion

San Pedro 422, Puerto Varas, Chile; tel: 56-65-232-747; fax: 56-65-235-938; e-mail: aquamotn@tel sur.cl or info@aquamotion.cl

Graded for various levels of difficulty, these multiday adventures in the Lake District include rafting, photo safaris, nature treks, volcano climbing, fly-fishing, horseback riding, and glacier excursions.

Campo Aventura

San Bernardo 318, Puerto Varas, Chile; tel: 56-65-232-910; e-mail: outsider@telsur.cl

This outfitter specializes in horseback trekking in the region and runs an outback camp and nature-study trail in the Cochamó Valley.

Cascada Expediciones

Orrego Luco 054, Providencia, Santiago, Chile; tel: 56-2-234-2274 or 56-2-232-7214; fax: 56-2-233-9768; e-mail: info@cascada-expediciones.com

Multiday adventures and shorter excursions throughout the Lake District include forest treks, snowshoeing, horseback riding, hiking, rafting, and mountain biking.

¡Ecole! Adventures International

P.O. Box 2453, Redway, CA 95560; tel: 800-447-1483; fax: 707-923-3001; www.asis.com/ecole

This company's ecotourism adventures in Chile's Lake District include forest and volcano treks, whitewater rafting, horseback riding in the mountains, fishing, and biking. Packages include stays at Hostería ¡École! in Pucón.

Excursions

Chiloé National Park

CONAF, Calle Gamboa 424, Castro, Chiloé, X Region, Chile; tel/fax: 65-63-22-89; e-mail: C247hrrm@conaf.cl

Located south of Puerto Montt, the Chiloé archipelago is renowned for its historic fishing villages, rich indigenous culture, and splendid scenery. Much of its wildest country is encompassed by Chiloé National Park, where modern-day travelers can follow in the footsteps of Charles Darwin (who visited in 1834–35) through a belt of evergreen coastal rain forest to vast, deserted beaches. The small, black Chilote fox, miniature pudu deer, long-snouted rat opossum, and monito del monte are just a few of the notable endemics; other residents include sea otters, sea lions, and penguins.

Los Glaciares National Park

Intendencia, Parque Nacional Los Glaciares, Avenida del Libertador 1302, El Calafate 9405, Provincia de Santa Cruz, Argentina; tel: 54-902-91005.

Near the southern tip of Argentina, great glaciers grind down granite slopes and across the plains into immense mountain lakes, where the creaking of ice carries for miles across the gelid waters. Visitors can walk or boat to the snouts of these spectacular rivers of ice and hike into the surrounding countryside, where majestic peaks rise above thick forests of ancient beech.

Torres del Paine National Park

National Forestry Corporation, José Menendez 1147, Punta Arenas, Chile; tel: 56-61-223-420; fax: 56-61-243-498.

Thrusting skyward from the snow-encrusted slopes of Torres del Paine is one of South America's natural wonders: the group of three rock towers that gives this southern Andean park its name. These stunning peaks, which take on an orange-brown hue in the late afternoon sun, aren't the only attraction. Backcountry hikers are rewarded with astounding views of glaciers, icy lakes, and ragged mountain ranges. Despite the chilly climate, wildlife abounds, including foxes, condors, swans, flamingos, and llama-like guanacos.

Northern Vietnam

CHAPTER 15

By the time North Vietnamese troops crashed through the gates of the Presidential Palace in Saigon on April 30, 1975, three decades of armed conflict on Vietnamese soil had created an environmental disaster. American armed forces had dropped thousands of napalm bombs and sprayed more than 19 million gallons (72 million liters) of Agent Orange and other potent herbicides over the countryside, resulting in the destruction of an estimated 5.4 million acres (2.2 million hectares) of forest and the loss of untold numbers of animals. Since then, logging and slash-and-burn agriculture have also taken a heavy toll on the environment, and the country's total forest cover has dwindled from 43 percent in 1943 to around 19 percent today. Yet, in recent years various conservation and large-scale reforestation programs have been implemented, and in some areas plant and animal populations are slowly beginning to recover. ◆ Researchers estimate that Vietnam still harbors about 12,000 plant species, 260 species of reptiles and amphibians, and more than 770 bird and 275 mammal species, including at least three large mammal species that eluded scientific discovery until the 1990s. This astonishing diversity, which exists in an area only half the size of Texas, can be partly attributed to the varied terrain. A narrow, S-shaped slice of Indochina that extends over 1,000 miles (1,600km) from north to south, Vietnam includes two major river deltas, more than 2,000 miles (3,200km) of coastline, a mountainous interior, and a mix of tropical and subtropical weather patterns. These support a remarkable variety of habitats, ranging from coral reefs and

Scattered pockets of wilderness shelter diverse bird life, endangered primates, and rare mammals that have only recently been discovered.

Limestone islands jut from the waters of Ha Long Bay. The Cat Ba archipelago encompasses more than 350 islands peppered with isolated beaches and grottoes and bristling with dense vegetation.

evolve independently from others in the region, leading to a greater variety of species in a relatively small area.

Rising from the Ashes

Following the war, Vietnam's Ministry of Forestry, with technical and financial assistance from the World Wide Fund for Nature, the World Conservation Union, and other environmental groups, implemented an ambitious management plan that has set aside more than 7,500 square miles (19,400 sq km) of protected wilderness – about six percent of the country. This currently includes 10 national parks and 49 nature reserves. More recently, the government initiated a project to plant more than 500 million trees in an attempt to reverse the ongoing diminution of its forests.

Ironically, the years of war probably helped to preserve flora and fauna in remote wilderness areas by retarding economic development during the second half of the 20th century – a time when other Southeast Asian nations, such as Thailand and Malaysia, were rapidly exploiting their natural resources. Of course, limited development also means limited infrastructure, and access to many of Vietnam's preserves remains difficult. But with improving transportation and growing private-sector involvement in tourism, the country has recently emerged as an important destination for nature travelers. In particular, several national parks in northern Vietnam offer exciting opportunities for visiting rain-forest habitats and observing diverse and unusual wildlife.

High Country Refuges

Vietnam's oldest and most user-friendly national park, **Cuc Phuong**, lies only 100 miles (160km) from **Hanoi**. When the park was established under North Vietnamese president Ho Chi Minh in 1962, few people lived in

mangroves to more than 30,000 square miles (77,500 sq km) of forests, including deciduous montane, temperate conifer, broadleaf, and lowland dipterocarp forests. Most of the country's surviving rain forest is confined to upland areas, the plains having been cleared for agriculture, and it's here that biodiversity is particularly pronounced. This could be the result of intermittent periods of cooler, drier weather during the ice ages of the Pleistocene epoch, which may have left some plant and animal populations temporarily isolated in pockets of surviving forest. This fragmentation would have allowed separate population groups to

Butterflies (above) are particularly abundant in early spring.

Traditional ways of life (left) persist among the northern hill tribes.

White-cheeked gibbons (bottom) establish their territory with loud, melodic calls, often sung as a "duet" with their monogamous mates.

this mountainous region. Since then, however, migrants from the densely populated **Red River Delta** to the north have encroached on adjacent lands, prompting the description of Cuc Phuong as a "patch of green laid in an immense sea of human beings."

The park has around 55,000 acres (22,250 hectares) of forest, and with rainfall about 224 days of the year, most is seasonal evergreen forest or lowland tropical rain forest. The clearing of trees from buffer zones surrounding the preserve has taken its toll on native animal populations, but Cuc Phuong still shelters a number of rare mammals, including red-bellied squirrels, Delacour langurs (a subspecies of the Francois' leaf monkey), and small populations of leopards and tigers. These threatened species have survived by seeking refuge in the most inaccessible areas of the park and are therefore rarely seen. However, hikers on Cuc Phuong's extensive trail system are sure to see plenty of bird life and butterflies amid the massive, centuries-old trees.

The 3.7-mile (6-km) loop trail from the visitor center leads through stands of primal rain forest, including magnificent examples of the dipterocarp *Parashorea stellata*, which can grow as high as 230 feet (70m), and massive, tangled vines. Halfway along the trail you'll encounter a particularly venerable example of the deciduous tree *Terminalia myriocarpa*, which has been enshrined with its own special viewing platform. Keep an eye out for red jungle fowl (the wild ancestor of the domestic chicken) and gray peacock pheasants in the understory, and pied hornbills and red-headed trogons on higher perches. If you're lucky, you may spot a tree squirrel scurrying

along a high branch or a spotted deer nibbling on foliage. In April and May, huge numbers of butterflies throng these forests.

Visitors can also join guided hikes to remote villages of indigenous Hmong people – one of the many groups that add to Vietnam's diverse ethnic heritage – and tours of Cuc Phuong's remarkable limestone caves, which contain evidence of prehistoric human occupation. And if the park's mammals have eluded you, you can take a closer look at some of them at the five-acre **Endangered Primate Rescue Center**. Established in 1993, it cares for captive monkeys confiscated from poachers and black-market traders, with the ultimate goal of reintroducing the animals to the wild.

Also accessible on a short excursion from Hanoi is **Ba Be National Park**, a 200-square-mile (500-sq-km) reserve located 150

passage inhabited by bats and traversed by a navigable waterway.

Ba Be is also home to small communities of Dai and Hmong people, and visitors can make arrangements at park headquarters to stay a night in the village of **Pac Ngoi**, less than half an hour away by boat, where they will be lodged in an authentic Dai stilt house.

Surf 'n' Turf

About 100 miles (160km) east of Hanoi at **Ha Long Bay**, the warm waters of the **Gulf of Tonkin** meet the karst formations of northeastern Vietnam to form a dramatic coastal landscape dotted with hundreds of steep limestone islands. In 1986, the eastern half of the largest island in the archipelago, **Cat Ba**, was declared a national park along with 20 square miles (52 sq km) of the adjacent marine environment and offshore islands. A visit to Cat Ba offers nature travelers a chance to explore lowland rain forest as well as coastal mountains, freshwater lakes, fecund mangrove forest, sandy beaches, and coral reefs – all in one reasonably compact area.

Many of the forest trails are unmarked and some can be challenging, so it's wise to hire a guide. Birds, including white swallows and tigrine doves, are abundant, and there's a chance of spotting Tonkin snub-nosed monkeys perched on trees high up on the precipitous limestone slopes. Longer excursions usually explore the wild southeastern corner of the park, where walkers can visit and stay overnight at the remote village of **Viet Hai**.

Visitors can also hire boats for day trips into the maze of islands and mangroves in

miles (240km) north of the capital, which contains Vietnam's largest natural lake. Ba Be Lake cuts a scenic swath between steep, jagged limestone formations cloaked with montane forest. This environment is home to 400 plant species, 111 kinds of birds, and 64 mammal species, including 33 varieties of bats and a small population of rare Tonkin snub-nosed monkeys. As at Cuc Phuong, encounters with large mammals are rare, but the lake and adjoining rivers provide effortless access to magnificent wilderness.

The best way to sample the scenery is to hire a boat and guide near park headquarters. As you drift along the verdant waterways, past towering limestone cliffs, caves, forests, and waterfalls, rhesus macaque monkeys leap and chatter among the high branches of the lakeside trees and squawking parrots hurtle overhead. For a taste of adventure, head for **Hang Puong** at the north end of the lake, a 1,000-foot-long (305-m) subterranean

Hikers (top) explore Cat Ba National Park. Trails can be strenuous and confusing; it's advisable to hire a guide.

The Rheinard's pheasant (left) is found only in the rain forests of Vietnam and Malaysia.

nearby **Lan Ha Bay**. Snorkelers will find the reefs off Cat Ba teeming with hard and soft corals, marine invertebrates, and more than 100 species of saltwater fish. Several species of dolphins and sea turtles are also present but seldom seen.

Coastal Colony

Three hundred miles (480km) to the south in Vietnam's narrow midsection, the much smaller **Bach Ma National Park** sits atop coastal mountains in an area that once served as a French colonial summer resort. The old hill station is now in ruins, but modern-day travelers are increasingly making the short journey inland from the coastal town of **Phu Loc** to explore Bach Ma's 85 square miles (220 sq km) of evergreen forest. With peaks reaching almost 5,000 feet (1,500m) above sea level and a blend of flora from the tropical south and subtropical north of Vietnam, Bach Ma is particularly rich in plant life, and more than 500 species of vascular plants grow here. It is also fertile ground for ornithologists, with 233 species of birds on record, and there are at least 55 mammal species.

Facilities remain fairly primitive – accommodations and trails are still under development – but providing you take a guide and are well-prepared, walking in Bach Ma can be a memorable experience.

Caves (left) honeycomb the limestone islands of Ha Long Bay, providing habitat for bats as well as a variety of marine invertebrates such as starfish and crabs. Some hold evidence of early human habitation.

Rice fields (below) surround isolated patches of forest in the valleys of the northern highlands.

Pathways wind through lush rain forest, past bubbling streams and jagged peaks. Black gibbons, macaques, and Douc langurs call from the canopy, and jungle fowl and pheasants forage on the forest floor. And although you are unlikely to spot one, you can revel in the knowledge that these same trails are trodden by some of the country's last remaining clouded leopards.

Experiences such as these underline the crucial role that national parks and other reserves play in the preservation of Vietnam's remarkable habitats and wildlife. As the country continues to recover from a war-torn past, these protected areas offer hope that growing numbers of visitors will be able to enjoy this country's ecological treasures while contributing to their long-term survival.

DETAILS

How to Get There

Hanoi is the principal gateway to northern Vietnam, with frequent flights from major cities in Asia. Danang in central Vietnam has a small airport that receives a limited number of flights from outside the country.

When to Go

Northern Vietnam has a distinct winter, with temperatures sometimes dropping to 32°F (0°C) and plenty of rain from November to March or April. Summer is hot, with occasional typhoons. Altitude has a significant effect on temperature and, in some cases, on precipitation, so travelers visiting the highland areas (including most of the national parks) should always be prepared for variable weather conditions.

Getting Around

Vietnam is not an easy "do-it-yourself" destination: away from the major tourist routes, getting around can be difficult, with little or no public transportation available in many areas. For this reason, travelers bound for national parks and nature reserves should consider joining a group tour or arranging guides and transportation through a tour operator. For longer journeys, a slow but affordable north-south rail system is available, as well as an extensive network of domestic flights. Ferry service links the island of Cat Ba to the town of Hai Phong.

INFORMATION

Vietnam National Administration of Tourism

80 Quan Su, Hanoi, Vietnam; tel: 84-4-825-2246 or 84-4-825-7072; fax: 84-4-826-3956; e-mail: titc@vietnamtourism.com; www.vietnamtourism.com

This agency provides information on general tourism, Vietnam's national parks, and lodging.

INTERNET RESOURCES

Destination Vietnam

www.destinationvietnam.com

Vietnam Adventures

www.vietnamadventures.com

Vietnam Online

www.vietnamonline.net/

CAMPING

Camping is not advisable in Vietnam's national parks.

LODGING

PRICE GUIDE – double occupancy

$ = up to $49 $$ = $50–$99

$$$ = $100–$149 $$$$ = $150+

Bong Sen Hotel

117-123 Dong Khoi Street, District 1, Ho Chi Minh City, Vietnam; tel: 84-8-829-1516; fax: 84-8-829-8076.

This 136-room hotel is in the middle of the Dong Khoi shopping district and day-trip distance from Nam Cat Tien National Park. Amenities include a health club. $$–$$$$

Caravelle Hotel

19 Lam Son Square, District 1, Ho Chi Minh City, Vietnam; tel: 84-8-829-3704; fax: 84-4-829-9902; e-mail: caravellehotel@bdvn.vnd.net

This hotel in the center of the city has 335 rooms, including suites and apartments. Day trips include Nam Cat Tien National Park. $$$–$$$$

Especen

79-E Hang Trong Street, Hanoi, Vietnam; tel: 84-4-826-6856; fax: 84-4-826-9612; e-mail: especen@fpt.vn

Ten small inns around the Old Quarter offer 66 spare but clean rooms with private baths. Cuc Phuong and Ba Be National Parks are in the area. $

Hai Au Hotel

177 Tran Phu Street, Danang, Vietnam; tel: 84-511-822-722; fax: 84-511-824-165.

This modern hotel with air-conditioned rooms is near Bach Ma National Park. $$

Huong Giang Hotel

51 Le Loi Street, Hue, Vietnam; tel: 84-54-822-182; fax: 84-54-823-424.

Set on the Perfume River, this hotel has 42 air-conditioned rooms with refrigerators. Amenities include a restaurant, tennis courts, and boat trips. Bach Ma National Park is nearby. $$–$$$$

National Parks

Vietnam National Administration of Tourism, 80 Quan Su, Hanoi, Vietnam; tel: 84-4-825-2246 or 84-4-825-7072; fax: 84-4-826-3956; www.vietnamtourism.com

To arrange lodging, it's best either to travel with a group tour or to contact tour agents in Hanoi or Ho Chi Minh City. Because there is limited lodging near or in Vietnamese national parks, tour groups generally take day trips to the parks from larger towns and cities. Those who wish to stay at the parks are typically limited to basic government-run park lodges or rustic guest houses and small hotels in nearby towns.

TOURS AND OUTFITTERS

Ann's Tourist Company

58 Ton That Tung, Ben Thanh Ward, District 1, Ho Chi Minh City, Vietnam; tel: 84-8-833-2564; fax: 84-8-832-3866; e-mail: anntours@yahoo.com

Culture and adventure tours travel throughout Vietnam, including Nam Cat Tien National Park.

Asian Trails

Mercury Tower, 15th Floor, 540 Ploenchit Road, Bangkok 10330, Thailand; tel: 66-2-658-6080; fax: 66-2-658-6099; e-mail: info@asiantrails.com

A variety of tours and day excursions visit destinations throughout Vietnam and Southeast Asia.

Asia Transpacific Journeys

2995 Center Green Court, Boulder, CO 80301; tel: 303-443-6789 or 800-642-2742; fax: 303-443-7078; e-mail: travel@southeastasia.com

Group trips and custom programs range from strenuous to relaxing and include scuba diving, rafting, trekking, and cultural home stays. This outfitter works in Vietnam, Papua New Guinea, Australia, and New Zealand.

Diethelm Travel

218 Ba Trieu Street, Hanoi, Vietnam; tel: 84-4-934-4844; fax: 84-4-934-4850; e-mail: dtvl@netnam.vn

Package tours throughout Vietnam and Southeast Asia include coach trips and cruises.

Exotissimo Travel

Saigon Trade Center, 37 Ton Duc Thang Street, District 1, Ho Chi Minh City, Vietnam; tel: 84-8-825-1723; fax: 84-8-829-5800; e-mail: richard@exotissimo.com

Cultural and historical tours include a trip that visits villages of traditional people.

Global Spectrum

1901 Pennsylvania Avenue, N.W., Suite 204, Washington, DC 20006; tel: 202-293-2065 or 800-419-4446; fax: 202-296-0815; e-mail: gspectrum@gspectrum.com

Ranging from eight to 30 days, Global Spectrum trips include cultural, hiking, rafting, kayaking, photography, culinary, and customized experiences. Tours can be extended to Laos, Cambodia, and Myanmar.

Excursions

Nam Cat Tien National Park

Vietnam National Administration of Tourism, 80 Quan Su, Hanoi, Vietnam; tel: 84-4-825-2246 or 84-4-825-7072; fax: 84-4-826-3956; e-mail: titc@vietnamtourism.com; www.vietnamtourism.com

Situated 100 miles (160km) north of Ho Chi Minh City, Nam Cat Tien is best known as one of the last remaining refuges of the extremely rare Javan rhinoceros. Founded in 1992, the park was merged in 1998 with neighboring Cat Loc Rhinoceros Reserve to create a 300-square-mile (780-sq-km) rhinoceros stronghold. The park is also home to elephants, tigers, gaur oxen, a wide range of primates, 260 bird species, and more than 600 plant species.

Wolong Nature Reserve

Wolong Nature Reserve Administration, Wenchuan County, Sichuan Province, 623006, China; tel: 86-837-624-6618 or 86-837-624-6615; fax: 86-837-624-6614.

In 1975, the Wolong Nature Reserve was established in southern China's Sichuan Province to preserve the dwindling habitat of the endangered giant panda. While panda sightings are rare in the 800 square miles (2,100 sq km) of alpine and subalpine forest, the area is rich in flora and fauna, including some 3,000 plant species and about a fifth of all animal species found in China.

Yokdon National Park

Vietnam National Administration of Tourism, 80 Quan Su, Hanoi, Vietnam; tel: 84-4-825-2246 or 84-4-825-7072; fax: 84-4-826-3956; www.vietnam tourism.com

Located on the Cambodian border, 240 miles (386km) north of Ho Chi Minh City, Yokdon is Vietnam's largest national park, with a total area of 22,500 acres (9,100 hectares). It protects a large tract of ecologically vital dipterocarp and evergreen rain forest that is home to tigers, leopards, and wild elephants. Visitors can join elephant safaris and organized hikes, and visit the villages of indigenous M'nong, Giarai, and Ede people.

Khao Yai
National Park
Thailand

CHAPTER **16**

Dusk is falling rapidly in **Khao Yai National Park** and the mosquitoes are out in force. Yet the small group of people standing silently in a tangle of rain forest on the park's northeastern edge seem oblivious to the insects' whining presence. Their eyes are fixed on a nearby cliff, clearly visible through a break in the canopy, and the dark hollows and recesses of the caves that pock its face. ◆ A crested serpent-eagle soars into view and begins to patrol the airspace above the cliff. Binoculars are lifted to straining eyes; necks are craned to breaking point. Suddenly, the eagle swoops into a dive as a burst of tiny black specks erupts from the largest cave and scatters into the purpling sky. Bats! The eagle soars into view again, its talons empty – for now. Soon, a steady trickle of wrinkle-lipped bats emerges, thickens, and becomes an undulating, seemingly endless black ribbon. As they flutter over the forest canopy, searching for the insects and fruits that constitute their nightly feed, the bats' high-pitched cries echo from the cliff face.

Thundering cascades plummet into forested valleys, where the myriad colors of butterflies, birds, and orchids enliven the dense foliage.

◆ The eagle attacks again, yet still the bats pour from the dark recesses of their daytime roost. Some 40 minutes and hundreds of thousands of bats later, the spectacle shows no sign of abating. But against the darkening sky, the shapes of the bats become increasingly difficult to discern. Reluctantly, the spectators depart. ◆ Night has come to the jungle, but much of the wildlife in Thailand's most popular national park has just woken up. ◆ Established in 1962, Khao Yai, situated 125 miles (200km) northeast of Bangkok, is Thailand's oldest national park. Within its 837 square miles (2,168 sq km)

White-handed gibbons use their long arms to swing through the canopy. They eat mostly fruit and leaves, and live in small family groups consisting of a monogamous male and female and two or three offspring of varying ages.

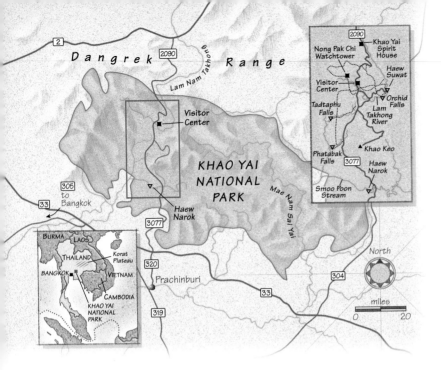

tropical rain forest (covering nearly 70 percent of the park); dry evergreen, mixed deciduous, and hill evergreen forests; plus savanna and second-growth forest in areas where agriculture and logging occurred before protection. Sustained by a monsoonal climate and an average annual rainfall of 89 inches (226cm), the forests shelter the headwaters of five major rivers, which swell to bursting in the rainy season, feeding more than 20 waterfalls. Rain also triggers the mass birth of what are perhaps the park's least popular animals – leeches. Taking them in stride is part of the rain-forest experience.

Sights and Sounds

Despite its monsoonal climate, Khao Yai is a park for all seasons, and trekking is one of its most rewarding activities. More than 30 miles (48km) of trails, many formed by wildlife, thread through the jungle. Guides are essential on all long-distance treks and advisable even on shorter routes, some of which are unmarked.

A number of trails, ranging in length from a half mile to five miles (1–8km), begin near the visitor center, which provides a useful introduction to Khao Yai's wildlife and habitats through displays (many in English) and maps. One of the best trails for spotting wildlife is the 2.1-mile (3.4-km) trail from KM 33, a distance marker on the main road, to **Nong Pak Chi Watchtower**. As you weave through towering dipterocarps, sops (*Altingia excelsa),* ma-mues (*Choerospondias axillaris),* and red cedars draped in mosses, lichens, climbers, and epiphytes, all may appear quiet; but for those with sharp eyes, signs of life are everywhere. Animal tracks, for example, abound. Among the species leaving evidence of their passage in the moist earth

lie one of mainland Asia's largest tracts of intact rain forest and an astonishing number and variety of plants and animals, including more than 70 mammal species, 74 reptile and amphibian species, more than 320 bird species, between 2,000 and 2,500 plant species, and thousands of insect species. About 250 elephants – the country's largest wild population – make their home in the park, as do about 50 tigers.

Khao Yai occupies the western tip of the **Dangrek Range**, which forms the southwest rim of the **Korat Plateau**. Its mountainous terrain, varying from 820 to 4,430 feet (250–1,350m), supports five vegetation zones:

Great hornbills (opposite) have odd nesting habits. The female is sealed into a cavity with mud and is fed by the male until her eggs hatch.

Sambar (right) are crowned with prominent three-tined antlers.

Asian elephants (bottom) are not as large as their African cousins, with smaller ears and a single fingerlike protuberance at the tip of their trunks.

racket-tailed drongo is perched nearby. And if you hear a loud whooshing noise like a steam locomotive, look up: a great hornbill – at up to four feet (1.2m) long, the largest and most impressive of the park's four hornbill species – may be flying overhead. The distinctive sound of the hornbill's flight results from a lack of underwing coverts, which allows air to pass through the wings.

Figs, particularly the strangling variety, are ubiquitous, providing a year-round source of fruit. One of the more impressive specimens, estimated to be about 500 years old, can be seen on a short detour about halfway along the path.

At Nong Pak Chi, the trail exits the forest abruptly, emerging onto rolling grassland. Here, a 65-foot-high (20-m) watchtower overlooking a large water hole and salt lick offers spectacular views as well as a prime opportunity for wildlife spotting. Elephants are known to frequent the salt lick, and sambar and barking deer often graze near the treeline. Birds abound: look out for great, wreathed, oriental pied, and brown hornbills, gray wagtails, black-naped orioles, and Indian rollers.

Nocturnal species can be viewed on

are sambar, barking deer, wild dogs, hog badgers, civets, and even elusive tigers and gaurs – which, at up to 6½ feet (2m) tall at the shoulder, are the world's largest species of wild ox. Deep claw marks on tree trunks indicate the recent presence of an Asiatic black bear. An excellent climber, the bear will not hesitate to scramble to the top of a 100-foot (30-m) tree to retrieve fruit or, even better, a beehive filled with honey.

Early-morning walkers may be greeted by the mournful cries of the white-handed gibbon, whose song can be heard from more than a mile away. With luck, you will spot these critically endangered animals high in the canopy, perhaps displaying their amazing acrobatic ability as they swing from branch to branch. Most walkers will hear, even if they don't immediately see, Khao Yai's prolific bird life. The white-crested laughing thrush announces its presence with scolding cackles and a chorus of hysterical laughter. What may sound like a giant cicada is actually the greater flameback, a member of the woodpecker family, while harsh whistles, ascending in tone, indicate the greater

spotlighting tours, which depart from headquarters twice each evening and involve riding in the back of a truck as it makes a slow 7½-mile (12-km) loop through forest and grassland. Although tigers rarely make an appearance, and elephants are only occasionally seen lying on the road, soaking up heat trapped in the asphalt, sightings of sambar and barking deer, civets, owls, porcupines, and snakes like the white-lipped pit viper are common.

Around the Falls

The power and beauty of Khao Yai's many waterfalls at the height of the rainy season are truly a sight to behold, and these great cascades are often happy hunting grounds for plant lovers and wildlife watchers alike. A word of warning: visitors should keep their distance from the falls and take care on slippery trails nearby. This is particularly the case at **Haew Narok**, the park's highest waterfall – about 12 miles (19km) south of park headquarters – which drops 500 feet (150m) in three stages. Tourists have slipped and fallen to their deaths here, and in August 1991 eight elephants were swept over the falls and drowned. Dangerous sections of the main trail are now closed during the rainy season, but caution is still required, especially on the steps to the viewing platform. It's worth the effort, however, as from close quarters the white water and billowing spray create an exhilarating spectacle.

Where there is water, there are bound to be butterflies, and a myriad of the jewel-bright insects, including the chocolate pansy, Paris peacock, royal assyrian, and great orange tip commonly lend their fragile beauty to this and other waterways. The forest around Haew Narok is also home to king cobras, at up to 20 feet (6m) long the largest venomous snake in the world. Encounters are rare, and despite its fearsome reputation, no bites have ever been recorded in Khao Yai.

Less spectacular than Haew Narok, but equally popular due to its year-round plunge pool, is 80-foot-high (24-m) **Haew Suwat Waterfall**, reached via an eight-mile (13-km) drive or a fairly strenuous five-mile (8-km) walk along an often slippery path from park headquarters. The area around Haew Suwat is pileated gibbon territory. Like its white-

Kaeng Krachan National Park

Travelers keen to explore more of Thailand's rich rain-forest habitats should head for the country's largest national park, **Kaeng Krachan**. Located 125 miles (200km) southwest of Bangkok, it is a paradise for hikers and naturalists, offering some of the country's best trekking and most exotic animals.

Relatively undeveloped, Kaeng Krachan encompasses mountains, steep cliffs, caves, waterfalls, grasslands and a 17-square-mile (44-sq-km) reservoir. Some 90 percent of its 1,125 square miles (2,915 sq km) is virgin woodland, most of it rain forest. This undisturbed world is home to at least 250 bird, 300 butterfly, and 40 mammal species, including wild elephants, palm civets, Asiatic black bears, Malayan sun bears, Malayan tapirs, and clouded leopards.

A day-long trek, or two-hour drive, to the summit of **Khao Phanoen Thung** – at 3,960 feet (1207m), the park's highest peak – is obligatory. Early in the morning, the view of the valley, in which densely forested peaks often appear to rise like islands from a sea of fog, is an unforgettable sight. Another highlight is the 2½-mile (4-km) trek to the 18-tiered **Tothip Falls**. Along the way, look out for white-handed gibbons and black giant squirrels, which may be heard crashing about the canopy. Despite its size – up to 32 inches (80cm) – the giant squirrel moves with surprising swiftness, often leaping gaps of 20 feet (6m) or more.

For a less strenuous outing, rent a boat or join a cruise to explore the scenic reservoir, which is ringed by mountains and dotted with wooded islands. Abundant waterbirds and waders include a small community of endangered woolly-necked storks, while false gavials, members of the crocodile family, inhabit remote coves.

A gibbon infant (opposite, top) clings to its mother.

Exuberant plant life (opposite, bottom) crowds the understory.

The clouded leopard (below), an elusive arboreal cat, inhabits the high country of Kaeng Krachan.

Indian rollers (bottom) are one of the region's most colorful birds.

handed cousin, the pileated gibbon sports a fringe of white fur around its leathery face, but it is distinguished by a white beard that splays out on both sides of its face.

Orchid lovers should follow the 1.4-mile (2.3-km) path along the **Lam Takhong River** from the parking lot at Haew Suwat to the aptly named **Orchid Falls**. Those visiting in May will be treated to a brilliant display of blooming *Renanthera coccinea*, which adorn many trees in the area. Along the way, look out for impressive Indo-Chinese water dragons, resting on tree branches overhanging the water, and gliding lizards cleverly camouflaged against the lichen-encrusted trunks.

Several signs on the main road to park headquarters entreat visitors not to feed the monkeys. The message appears to have been less than effective because an additional sign has now been posted: "Monkeys: don't take food from humans." A legacy of the illicit offerings is that pig-tailed macaques are

particularly evident along this stretch of road.

Other illegal activities have had a more destructive effect. Logging and poaching are an ongoing problem despite the presence of some 20 park substations; countermeasures include the construction of a road around the park's perimeter, which will make surveillance easier. Poachers hunt animals for food and to sell to the wildlife trade; loggers target trees such as the eagle-wood, which is prized for its fragrant timber.

Rangers are not the park's only guardians, however. Just inside the northern entrance stands the **Khao Yai Spirit House**, where offerings are made to the spirit who protects the forest and its wildlife. Locals greet it with a *wai*, a prayerlike gesture, each time they pass by. Should you feel the urge to do likewise, give in to it. The environment in this particular spirit's keeping is natural heritage of the highest order. Every effort should be made to keep it that way.

DETAILS

When to Go

Thailand's climate is defined by three distinct seasons: the cool season (November to February), hot season (March to May), and rainy season (June to October). There is no "best time" to visit Khao Yai; the park is accessible year-round. Orchids bloom between April and June, high-mountain flowers between December and February; waterfalls are fullest between June and November, and wildlife is most visible in April and May, although birds are present year-round. The average temperature is 73°F (23°C), though nighttime cool-season temperatures can drop to 50°F (10°C).

How to Get There

Bangkok International Airport, a hub for numerous major airlines, is about 125 miles (200km) from Khao Yai. Car rentals are available. Buses to Pak Chong, the gateway to Khao Yai, regularly depart Bangkok from the Northern Bus Terminal. From Pak Chong, songthaews (small pickup trucks) can be taken to the park entrance. Trains to Pak Chong depart from Bangkok's Hualamphong Station. For those without their own vehicle, a number of commercial tours are available from Bangkok.

INFORMATION

National Parks Division, Royal Forestry Department

61 Paholyothin Road, Bangkhen, Bangkok 10900, Thailand; tel: 66-2-579-5269 or 66-2-579-4842.

Tourism Authority of Thailand (TAT) Northeastern Office: Region 1

2102–2104 Mittraphap Road, Tambon Nai Muang, Amphoe Muang, Nakhon Ratchasima 30000, Thailand; tel: 66-44-213-666; fax: 66-44-213-667; e-mail: tatsima@tat.or.th; www.tat.or.th

Tourism Authority of Thailand (TAT) Central Office: Region 2

500/51 Phetkasem Road, Amphoe Cha-am, Phetchaburi 76120, Thailand; tel: 66-32-471-005 or 66-32-471-502; fax: 66-32-471-502; e-mail: tatphet@tat.or.th; www.tat.or.th

This office can provide information about Kaeng Krachan.

CAMPING

Khao Yai National Park

61 Paholyothin Road, Bangkhen, Bangkok 10900, Thailand; tel: 66-2-579-5269, 66-2-579-4842, or 66-2-579-5734.

Pha Kluai Mai (Orchid) Camping Ground offers showers, toilets, a restaurant, and a souvenir shop selling basic supplies. Reservations should be made in advance.

LODGING

PRICE GUIDE – double occupancy

$ = up to $49 $$ = $50–$99

$$$ = $100–$149 $$$$ = $150+

Juldis Khao Yai Resort

54 Moo 4, Thanarat Road (Km 17), Thambol Moo-Sri, Pak Chong, Nakhon Ratchasima 30130, Thailand; tel: 66-44-297-297; fax: 66-44-297-291; e-mail: juldis@korat.a-net.net.th; www.khaoyai.com

The Juldis resort offers luxurious suites and cozy bungalows, all with private baths. Guests can choose between Thai and European cuisine in the Chommanade Restaurant or the Steak House. Amenities include a swimming pool, pub, lobby bar, and tennis court. Activities include canoeing, cycling, and horseback riding. $–$$$$

Jungle House Resort

132 Moo 5, Thanarat Road (Km 19.5), Pak Chong, Nakhon Ratchasima 30130, Thailand; tel/fax: 66-44-297-183.

Set on 21 forested acres (9 hectares) by the Lam Takhon River, accommodations range from air-conditioned rooms to traditional Thai houses. Facilities include an open-air restaurant and barbecue area. Elephant rides are available. Rafting trips down the Lam Takhon River (outside the park boundaries) and guided tours of the park can also be arranged. $

Khao Yai Garden Lodge

135/1 Thanarat Road (Km 7), Pak Chong, Nakhon Ratchasima 30130, Thailand; tel: 66-44-365-178; fax: 66-44-365-179; www.khaoyai-garden-lodge.de

This lodge is set in a garden with more than 200 orchid species. Fan-cooled rooms with shared bath and more luxurious air-conditioned rooms with private bath are available. Facilities include an aviary filled with butterflies and small birds, and a swimming pool. Tours to Khao Yai are offered by the affiliated Khao Yai Wildlife Tours. $

Khao Yai National Park

61 Paholyothin Road, Bangkhen, Bangkok 10900, Thailand; tel: 66-2-579-5269 or 66-2-579-5734.

Basic lodgings are available and should be booked in advance. Simple, inexpensive dormitory-style accommodations, with showers and toilets, are available at Yaowachon Camp and Kong Kaew Camp. Bedding is not supplied, but blankets and pillows can be rented from the park headquarters for a small fee. $

Klong Sai Resort Khao Yai

42 Thanarat Road (Km 20), Pak Chong, Nakhon Ratchasima 30130, Thailand; tel: 66-44-297-112 or 66-44-297-118; fax: 66-44-297-119.

Densely forested hills form a scenic backdrop to this peaceful resort set on landscaped grounds. Each air-conditioned room has a private balcony or a large living area, satellite TV, and telephone. Amenities include a swimming pool and restaurant. Activities include fishing, camping, and nature walks. Tours of the park can be arranged. $–$$

TOURS AND OUTFITTERS

One-hour spotlighting tours depart from park headquarters each night at 7 P.M. and 8 P.M.; reservations should be made before 6 P.M. Rangers can also be hired as guides.

Eco–Life

513/701 Rattanakosin 200, Prachatipat, Thanyaburi, Pathumtani 12130, Thailand; tel: 66-2-567-2039 or 66-2-958-4305; fax: 66-2-958-4305; e-mail: ecolife@samart.co.th

Two-day tours to Khao Yai include hiking through forests, visits to waterfalls, night safaris, and wildlife watching. Visitors can choose between camping or bungalow accommodations.

Khao Yai Wildlife Tours

P.O. Box 27, Pak Chong, Nakhon Ratchasima 30130, Thailand; tel: 66-44-365-178; fax: 66-44-365-179; e-mail: khaoyaigarden@hotmail.com; www.khaoyai-garden-lodge.de

One-and-a-half- to three-day tours of Khao Yai National Park are led by experienced guides. Tours include a visit to the bat cave, a spotlighting tour, and a wide range of treks.

Nature Trails

49 Ramkamhaeng 64, Huamak, Bangkapi, Bangkok 10240, Thailand; tel: 66-2-7350-644; fax: 66-2-7350-638; e-mail: ntrails@samart.co.th or ntrails@ksc.th.com

Experienced tour guides lead three-day hiking trips to Khao Yai and Kaeng Krachan National Parks.

Excursions

Khao Phanom Bencha National Park

National Parks Division, Royal Forestry Department, 61 Paholyothin Road, Bangkhen, Bangkok 10900, Thailand; tel: 66-2-579-5269 or 66-2-579-4842.

This small but exquisite park near the coastal town of Krabi protects ragged, forest-cloaked mountains crowned by 4,430-foot (1,350-m) Phanom Bencha. Short walks lead to several picturesque cascades and to Khao Phung Cave, where colorful mineral deposits create an enchanting subterranean world. Two longer hiking trails permit wider exploration and increase your chances of spotting elusive mammals such as barking deer, leaf monkeys, and gibbons, as well as some of the 156 bird species present.

Khao Sok National Park

61 Paholyothin Road, Bangkhen, Bangkok 10900, Thailand; tel: 66-2-579-5269 or 66-2-579-5734.

Encompassing dense rain forest with waterfalls, dramatic limestone cliffs, caves, narrow gorges, and a vast, island-studded lake, Khao Sok is one of Thailand's most spectacular parks. Located in the western part of Surat Thani Province on the Thai peninsula, this 250-square-mile (648-sq-km) preserve shelters an abundance of wildlife, including wild elephants, pig-tailed macaques, serows, gaurs, leopards, tigers, and Malayan sun bears, as well as more than 180 bird species. Botanical wonders abound: the rare rafflesia – the world's largest flower, with blooms measuring 32 inches (81cm) in diameter – is found here, as is the giant rattan, which has a stem measuring four inches (10cm) in diameter.

Thaleban National Park

61 Paholyothin Road, Bangkhen, Bangkok 10900, Thailand; tel: 66-2-579-5269, 66-2-579-4842, or 66-2-579-5734.

Along Thailand's southern border with Malaysia, travelers can visit a well-preserved slice of true Sundaic rain forest at Thaleban National Park. Huge old-growth dipterocarp trees tower over the 75-square-mile (194-sq-km) preserve, providing natural habitat for a wide range of rarely seen forest creatures, including hornbills, gibbons, macaques, gaurs, and the small but formidable Malayan sun bear, which feeds on bees and honey by ripping into hives with its powerful claws.

Borneo
Malaysia and Indonesia

Standing atop **Mount Kinabalu** in **Malaysian Borneo**, you are surrounded by rock and open sky. Beneath the jagged peaks, the slopes are bare granite, worn smooth by glaciers during the last ice age and cracked by subsequent weathering. Here and there, clumps of sedges and mats of mosses have gained a foothold in hollows, and one or two hardy orchids sprout in sheltered crevices. Otherwise, there are few signs of life. On this cold, barren perch – at 13,455 feet (4,101m), the highest point on the Malay Archipelago – it's easy to forget that the mountain rises from a totally different environment, that, far below, towering dipterocarp trees shelter more than 1,200 species of wild orchids, 40 kinds of oak trees, 25 species of rhododendrons, an array of carnivorous pitcher plants, and the world's largest flower, the rafflesia. And it takes a leap of the imagination to picture the rain forest's animal inhabitants: the barking deer that forage in clearings, the squirrels that scurry through the understory, the multihued birds that throng the canopy.

Rugged terrain and dense vegetation have long held development at bay, making this island a stronghold for rain-forest species.

◆ The slopes of Mount Kinabalu are, in fact, part of one of the oldest and most biologically diverse tropical ecosystems on Earth. They crown the mountainous island of Borneo, which is situated to the east of the Malay Peninsula in the South China Sea and politically divided among Indonesia, Malaysia, and the tiny but wealthy sultanate of Brunei. Borneo's diverse habitats range from dank peat swamps to limestone mountains honeycombed with caves, but most of the island is swathed in some of the world's oldest and tallest rain forests. Extensive logging has had a drastic impact – the east Malaysian

Orangutans are solitary by nature, gathering only briefly to mate. Their long digits and opposable thumbs and big toes are an adaptation to life in the treetops.

connecting the islands of Borneo, Java, and Sumatra to the Asian mainland. The consequent mingling of plant and animal communities, followed by periods of isolation when the sea again separated the islands, is thought to have fostered further diversification.

Layers of Life

Near the northern tip of Borneo in Sabah, **Kinabalu National Park** offers well-developed visitor accommodations and an accessible cross-section of Bornean wildlife. Poachers have reduced populations of larger animals in the park, but there's no better place to view the island's astonishing array of plants.

Hikers can explore several miles of easy trails near park headquarters, as well as a **Mountain Garden** that brings together notable plant species found throughout the preserve. Farther east, **Poring Hot Springs**, a group of five geothermal mineral springs that emerge from the lower mountain, is a

state of **Sabah**'s rain-forest cover, for example, plummeted from 86 percent of the land in 1953 to just 41 percent in 1991 – but with so much rugged terrain and a relatively low population density, much remains. A trove of biological treasures and a precarious haven for rain-forest flora and fauna, Borneo supports some 11,000 plant species, more than 500 kinds of birds, and a remarkable array of reptiles, amphibians, rodents, and insects. Tigers are not native to Borneo, but tapirs, rhinoceroses, Asian elephants, and other large mammals are present, as are several notable primate species, including orangutans, which are found only in Borneo and Sumatra.

A variety of factors has given rise to this extraordinary diversity. Archaeological evidence suggests that during the most recent ice age, when advancing glaciers in the Northern Hemisphere consumed much of the world's freshwater supply and the rain forests of South America and sub-Saharan Africa gave way to dry savanna, the islands and coastal zones of Southeast Asia retained a relatively steady level of moisture that supported rain-forest communities. At the same time, rising and falling sea levels periodically drained the Java Sea, temporarily good base from which to explore the lowland dipterocarp forest that covers a third of the park's 290 square miles (750 sq km), up to an elevation of about 3,000 feet (900m). Easy trails winding between great buttressed tree trunks provide a snake's-eye view of this classic tropical rain forest, where curtains of vines hang between the trees and a thick upper canopy blocks the sunlight, inhibiting the growth of dense vegetation on the forest floor. Keep an eye out here for mountain tree shrews and the Bornean mountain ground squirrel on and just above the ground, as well as tree frogs and giant stick insects amid the foliage.

It's worth hiring a guide or joining one of the regular guided walks to increase your chances of making further discoveries. For example, staff members keep track of rafflesias that are currently in bloom. This parasitic plant without leaves, roots, or stems grows as a bud attached to a particular kind of forest vine. When the bud is fully developed, it blossoms into a striking red flower three feet (1m) in diameter. This emits an

The giant atlas (opposite) is one of the world's largest moths; its wingspan measures up to 10 inches (25cm) across.

A long-tailed macaque (left) gets a closer look at a visitor's camera.

Mount Kinabalu (below) rises majestically above farmland at the edge of the national park.

odor like the smell of rotting meat to attract carrion flies, which then unwittingly assist with pollination.

For a startlingly different perspective on Kinabalu's rain forest, take to the canopy walkway, also at Poring Hot Springs. This allows visitors to "hike" through the treetops and observe the birds, insects, and epiphytes that flourish high above the forest floor. Especially early and late in the day, the canopy is full of the colors and chatter of bulbuls, trogons, and laughing thrushes. Glance down and you may spot the flashing iridescent-green wings of a spectacular Rajah Brooke birdwing butterfly.

The trek to the top of Mount Kinabalu is a strenuous two-day undertaking but requires no special mountaineering skills,

Kinabalu friendly warbler flitting through the ferns. These forests are also home to various insectivorous *Nepenthes* or pitcher plants, which trap their six-legged victims in reservoirs filled with digestive enzymes. Ten different pitcher plants grow on Kinabalu, including the Rajah Brooke, whose pitchers are large enough to drown small rodents. Keep an eye out too for the giant red Kinabalu leech, which grows to almost a foot long and feeds on a particular species of blue earthworm.

After a brief overnight stop in huts above 10,000 feet (3,000m), most climbers press on toward the summit zone by flashlight in the predawn hours. Here, colder temperatures, strong winds, and intense sunlight force plant and animal species to seek shelter. Look in crevices or the lee of large boulders for heath rhododendron, Low's buttercups, and delicate necklace orchids. The air is thin, making the trek difficult for travelers who have recently arrived from sea level, but if you make it to the top you'll be rewarded with a glorious high-altitude sunrise before beginning the long descent.

just warm clothes, a good pair of hiking boots, and a reasonable level of physical fitness. The summit trail begins 6,000 feet (1,800m) up the mountain in a temperate montane forest of oaks (more than 40 species have been recorded here), chestnuts, and laurels, with dense undergrowth sustained by sunlight filtering through gaps in the canopy. Climbing higher, you soon pass into a cooler cloud forest of gnarled, moss-covered trees. Look in their shade for the pink flowers of Kinabalu balsam and the golden blossoms of Low's rhododendron, and watch for birds such as the

Caves, Crags, and Headhunters

Like Mount Kinabalu, **Gunung Mulu National Park** in the Malaysian state of **Sarawak** encompasses a wide range of forest habitats, including dipterocarp and montane forest, as well as lowland swamps,

A suspension bridge (top) at Mount Kinabalu lets hikers get a close-up view of the canopy and its inhabitants.

A giant forest gecko (left) makes a meal of a cicada.

limestone crags, and an extensive network of caves. The area is also home to some of Borneo's diverse indigenous cultures, notably the Iban people, Sarawak's largest ethnic group, and the traditionally nomadic Penan, who gained international attention in the 1980s by mounting high-profile protests against logging operations in their native forests. Trekkers may still encounter a few Penan nomads at Gunung Mulu, though the Malaysian government has now settled most of them in permanent villages, including one community near park headquarters.

Gunung Mulu's 210 square miles (540 sq km) of mountainous terrain offer a range of options for visitors, including easy hikes on marked trails near park headquarters, river-boat rides, cave tours, and strenuous multi-day treks that penetrate deep into the forest.

These longer treks offer the best opportunities for wildlife viewing, but even in the more accessible areas, some of the park's 1,500 species of flowering plants (including 170 wild orchids and 10 species of pitcher plants), 262 bird species (including all 10 Bornean native hornbills), and 67 different mammals may be seen.

Local guides are required for the three principal trekking routes at Gunung Mulu: the **Pinnacles Trek**, the **Gunung Mulu**

Protected Primates

Gaze into the sentient eyes of Asia's only indigenous great ape and you'll understand why the Malays chose to call this shaggy red primate *orang utan*, or "person of the forest." In fact, modern taxonomy places the orangutan in the Pongidae family along with chimpanzees and gorillas – all close relatives of *Homo sapiens*. Sadly, our close kinship to these magnificent creatures has not prevented the destruction of their native habitat in the lowland forests of Borneo and Sumatra, and their survival is under serious threat.

Rafflesia (top), the world's largest flower, is a parasite that attaches itself to a vine. It is pollinated by flies, which it attracts by imitating the smell and appearance of rotting meat. The bloom lasts only a few days.

Since the 1960s, the **Sepilok Orangutan Rehabilitation Centre** at **Sepilok Forest Reserve** in eastern Sabah has provided a sanctuary for displaced, orphaned, and injured orangutans. The animals are treated at the center's veterinary clinic, then gradually reintroduced to life in the wild within the reserve. Some return regularly to feeding platforms near the visitor center, where they munch on bananas and other tropical fruits set out by the staff and can be observed by visitors.

Rescued orangutans (left and below) are taught to fend for themselves at the Sepilok Orangutan Rehabilitation Centre.

Orangutans are solitary creatures that spend their lives high above the forest floor. By day, they browse on arboreal fruits; at night, they sleep in treetop nests constructed of leaves and branches. Given their reclusive habits, a visit to Sepilok may be your only chance to see one outside of a cage.

Several other primates inhabit Sepilok, including three species of leaf monkey, two species of macaque, the Bornean gibbon, and the rare proboscis monkey, which is found only in the lowland forests of Borneo. One common Malay name for this creature – *orang belanda*, or "Dutch person" – equates the proboscis monkey's large nose with the generous schnozzes of the European colonists who once governed the island.

Summit Trek, and the Headhunters Trail. Even with the assistance of guides, these outings are not for the faint of heart. Hikers must be physically and mentally prepared for treacherous trails, intense heat and humidity,

Sumatran rhinos (left) often spend hours wallowing; mud protects them from biting insects and parasites.

Mueller's gibbons (bottom) are primarily fruit eaters but will also consume flowers, leaves, and insects.

wet weather, and armies of leeches. The rewards, however, are great.

The three-day Pinnacles Trek begins with a riverboat ride to the trailhead and a three-hour hike through virgin rain forest to the **Melinau Gorge** wilderness camp, which has showers, toilets, and covered sleeping quarters. Along the way, you may be lucky enough to catch sight of a spectacular rhinoceros hornbill, with its huge yellow bill and prominent casque. The destination on day two is a ridge on **Gunung Api** overlooking a remarkable "forest" of sharp limestone crags that jut more than 100 feet (30m)

above the trees. It's an exhausting and hazardous four-hour climb, including a final ascent of an almost vertical slope fitted with fixed ropes and ladders, but trekkers are rewarded with sightings of rare plant and animal life, including orchids and pitcher plants at the trailside, as well as a magnificent view of the pinnacles themselves. After a second night in camp, participants retrace their steps.

At almost 8,000 feet (2,450m), Gunung Mulu is the highest peak in the park, and as on Mount Kinabalu, climbers traverse several vegetation zones as they ascend the mountain. The trek to the summit and back typically takes four days, with overnight accommodations at primitive camps. As you hike through the forest on the lower slopes, listen for the whooping calls of female Bornean gibbons, which define their territory with song, and the high-pitched buzz of male cicadas, which sing to attract mates. Pay careful attention and you'll notice that the cicada calls change every few minutes as each of the many subspecies briefly takes center stage. This cooperative use of bandwidth prevents the cacophony that would result if all subspecies called simultaneously. It is said that the daily cycle of cicada calls is so precise that the Penan people use them to tell the time with astonishing accuracy.

The Headhunters Trail combines forest trekking and riverboat travel with an overnight stop at an Iban longhouse. The trail is named for Kayan war parties that once paddled up the **Melinau River**, then dragged their dugout canoes through the jungle to the **Terikan River** to launch raids on the people of Limbang. You're not likely to lose your head here these days, but the ancestors of today's Iban were fierce head-hunters themselves, and the longhouse visit offers an engaging glimpse of village life.

Going Underground

Persistent heavy rainfall has gradually eaten away at the soft limestone that underlies much of Gunung Mulu National Park, leaving a complex network of underground chambers. One of them, the **Sarawak Chamber**, is the largest natural subterranean chamber ever found. To make the system more accessible, the park service has outfitted four "show caves" with wooden walkways and electric lights, and, for a small fee, local guides will show you the way.

A short hike from park headquarters is the entrance to **Deer Cave**, one of the longest underground passages in the world. Strolling through this and neighboring **Lang's Cave**, you'll see massive chambers, high waterfalls, stalactites and stalagmites, and other beautifully formed limestone deposits. When you smell the litter of bat guano on the floor, look up and you'll see dense populations of mainly wrinkle-lipped bats clinging to the ceiling and swooping through the air above your head. The droppings provide the basis for a sunless food chain that supports insects, spiders, fish, and other small life-forms specifically adapted to the cave environment. One of the most impressive sights in the park occurs around sundown, when hundreds of thousands of bats pour out of Deer Cave to feed on nocturnal insects. As the stream of dark bodies flows into the night, bat hawks and crested goshawks swoop in to snag a few of the flying mammals for supper.

As you explore this remote subterranean realm, think back to the windswept heights of Mount Kinabalu and the myriad tropical ecosystems in between. You'll be struck by the richness of Borneo's ecological treasures and have a dizzying sense of just how magnificently inventive nature can be.

Carnivorous pitcher plants (above) drown and digest insects in their vase-shaped reservoirs.

Langanan Falls (below) spills over a rocky ledge at Poring Hot Springs.

DETAILS

How to Get There

Most travelers arrive from regional gateways such as Singapore, Kuala Lumpur, Jakarta, and Denpasar. Indonesian and Malaysian domestic carriers serve all major tourist destinations on the island.

When to Go

Monsoons bring tropical showers to Borneo during much of the year, with the heaviest rainfall from October to February. Hot and humid conditions persist year-round, with temperatures rarely dropping below 68°F (20°C) even at night and generally climbing to 85°F (30°C) or higher during the day. Higher altitudes are an exception; temperatures there can drop considerably.

Getting Around

Road conditions and public transportation networks vary widely in Borneo. While good paved roads and inter-city buses serve some areas, travelers should expect rough roads and limited transportation throughout much of the island. For longer trips, domestic air connections may be the best option. Passenger boats, ranging from large motor launches to dugout canoes, operate on many of Borneo's navigable rivers.

INFORMATION

Gunung Mulu National Park

National Parks and Wildlife Office, 1st Floor, Wisma Sumber Alam, 93050 Kuching, Sarawak, Malaysia; tel: 60-82-442-180; or National Parks and Wildlife Office, Forest Department, 98000 Miri, Sarawak, Malaysia; tel: 60-85-436-637.

Mount Kinabalu National Park

Sabah Parks, P.O. Box 10626, 88806 Kota Kinabalu, Sabah, Malaysia; tel: 60-88-211-585 or 60-88-211-652.

Sabah Tourism Promotion Corporation

Mail Bag 112, 88999 Kota Kinabalu, Sabah, Malaysia; tel: 60-88-212-121.

Sarawak Tourism Board

Shoplots 3.43 and 3.44, Level 3, Wisma Satok, Jalan Satok/Kulas, 93400 Kuching, Sarawak, Malaysia; tel: 60-82-423-600; www.sarawaktourism.com/

Sepilok Orangutan Rehabilitation Centre

Sabah Wildlife Department, W.D.T. 200, 90000 Sandakan, Sabah, Malaysia; tel: 60-89-531-180.

Tourism Malaysia

17th Floor Menara Dato Onn, Putra World Trade Center, 45 Jalan Tun Ismail, 50480 Kuala Lumpur, Malaysia; tel: 60-3-293-5188.

CAMPING

Many of the parks in Borneo have official campgrounds and permit camping in non-designated sites in the backcountry. Overnight visitors also commonly stay in lodges, cabins, or huts inside the parks. It is advisable to reserve ahead for these accommodations.

LODGING

PRICE GUIDE – double occupancy

$ = up to $49 $$ = $50–$99
$$$ = $100–$149 $$$$ = $150+

Gunung Mulu National Park

National Parks and Wildlife Office, Forest Department, 98000 Miri, Sarawak, Malaysia; tel: 60-85-436-637.

Lodging inside the park includes chalets, hostel rooms, and guest houses at park headquarters.

Kinabalu Gold Resorts

Lot 3.46, Third Floor, Block C, Kompleks Karamunsing, Locked Bag No. 179, 88744 Kota Kinabalu, Sabah, Malaysia; tel: 60-88-257-941 or 60-88-245-742; e-mail: nature@kinabalu.net

While some privately operated lodges are available near Mount Kinabalu National Park, it's best to book accommodations within the park by contacting Kinabalu Gold Resorts. Options include basic dormitory-style beds, lodges and chalets, cabins of various sizes, and primitive mountain huts on the summit trail. $–$$$

Royal Mulu Resort

Melinau River, Mulu 98008 Miri, Sarawak, Malaysia; tel: 60-85-421-122; fax: 60-85-421-099.

Hugging the Melinau River near Gunung Mulu National Park, this resort's longhouses are linked by a series of wooden walkways and contain 188 rooms with private baths. $$$–$$$$

Sepilok Jungle Resort

Labuk Road, P.O. Box 2082, 90723 Sandakan, Sabah, Malaysia; tel: 60-89-533-031; fax: 60-89-533-029; e-mail: sepilokjr@yahoo.com

Guests at the resort can hear or see gibbons, hornbills, fruit bats, and butterflies. There is a choice of dormitory rooms with shared bathrooms and standard, family, and deluxe rooms with private bathrooms (some with air conditioning). Malaysian cuisine is served. The Sepilok Orangutan Rehabilitation Centre is within walking distance. $

Sepilok Nature Resort

Pulau Sipadan Resort and Tours, 484 Bandar Sabindo, P.O. Box 61120, 91021 Tawau, Sabah, Malaysia; tel 60-89-765-200; fax: 60-89-763-575 or 60-89-763-563; e-mail: info@sipadan-resort.com

Adjacent to the Sepilok Orangutan Rehabilitation Centre, this resort has 20 rooms with attached bathrooms and private verandas overlooking the forest. Included are nature activities such as a tour of the orangutan center. $$–$$$

TOURS AND OUTFITTERS

Api Tours

P.O. Box 12853, 88831 Kota Kinabalu, Sabah, Malaysia; tel: 60-88-424-156 or 60-88-420-123; fax: 60-88-424-174 ; e-mail: apitour@po.jaring.my

Able to customize packages, Api runs half- and full-day excursions, mountain treks, whitewater rafting, jungle, and wildlife adventures, and cultural tours.

Borneo Adventure

55 Main Bazaar, 93000 Kuching, Sarawak, Malaysia; tel: 60-82-245-175, 60-82-410-569 or 60-82-415-554; fax: 60-82-422-626 or 60-82-234-212; e-mail: bakch@borneoadventure.com

Guides specialize in rain-forest, cultural, and historical tours and adventures in Sarawak and Sabah. Special-interest tours focus on endangered species, education, shamans, and bird-watching.

Borneo Nature Tours

Block 3, Ground Floor, MDLD 3285, Fajar Centre, P.O. Box 61174, 91120 Lahad Datu, Sabah, Malaysia; tel: 60-89-880-207 or 60-89-880-206; fax: 60-89-885-051; e-mail: bntkk@ysnet.org.my

Rain-forest tours include night drives, day trips to a biological field station, bird-watching, and guided nature walks with experienced naturalists. Travelers stay at Borneo Rainforest Lodge.

Field Guides

9433 Bee Cave Road, Building 1, Suite 150, Austin, TX 78733; tel: 800-728-4953 or 512-263-7295; fax: 512-263-0117; e-mail: fgileader@aol.com

A 21-day bird-watching tour of Malaysia includes visits to the Sukau, Sepilok, and Kinabalu reserves, offering everything from lowland rain forest to montane wilderness.

Excursions

Bali

Indonesian Tourism Promotion Board, Bank Pacific Building, Ninth Floor, 8 Julun Jenderal Sudirman, Jakarta 10220, Indonesia; tel: 62-21-570-4879; fax: 62-21-570-4855; e-mail: itpb@indosat.net.id; www.tourismindonesia.com/

Ever since the 1930s, the island of Bali has worked its particular magic on visitors from around the world, and while large areas in the south have been transformed by extensive tourism, much of the island has retained its rural charm. Exquisite beaches ring the coast, terraced rice paddies cover much of the mountainous interior, and numerous temples throughout Bali reflect the island's unique cultural heritage, which integrates spirituality and artistic sensibility into all aspects of daily life.

Komodo National Park

Komodo National Park, Jl. Labuan Bajo, West Flores, East Nusa Tenggara 36554, Indonesia; tel: 62-384-41004; fax: 62-384-41006.

This arid and rugged national park encompassing the islands of Komodo, Rinca, Padar, and Gili Motong is the domain of the world's biggest lizard, the Komodo dragon. A nine-foot (3-m), 200-pound (90-kg) carnivore, the Komodo feeds on prey as large as monkeys, wild boar, and small deer. Viewing these formidable creatures (at its best from June to September) is strictly controlled by park guides, who can also organize hikes into the surrounding savanna and montane forest to observe other endemic reptiles, macaques, fruit bats, and up to 150 species of birds, including the imperial pigeon, sulfur-crested cockatoo, and orange-footed scrubfowl.

Tanjung Puting National Park

Tanjung Puting National Park, Jl. Malijo No. 03, Madurejo, Pangkalan Bun, Kotawaringin Barat, Central Kalimantan, Indonesia; tel: 62-532-22340.

At the southwestern edge of Borneo, "blackwater" rivers slide silently through lowland swamps, their mirrorlike surfaces reflecting a tangle of tropical vegetation dominated by mangroves, heath forest, and rain forest. The park protects more than 1,160 square miles (3,000 sq km) and is a vital refuge for clouded leopards, sun bears, civets, more than 220 bird species, and seven kinds of primates, including orangutans, many of which were rehabilitated at the park's renowned Camp Leakey Research Station.

Papua
New Guinea

Just a few steps from the banks of the **Sepik River**, the forest is a fantasia of feathery bamboo, tangled vines, and massive hardwood trees flanged at their bases like rockets. Creepers climb every upright surface; the roots of strangler figs reach groundward from the canopy. Huge primeval palms burst upward like fountains; gardens of orchids flourish on every branch. You can almost sense the vegetation growing around you. ◆ High above, the canopy resounds with the calls of birds and other unseen creatures, but at ground level all seems silent and still. Slowly, however, forest dwellers reveal themselves. A swaying vine turns out to be a brilliantly costumed tree python – so green as to be almost iridescent – curled in sinuous coils around a branch. A massive hornbill plummets from a concealed perch and flies off **Bountiful wildlife and** with mighty wingbeats that echo like **intriguing indigenous cultures** a steam locomotive chugging through the **await visitors to some of** tunnel-like forest. And what resembles a **the largest tracts of primal** torn sheet of brown-and-white tissue drifting **rain forest in Southeast Asia.** on a breeze is actually a Queen Alexandra birdwing, the largest butterfly in the world. ◆ Nature does nothing by halves in **Papua New Guinea**. Occupying the eastern side of New Guinea, the second-largest island in the world, as well as 600 or so offshore islands, this nation possesses some of the wildest terrain and the most fascinating wildlife on the globe. ◆ Situated just below the equator, New Guinea is exposed to moisture-laden winds for most of the year. These push sodden air up the island's rugged mountain backbone, where the air condenses, forming giant thunderheads. Regular deluges drop as much as 600 inches (1,525cm)

The spotted cuscus, a marsupial with a prehensile tail, is found mostly in lowland tropical forests. It is an arboreal creature, moving slowly through the canopy at night, feeding on fruit, leaves, eggs, and nestlings.

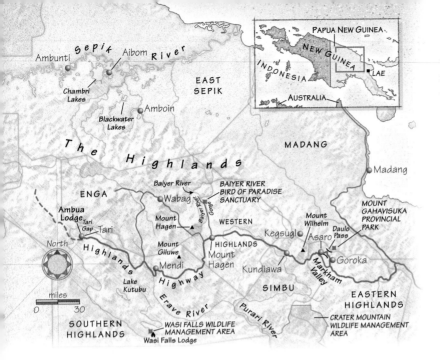

them 46 kinds of parrots – more than any other country. And its 250 species of mammals include approximately 70 marsupials, ranging from cuscuses and possums to wallabies and tree kangaroos. Moreover, Papua New Guinea is a bonanza of the bizarre: it has the world's only known toxic bird (a species of pitohui, which has poisonous feathers), egg-laying mammals that suckle their young (two species of long-beaked, spiny echidnas), and bedazzling birds that perform elaborate courtship dances (numerous birds of paradise).

Although wildlife is abundant, parks and reserves are few and far between, and access to protected areas is limited by the ruggedness of the terrain. Travel often involves short flights, multiday tours on riverboats, or extended hikes along jungle trails. Two of the most accessible areas are the Sepik River in the northwest and the Highlands region of the interior.

of rain a year, and during downpours, small streams become seething torrents, bounding down the mountains in angry leaps, then spilling their coffee-colored waters across the surrounding plains. Such an abundance of water has resulted in dense and varied vegetation. Despite accelerating deforestation, three-quarters of Papua New Guinea is still covered by primeval tropical rain forest, cool mid-mountain forest, and cloud forest, which are in turn home to an astounding diversity of plant and animal life.

The country has at least five percent of the world's floral species, a staggering abundance that includes more than 250 kinds of rhododendrons and 2,500 types of orchids. It also boasts more than 650 bird species, among

Along the Sepik

Sepik is said to mean "big river," an appropriate name for this sluggish waterway that begins life high in the central mountains and coils like a serpent for 750 miles (1,200km) across the northwestern plains. A liquid highway for isolated communities, it borders swamps, wetlands, grasslands (known locally as pitpit), and dense jungles equal in biological importance to those of the Amazon and Congo Basins.

Multiday cruises leave from the port of **Madang** on the coast and from various bases along the river, notably **Karawari Lodge**, near **Amboin**, and **Ambunti**. Most last three to seven days and explore the lower and middle reaches of the river. Shorter tours from bases such as Amboin and Ambunti tend to focus on the area around **Chambri** and **Blackwater Lakes**, the Sepik's cultural heartland. In the wet season, this area is a maze of wide waterways flush with waterfowl; in the dry season, the waters recede and boats have to negotiate narrow, muddy channels.

A Sepik River cruise (opposite) is the easiest way to sample the island's wildlife and native cultures.

Azure snout weevils (left), seen here mating, are just one of thousands of colorful and bizarre insect species found on New Guinea. Weevils feed by boring their snouts into plant tissue.

A jungle clearing (below) reveals a waterfall in the remote and densely forested Highlands.

As you drift along the great river, sea eagles wheel overhead, kingfishers dart from the banks, scarlet and yellow snapper turtles scuttle just under the water's surface, and egrets and royal spoonbills scour the shoreline. Look carefully and you may spot a crocodile lurking in the river, as motionless as a log. The fish-eating New Guinea species rarely exceeds 14 feet (4m), but its gargantuan saltwater relative, which can reach 20 feet (6m), is another story. Travelers should take great care near riverbanks: more than one person has gone for a swim, heard the water behind them explode, and turned to get a glimpse down the gullet of a giant croc a split-second before its jaws slammed shut on them.

River trips also provide an intriguing insight into the Sepik's rich indigenous culture. Although creeping westernization has subtly altered local lifestyles, many ancient traditions endure. The men still hew long, narrow dugout canoes with fearsome crocodile jaws carved on the prow. Boys undergo

Tree kangaroos (left) are adapted to life in the branches. Unlike terrestrial kangaroos, their hind legs move independently, and they have sharp claws for climbing.

The green tree python (bottom) lures prey by dangling its tail.

niches, including the Sepik blue, whose spiked red flowers can grow to 24 inches (60cm), and the *Vandopsis* orchid, whose blooms trail in great sprays up to 10 feet (3m) long. The air is filled with the coarse cries of palm cockatoos, the raucous screeches of parrots barreling overhead in jet-fighter formation, and the liquid notes of honeyeaters. With luck, you may come across a tiny pygmy parrot, the world's smallest at just three inches long (7.5cm); a stunning, neon-blue Ulysses butterfly; or a Hercules moth, one of the largest moths in the world, with a wing area of about 40 square inches (260 sq cm).

initiation ceremonies involving the carving of marks resembling those on the backs of crocodiles into their skin. And in some remote villages, people still venerate the dead by embalming corpses and hanging them to dry in the rafters of their homes like smoked kippers.

Every cruise upriver is a magical mystery tour of homespun art. Each village has a *haus tambaran*, a thatched communal spirit house featuring massive drums and ritual flutes, ornate carvings, masks, and shields. Some settlements are associated with particular artifacts and styles: Aibom, for example, is known for its pottery, the Chambri Lakes villages for their elongated masks.

Most tours also offer opportunities for viewing the Sepik's spectacular swamp forests, and some allow time for detours inland. Hiking through the dank, heavy jungle air can be like pushing your way through a soggy curtain, and you have to be wary of the jungle's hazards – the lethally barbed lawyer vines, or rattans, that climb the trees; the leeches that slither along the trails and reach out from bushes; the mosquitoes that whine around your ears. But the delights are myriad. The trees are festooned with vines, including D'Alberti's creeper, stippled with flowers as red as bright lipstick. Orchids bloom in shady

Highland Highs

Equally intriguing but contrasting terrain can be found in the island's remote interior uplands, the **Highlands**. Although this

hectare) mountain reserve traversed by marked trails, which includes a botanical sanctuary where you can see a wide range of native plants. To the south, **Crater Mountain Wildlife Management Area**, a 1,000-square-mile (2,600-sq-km) preserve where trails are currently under development, is a good place to spot tree kangaroos. These somewhat clumsy climbers ascend trees much the way a repairman shimmies up a telegraph pole, using their formidable sharp-toed feet as cleats. They bound along the branches with relative ease, leaping between trees as much as 10 feet (3m) apart and using their tails as stabilizers when they land with a thud.

From Goroka, the road continues up to **Asaro**, famous worldwide for its "mud men," warriors who daub themselves with clay and don carved mud masks resembling

cloud-shrouded region is one of the most densely populated parts of the country, it was not explored by Europeans until the 1930s. Within its serried ranges rising from lush fertile valleys and smothered with tangled forest, the first westerners found tribespeople who had been farming the region for thousands of years, yet had had virtually no contact with the outside world. None had ever seen a wheel, let alone a car or a truck, and cannibalism was a widespread practice.

Today, the highlanders still live in widely scattered communities, but a highway now claws its way up the mountains from the coastal town of **Lae** and bores westward through ever more rugged valleys, allowing relatively easy access to sights and trails. Exhilarating mountain paths wind through forests and over traditional vine bridges to villages and isolated homesteads surrounded by carefully cultivated patches of kaukau (sweet potato) and coffee. A word of warning: much of the region (particularly Enga province) is volatile, and independent hikers should always consult local police before setting off.

Nestled in the Markham Valley, **Goroka** is the center of the Eastern Highlands and a good base for exploring. About seven miles (11km) to the north lies **Mount Gahavisuka Provincial Park**, a 200-acre (80-

Bright color (top) attracts pollinators to a wax ginger flower, which flourishes in the shade of the understory.

The greater bird of paradise (right), about the size of a crow, is known for its luxuriant plumage and extravagant courtship displays.

The Wigmen

Throughout the Western and Southern Highlands, men sport elaborate head-dresses made from human hair and adorned with feathers and flowers. Though some groups wear them on a more regular basis, these "wigs" are generally reserved for ceremonial gatherings. Each tribe has its own style: the Huli wear crescent-shaped wigs with thick ends; in Mendi, the wigs take on a Napoleonic slant, rising on either side of the head; in Enga, they are disc-shaped and flat.

Wigs are passed down as family heirlooms and are believed to provide ancestral ghosts with a place of abode. Traditionally, the hair had to come only from males, but women and children now top up supplies. While weaving his wig on a vine-and-cane frame, a man may be required to live apart from his family for months and eschew sexual relations.

The wigs are most commonly worn at ceremonial gatherings known as sing-sings. Participants also wear *bilas*, or body decorations, including pig tusks, shells, and colorful pigments, often mixed with animal grease to obtain a glossy sheen. These decorations reflect tribal affiliations: Mount Hagen men, for example, wear the red flower of the kwita tree, which attracts birds and is thought to have a similar effect on women.

The most important sing-sing is the Highlands Show, held in alternate years in Goroka and Mount Hagen, at which different tribes try to outdo each other with impressive displays of dancing and singing. The throbbing of drums echoes through the valley as the participants stomp in rings, flick their hips to swing their grass skirts, or *purpurs*, and chant in choruses that rise and fall like the sound of waves in a great swelling sea.

A Huli man (below) dons an elaborate wig, face paint, and other finery for a sing-sing.

The Goliath butterfly (bottom) has a wingspan of up to 11 inches (28cm).

An Asaro mudman (right) reenacts a legendary battle.

Small but brilliant, the king bird of paradise (opposite, bottom) is found in lowland forests.

great earthenware diving helmets in order to reenact a legendary battle. Westward, the road writhes over the **Daulo Pass** and descends into populous **Simbu Province** and **Kundiawa**, the departure point for the climb to the summit of 14,794-foot (4,509-m) **Mount Wilhelm**, the highest mountain in Papua New Guinea. Best undertaken with a guide, the ascent begins at **Kegsugl**, 35 miles (56km) from Kundiawa, and usually takes two or three days.

At lower levels, the trail winds upward through lush forests and grassy valleys studded with cycads, giant primeval-looking ferns with fronds furled like fiddle-heads. In the cooler mid-mountain forests, oak trees predominate; above 10,000 feet (3,000m), hikers pass through beech forest swathed in gauzy mists and festooned with mosses, orchids, and old man's beard lichen, or usnea. Look here for shrubs such as the Malabar rhododendron, with its beautiful purple flowers. Near the summit, the forest gives way to alpine grassland and rocky scree, where stunted dwarf shrubs hunker low against the cold lash of sodden winds.

There's a good chance of spotting one of the island's three species of cassowary at lower elevations. These flightless forest-dwellers resemble an overstuffed turkey on stilts, with a shaggy coat of black feathers and a bald neck painted in primary colors. They may seem ungainly, but cassowaries can travel through the forests at high speed, clearing obstacles in great leaping bounds. Don't get too close. A cassowary can kill

with one kick of its powerful feet, each of which bears a long, slashing claw.

The grasslands of Mount Wilhelm are favored by ground-dwelling bowerbirds. The males of this genus are ardent seducers, given to wooing their mates with deft artwork. Avian Picassos, they use sticks and grasses to construct a display site, or bower, and then adorn it with flower petals, fruits, and mosses. Each bower encloses an intimate mating space, a real love nest, into which the female is induced by the male's evocative dancing.

A Paradise of Birds

The flamboyant courtships of the bowerbirds are outdone only by those of Papua New Guinea's remarkable birds of paradise. The true jewels of the rain forest, male birds of paradise boast a dazzling range of iridescent colors as well as decorative plumes and crests, which they employ along with elaborate displays to woo prospective mates. Often they perform side by side, attempting to outshine each other with increasingly complex moves. The purple-and-black magnificent bird of paradise, for example, builds up to a paroxysm of ecstasy, its spread wings shuddering as if jolted by electricity. Of the world's 43 species of birds of paradise, 38 inhabit Papua New Guinea and 36 are unique to the country.

The Western and Southern Highlands offer the best prospects for sighting these superb birds in the wild. At the **Baiyer River Bird of Paradise Sanctuary**, set amid 2,000 acres (800 hectares) of rain forest and river flats 35 miles (56km) north of **Mount Hagen**, and reached by road via the spectacular **Baiyer River Gorge**, you are almost guaranteed an eye-to-eye encounter. Farther west, beyond **Mendi**, the capital of the **Southern Highlands Province**, which sits wedged between limestone peaks and shadowed by the looming mass of **Mount Giluwe** (14,414ft/4,393m), the **Tari Gap** area is also renowned for its

excellent birding. South of Mendi, the virgin forests of the superbly scenic **Kutubu** region brim with birds of paradise and butterflies, best viewed in the **Wasi Falls Wildlife Management Area**, which can be reached on guided hikes from Wasi Falls Lodge and Ambua Lodge in **Tari**.

Tari is also the home of the Huli people, renowned for wearing remarkable "wigs" of human hair decorated with lichens, yellow everlasting daisies, cuscus fur, and the plumes and feathers of birds of paradise. The widespread use of such headdresses throughout the Western and Southern Highlands can be seen as a symbol of the Papuan people's long and close association with the rain forest, and their deep reverence for its magnificent wildlife.

DETAILS

How to Get There

Papua New Guinea's national airline, Air Niugini (tel: 675-327-3555; 714-752-5440 in the United States) offers international flights to Port Moresby from major Australian and Asian gateways. Milne Bay Air (tel: 675-325-2201) flies to Port Moresby from Cairns, in northern Australia.

When to Go

Papua New Guinea's climate is hot and humid year-round, with the wet season (December to March) and the dry season (May to October) subject to regional variation. Rainfall varies tremendously, from an average of 40 inches (101cm) in Port Moresby to more than 20 feet (6m) in some mountain areas. Temperatures along the Sepik River hover between 86°F (30°C) and 104°F (40°C) year-round but drop at higher altitudes. It can be chilly in the Highlands.

Getting Around

Air Niugini and Milne Bay Air fly to regional centers and upscale wilderness lodges throughout the country. Most land travel is aboard public motor vehicles that service informal bus routes. Vehicles are usually modern minibuses, but some are open-bed trucks. Rental cars are not recommended because of quirky local laws. On the Sepik, travelers with more time can take live-aboard cruises or motorized canoes from village to village.

INFORMATION

Embassy of Papua New Guinea

1779 Massachusetts Avenue, N.W., Suite 805, Washington, DC 20063; tel: 202-745-3680; fax: 202-745-3679; e-mail: kunduwash@aol.com

Papua New Guinea Tourism Promotion Authority

P.O. Box 1291, Port Moresby, PNG, tel: 675-320-0211; fax: 675-320-0223; e-mail: tourismpng@dg.com.pg; www.tiare.net.pg/tpa/home.html

CAMPING

There are no organized campsites, and camping is not advised for safety reasons.

LODGING

PRICE GUIDE – double occupancy

$ = up to $49 $$ = $50–$99

$$$ = $100–$149 $$$$ = $150+

Ambua Lodge

Trans Niugini Tours, P.O. Box 371, Mount Hagen, PNG; tel: 675-542-1438; fax: 675-542-2470; e-mail: travel@pngtours.com

Located at 7,000 feet (2,134m) in the Southern Highlands, Ambua has 40 guest units with modern bathrooms and views from 180-degree picture windows. $$$$

Bird of Paradise Hotel

P.O. Box 12, Goroka, PNG; tel: 675-732-1144; fax: 675-732-1007.

This hotel in the center of town offers 52 rooms and suites and two restaurants. $$$

Highlander Hotel

P.O. Box 34, Mount Hagen, PNG; tel: 675-542-1355; fax: 675-542-2000.

Sixty-eight rooms are available at this in-town hotel surrounded by gardens. Trans Niugini Tours operates from the hotel. $$$$

Haus Poroman Lodge

P.O. Box 1182, Mount Hagen, PNG; tel: 675-542-2250; fax: 675-542-2207.

Overlooking the Waghi Valley, separate lodges have modern rooms with a choice of private or shared bathrooms. $$

Karawari Lodge, Amboin

Trans Niugini Tours, P.O. Box 371, Mount Hagen, PNG; tel: 675-542-1438; fax: 675-542-2470, e-mail: travel@pngtours.com

Commanding a ridge overlooking lowland rain forest, Karawari is replete with regional art and offers cottages with modern bathrooms and mosquito-netted beds. $$$$

M/V *Sepik Spirit*

Trans Niugini Tours, P.O. Box 371, Mount Hagen, PNG; tel: 675-542-1438; fax: 675-542-2470; e-mail: travel@pngtours.com

This "floating lodge" cruises the Middle Sepik and accommodates 18 passengers in nine twin bedrooms, each with a private bathroom. Facilities include a dining room and observatory deck. $$$$

M/V *Melanesian Discoverer*

Melanesian Tourist Services, Coastwatchers Avenue, P.O. Box 707; Madang, 511, PNG; tel: 675-822-766; fax: 675-852-3543.

This 114-foot-long (35-m) catamaran operates four- to 17-night cruises into the heart of the Sepik River and is equipped with a helicopter for off-river exploration. The 18 twin lower berths, four suites, and four bunk cabins all have private bathrooms. $$$$

TOURS AND OUTFITTERS

Adventure Center

1311 63rd Street, Suite 200, Emeryville, CA 94608; tel: 510-654-1879 or 800-227-8747; fax: 510-654-4200.

A wide range of Highland treks, rafting, and Sepik packages are available, including budget plans.

Field Guides

9433 Bee Cave Road, Building 1, Suite 150, Austin, TX 78733; tel: 800-728-4953 or 512-263-7295; fax: 512-263-0117; e-mail: fgileader@aol.com

This bird-watching specialist offers a 22-day Papua New Guinea package that includes the Sepik River, Variarata National Park, and the Tari Highlands.

Goroka PNG Highland Tours

P.O. Box 583, Goroka, Eastern Highlands Province, PNG; tel: 675-732-3302; fax: 675-732-1602.

Travelers see everything from birds of paradise and orchids to local pottery and traditional dance on bush walks, day trips, and cultural tours in the Highlands. Treks to Goroka and Mount Wilhelm are also available.

Melanesian Tourist Services

Coastwatchers Avenue, P.O. Box 707, Madang, 511, PNG; tel: 675-852-2766; fax: 675-852-3543.

Cruises along the Sepik include options for scuba diving and helicopter excursions. Other cruises explore Papua New Guinea's north coast, Irian Jaya, and New Ireland.

Sepik Adventure Tours

P.O. Box 248, Wewak, PNG; tel: 675-856-2525.

This locally owned company leads canoe trips along the Sepik. Birding tours and hikes can also be arranged.

Trans Niugini Tours

P.O. Box 371, Mount Hagen, PNG; tel: 675-542-1438; fax: 675-542-2470; e-mail: travel@pngtours.com

Specializing in treks in Papua New Guinea and Irian Jaya, guides lead hikes, dives, mountain climbs, rafting, motorized canoe expeditions, and Sepik cruises.

Wilderness Travel

1102 Ninth Street, Berkeley, CA 94710; tel: 510-558-2488; fax: 510-558-2489; e-mail: webinfo@wildernesstravel.com

Programs feature hiking, rafting, and Sepik River journeys.

Excursions

Baliem Valley, Irian Jaya

Indonesian Tourism Promotion Board, Bank Pacific Building, Ninth Floor, 8 Jalan Jenderal Sudirman, Jakarta 10220, Indonesia; tel: 62-21-570-4879; fax: 62-21-570-4855; e-mail: itpb@indosat.net.id; www.tourismindonesia.com

Irian Jaya, New Guinea's western half, is still largely untamed wilderness. The Baliem Valley, in the remote and rugged eastern highlands, is one such place. It's superb for trekking, renowned for its hidden villages occupied by the Dani, and was unknown to the outside world before 1938. Small in stature, the men are seldom seen without their bows and arrows, wearing nothing but gourds around their penises.

Solomon Islands

Tourism Council of the South Pacific, 203 Sheen Lane, London SW14 8LE, England; tel: 44-181-876-1938; e-mail: tcspuk@interface-tourism.com

The people of this mountainous archipelago off the eastern tip of New Guinea were brought to the world's attention by anthropologists Bronislaw Malinowski and Margaret Mead. Here pigs have greater value than cash, outriggers ply coral lagoons, and sharks are treated with totemic reverence. The isles have active volcanoes fringed by beaches and spectacular reefs with hundreds of coral-encrusted relics from World War II. The Western and Anarvon Islands harbor the world's largest nesting grounds for the endangered hawksbill turtle.

Torres Strait Islands

Tourism Queensland, G.P.O. Box 328, Brisbane, Qld 4001, Australia; tel: 61-7-3406-5400; fax: 61-7-3406-5329; www.qttc.com.au

Two dozen or so islands sprinkle the Torres Strait like stepping stones from the tip of Cape York Peninsula to within three miles (5 km) of the Papua New Guinea coastline. About one-third of the population of approximately 9,000 live on Thursday Island, the administrative center. On outer islands domestic pigs are reared for ceremonial feasts, and dugongs and turtles are caught for meat. The islands were once a major pearling center.

Wet Tropics
Australia

Deep within the heart of the tropical rain forest, where the tangle of lawyer vines, fan-palm fronds, and giant buttressed fig trees chokes out the sun's dawn rays, it is dark and refreshingly cool. Nocturnal residents have retired to their treetop roosts to slumber, leaving only birds like the wompoo pigeon and the double-eyed fig parrot to flit and chatter amid the branches. A giant white-tailed rat – one of Australia's largest rodents – rests contentedly in a tree hollow, oblivious to the procession of green tree ants trailing torn leaves across the trunk toward their own retreat. Nearby, a furtive orange-footed scrubfowl tends to a large mound of soil and plant matter in which its eggs are incubating. ◆ Suddenly, the scrubfowl scurries for cover as the undergrowth rustles and parts to reveal a bulky shadow. The interloper is a male cassowary, one of the world's largest (though flightless) birds. Standing up to six feet (2m) tall, it sports a tutu of glossy black plumage and a brilliant necklace of azure blue, purple, and orange skin, from which hang two elongated red wattles. Crowned by an imposing blade-shaped bony helmet, the cassowary is lord of all that it surveys. ◆ Stealthily, the bird stalks the forest floor, searching about the leaf litter for fallen fruit, fungi, snails, and insects. Then, an errant sound brings its browsing to an abrupt halt. Sensing the presence of a rival male, the cassowary stretches high on its powerful feet, fluffs up its feathers defensively, and issues a guttural grunt. Summoned by this warning, a striped black-and-cream fluff ball barely two feet (60cm) high – the male's solitary chick, which he will look after for

In Australia's largest tracts of tropical forest, brilliantly hued butterflies color the canopy, kangaroos scale the trees, and crocodiles prowl the waterways.

Licuala fan palms, known for their broad umbrella-like leaves, thrive in the filtered light of the understory in seasonal swamps and other wetlands.

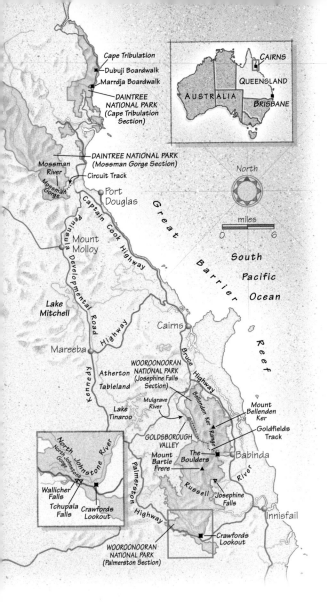

The greater glider (above) soars from tree to tree on winglike flaps of skin.

world of the **Wet Tropics** of northeastern Australia. A 164,372-acre (66,519-hectare), World Heritage-listed, rain-forest wonderland that extends 360 miles (580km) down the **Queensland** coast from **Cooktown** to **Townsville**, this garland of 19 national parks protects the greatest diversity of wildlife in Australia, with no fewer than 400 endangered species, 70 of them found nowhere else in the world. It is also staggeringly rich in plant life, including descendants of some of the oldest species on Earth. A living museum, the Wet Tropics has unlocked many long-held evolutionary secrets.

Rain-Forest Reconnaissance

While much of the Wet Tropics is rugged and remote, a plethora of both comfortable and challenging walking trails, scenic driving circuits, cultural tours, and nocturnal adventures, all within a few hours' drive of **Cairns**, opens a window on this most primeval of landscapes and the Aboriginal people it has sustained for thousands of years.

Visitors follow part of an age-old Aboriginal walking trail as they travel north from Cairns to remote and beautiful **Daintree National Park**, the jewel of the Wet Tropics. This park incorporates the country's largest tract of lowland rain forest and a mosaic of mountain forests, heaths, swamps, and coral foreshores in two distinct areas: the 161,785-acre (65,472-hectare) **Mossman Gorge** section at its southern extremity and the 42,237-acre (17,093-hectare) sliver of **Cape Tribulation** to the north, where the rain forest greets the **Great Barrier Reef** in a broad smile of inviting white sand.

Most of the Mossman section is inaccessible, except to experienced and well-equipped bushwalkers, but its defining feature, Mossman Gorge, is easily reached and the best starting point for a Daintree odyssey. Here, the pristine **Mossman River** carves a path through a steep-sided valley, tumbling over moss-cloaked granite in a series of cascading pools. The 1.7-mile (2.7-km) circuit trail, an easy amble, is the perfect introduction to its lush lowland rain forest and, especially on humid days, the forest's shade

nine months – abandons its hiding place, cheeps with alarm, and rushes to its father's skirted side. The protective parent prepares to defend itself and its young, but soon senses that the danger has passed, and father and chick return to their foraging.

Scores of curious creatures, ranging from cassowaries to tree kangaroos and giant purple pythons uncoiling to 23 feet (7m) in length, are secreted in the shady nether-

A float trip (right) on the North Johnstone River passes through Wooroonooran National Park.

Cassowary males (bottom) are devoted fathers, incubating eggs for two months and caring for chicks.

provides welcome relief from the oppressive heat.

Running parallel to the river, the trail passes boulders carpeted with emerald lichens, liverworts, and small lithophytes (plants that live on rocks), and trees like rose butternut, candlenut, pencil cedar, and Daintree penda adorned with rare orchids and large basket and bird's-nest ferns. The turquoise-winged Ulysses butterfly occasionally flutters by, but Australia's largest butterfly, the velvety green-and-black Cairns birdwing, prefers the heights of the rain-forest canopy.

Bird-watchers are rarely disappointed on this walk. Brush turkeys commonly scratch about the undergrowth and the pale-yellow robin and spectacled monarch both construct their nests here, decorating them with flakes of lichen and swatches of moss. During the warmer months, keep your eyes peeled for the buff-breasted paradise kingfisher, with its distinctive royal blue, orange, and black plumage and long white tail feathers, which eschews trees to nest in termite mounds.

The traditional custodians of the north Queensland forests, the Kuku-Yalanji Aborigines, had ingenious uses for a range of trees found within Mossman Gorge and their intimate understanding of rain-forest ecology gave them fascinating insights into food availability. For example, when the sticky bean tree was flowering, they knew it was time to dig incubating scrubfowl eggs from their mounds; when the wattle wore its vivid yellow

dress, the mullet were plump for spearing on the coast. In a reserve within Mossman Gorge, the Kuku-Yalanji share the secrets of their traditional rain-forest lifestyle during a short cultural tour.

Time Travelers

The forebears of the ribbonwood tree, found in the **Cape Tribulation** canopy, flourished perhaps 120 million years ago – long before people first set foot on the continent. At the time, Australia was part of the supercontinent Gondwana and draped in a velour-like cape of rain forest, sewn with cycads, mosses, ferns, and conifers. The appearance of the ribbonwood's ancestors heralded a major development – the evolution of our planet's first flowering plants. Only 18 plant families of this antiquity have been identified worldwide, 10 of them in the forest refuges of Daintree National Park, and within these families at least 50 species are found exclusively in the Wet Tropics. This botanical suite represents the greatest diversity of ancient flowering plants anywhere in the world.

Until its rediscovery in 1971, the ribbonwood (*Idiospermum australiense*) was known only

The common tree snake (right) hunts frogs and small reptiles, which it swallows head first.

A backpacker (below) takes a break at a remote cascade.

from a specimen collected in 1902. Today, little changed over the millennia, it still sports sweet-smelling cerise flowers during the dry season and can be seen along Daintree's **Marrdja Boardwalk**, just south of Cape Tribulation. Like some botanical time-tunnel, this pathway near Oliver Creek reveals relict cycads and zamia palms as well as more recent arrivals such as mangroves.

During drier spells, the forest rings with the calls of plump wompoo pigeons, and pairs of Victoria's riflebirds are occasionally seen engaging in a synchronized, swaying seduction. At higher altitudes, careful observers might notice the ornate bowers built on the ground by the golden bowerbird. These love nests may be up to eight feet

(2.4m) long and are furnished with lichens and freshly picked blooms. Lesser house-keepers like the yellow-spotted and bridled honeyeaters are more likely to be occupied feeding on insects and blossoms.

One of Daintree's few diurnal mammals lives in thicker rain forest nearby. The smallest and most primitive member of the kangaroo family, the musky-rat kangaroo emerges from thickets of the wait-a-while palm or rustles about the forest floor collecting leaves. Its distant cousin, the Bennett's tree-kangaroo, would never be so bold. A secretive animal, it leaves telltale scratches or mud marks on the trees it scales, but a sudden crash of branches and a flash of brown fur is usually all that is heard and seen of this creature as it alights from its treetop roost.

While wildlife is its major attraction, Cape Tribulation also caters to those travelers simply intent on beachcombing its stunning coastline, shaded by beach almonds and pandanus. About a quarter mile (400m) from the car park at the cape, north of Marrdja, a platform commands glorious views of the beach and ocean. Close by, the **Dubuji Boardwalk** leads visitors through fan palms that stand 50 feet (15m) high and resemble giant lime parasols, and past swamps to shoreline mangroves – sentries at the entrance to north **Myall Beach**.

A spotlighting tour is a great way to maximize your chances of seeing some of Daintree's nocturnal creatures and to experience its cloistered confines after dark. You'll undoubtedly hear the screeching of flying foxes as they drop from their daytime perches like ripe fruit to embark on a night's frenzied feeding. If you're lucky, you might come eye-to-eye with a rare or endangered possum such as the resident pygmy possum or the

The Ancient Croc

For many visitors, the highlight of a Wet Tropics adventure is glimpsing a living dinosaur that has changed little over the past 240 million years: the estuarine crocodile. This fierce creature is also one of Australia's most resilient, having survived the extinction of dinosaurs 65 million years ago as well as vast geological and climatic changes – not to mention decades of persecution by man. Crocodiles were hunted almost to extinction in Queensland for their leather, and although they were finally afforded protection in 1974, they remain on the threatened species list.

Growing to almost 20 feet (6m) in length, estuarine crocodiles typically inhabit tidal creeks and rivers, crawling up on the banks during the day to bask in the sun. They breed between October and April, and after mating, the female builds a nest of sedges and ferns near a coastal watercourse. She then lays about 50 eggs and guards the nest protectively until they hatch. The young spend only a short time with their mother before dispersing to begin life alone.

Although crocodiles never wander into the rain forest, all waterways in the Wet Tropics, except for shallow, fast-flowing streams, should be regarded as croc habitat. Travelers are advised not to swim in any rivers or creeks in the tropical lowlands, no matter how inviting they may appear.

Australia's saltwater crocodiles (below) are the biggest in the world and have been known to attack humans.

A male eclectus parrot (bottom), in bright green plumage, feeds its blue-and-red mate during the two- to four-week incubation period.

striped possum, a beautifully marked species that draws noisy attention to itself by tearing at dead wood in search of beetle larvae.

Riding the Rapids

It's a very different sound – rushing water – that greets more daring visitors to the heart of **Wooroonooran National Park**, between Cairns and **Innisfail**. Here, the fast-flowing **Russell River** hurries from its watershed in the **Bellenden Ker Range**, swirling cool and clear through isolated lowland forest to its meeting with the mighty South Pacific.

Uncoiling like a serpent in the shadow of Queensland's highest peak, 5,320-foot (1,620-m) **Mount Bartle Frere**, the Russell is one of the most easily accessible of the Wet Tropics' magical rivers and perfect for white-water rafting or kayaking.

Traveling the river, especially after the summer deluge, is an invigorating experience. Once the storms have abated, the Russell flows strong and high, swollen by an average annual rainfall of close to 19 feet (6m) in its mountainous catchment. Its meandering banks are fringed by overhanging crow's nest ferns and rain-forest giants including figs, tulip oaks, river cherries, and white beech. On some of their boughs, ornately patterned, non-venomous amethystine and carpet pythons bask in the sun.

A variety of fish, including sooty grunter, native catfish, and jungle perch, live in these waters, but visitors hoping for a fleeting glimpse of another of their inhabitants – the platypus – should explore the more tranquil backwaters, where this shy, egg-laying mammal prefers to swim and forage.

The best way to experience more of 196,365-acre (79,466-hectare) Wooroonooran, the largest rain-forest park in Queensland, is on foot. A network of graded trails invites visitors to sample the luxuriant vegetation in the **Palmerston** section of the park, south of the Russell River, which is renowned for its generous spill of waterfalls. From **Crawford's Lookout** on the **Palmerston Highway**, you can descend deep into **North Johnstone Gorge** to visit **Tchupala** and **Wallicher Falls**. More experienced and physically fit visitors can tackle the arduous 9.3-mile (15-km) trail that winds its way to the summit of Mount Bartle Frere, in the northern **Josephine Falls** section. This is a hazardous climb, hampered by slippery rocks and often poor visibility. But from progressively higher vantage points, tenacious walkers are rewarded with splendid views of the **Atherton Tableland**, **Bellenden Ker** (the state's second-highest peak), the **Mulgrave River Valley**, and the north Queensland coast.

A less challenging walk, to the north, takes you back in time along the historic 12-mile (19-km) **Goldfields Track**, an old prospecting route between Mount Bartle Frere and Mount Bellenden Ker. This journey of between seven and nine hours, linking the **Boulders Scenic Reserve**, near **Babinda**, and **Goldsborough Valley State Forest**, can be completed in either direction along a path noted for its monstrous king ferns, refreshing streams, gully crossings, and ridge-top views.

Especially beside creeks, walkers may be startled by the raucous screeches of sulfur-crested cockatoos or see smaller bush birds like the scrubwren or thornbill flitting through the forest understory. High in the canopy, the flashes of brilliant crimson belong to king parrots dining on seeds, fruit, leaf buds, and blossoms. Whatever the perspective, from treetops to leaf-strewn floor, the Wet Tropics is a true masterpiece – a verdant canvas lavishly painted with some of the world's most precious and vibrant wildlife.

Rain-Forest Resources

The Aboriginal people who lived for thousands of years amid the rain forests of northeastern Queensland devised a range of ingenious uses for their myriad plants. They realized, for example, that the Wet Tropics was a complete pharmacy. The sap of the candlenut tree could cure fungal diseases, and chewing and swallowing the young tips of the lawyer cane relieved the symptoms of dysentery. Heated sap from the leaves of the cordyline lily had general healing properties, while the large leaves of the cunjevoi could be pounded and applied to insect and snake bites.

Rain-forest plants also served more prosaic functions. Shields were cut from the buttresses of tree roots, and spear shafts and digging sticks were crafted from the wood of the black palm, which also yielded fiber to make bags and fishing nets. The Aborigines also made their shelters, or wuruns, entirely from local materials. Pliable lawyer vines or similar young saplings were curved to build the semicircular frame, which was then covered with a thatching of waterproof paperbark, fan-palm fronds, grass, and ginger leaves.

The local people also became aware of the powerful effects of certain chemicals contained within more than 30 plant species. For example, by placing the sap of the milky pine or the outer coating of the foambark in streams they found they could stupefy fish, which then floated to the surface for easy collection. Removing those same harmful toxins so that the plants could be eaten involved skillful preparation. The seeds of the black bean, for instance, were steamed for a day with wet candlenut leaves in an earthen oven, then finely sliced and placed in a river's gently flowing water to leach out the chemicals. After three to five days, the beans were safe for consumption.

Ceremonial garb (left) is fashioned from a variety of forest plants.

Northern blossom bats (right) roost alone or in small groups during the day and feed on nectar and pollen during their nighttime forays.

TRAVEL TIPS

DETAILS

How to Get There

Most flights from North America go to Sydney or Melbourne, but airlines also serve cities closer to the rain forests: Cairns or Townsville. Cairns is centrally located to most sites in the Wet Tropics, but Townsville offers opportunities to explore the south, including Hinchinbrook Island.

When to Go

While many people prefer the more stable weather conditions of the dry season, visitors should not discount the wet season, from November through May, when almost all annual rainfall occurs and the forest assumes a totally different atmosphere. Average temperatures range from 75°F (24°C) to 92°F (33°C), and tropical cyclones are common, rendering some roads impassable. In the dry season, temperatures range from 57°F (14°C) to 79°F (26°C) but drop to chilly lows at upper elevations.

Getting Around

Rental cars allow visitors to sample the 372 miles (600km) of roads throughout the Wet Tropics, including 40 scenic drives. Travelers should check road conditions before setting out, especially in the wet season. Four-wheel-drive vehicles are advisable in some areas. There are also scores of tour operators in the Wet Tropics, offering everything from ballooning to mountain biking.

INFORMATION

Daintree National Park

Mossman section: Queensland National Parks and Wildlife Service, Johnston Road, P.O. Box 251, Mossman, Qld 4873, Australia; tel: 61-07-4098-2188; fax: 61-7-4098-2279. Cape Tribulation section: PMB 10, PS 2041, Mossman, Qld 4873, Australia; tel: 61-7-4098-0052; fax: 61-7-4098-0074.

Queensland National Parks and Wildlife Service

10-12 McLeod Street, Cairns, Qld 4870, Australia; tel: 61-7-4052-3096; fax 61-7-4052-3080; www.env.qld.gov.au/environment/park

Tourism Tropical North Queensland Visitor Information Centre

51 The Esplanade, Cairns, Qld 4870, Australia; tel: 61-7-4051-3588; fax: 61-7-4051-0127; www.tnq.org.au

Wooroonooran National Park

Palmerston section: P.O. Box 800, Innisfail, Qld 4860, Australia; tel: 61-7-4064-5115; fax: 61-7-4064-5252. Josephine Falls section: P.O. Box 93, Miriwinni, Qld 4871, Australia; tel: 61-7-4067-6304; fax: 61-7-4067-6443.

CAMPING

There are scenic camping areas in national parks, state forests, and reserves in the Wet Tropics. Permits are required at Snapper Island in Daintree National Park and are available from the Environmental Protection Agency (tel: 61-7-4052-3096). Permits for bush camping in the Josephine Falls section of Wooroonooran National Park can be obtained from self-registration stands at the top of the Josephine Falls parking lot or at Junction Camp. There are also commercial campgrounds in nearby towns. Because crocodiles are abundant in the Wet Tropics, campers should pitch tents well away from deep pools.

LODGING

Bartle Frere House

Josephine Falls Road and Price Road, Bartle Frere, Qld 4871, Australia; tel: 61-7-4067-6309; e-mail: bfhouse@fastinternet.com.au

With rain forest on three sides and stunning views of Wooroonooran National Park, Bartle Frere House has two motel-style rooms – one queen and one double – no electricity, and shared facilities. Campsites are surrounded by rain forest. $

Crocodylus Youth Hostel

Lot 5, Buchanan Creek Road, Cow Bay, Cape Tribulation, P.M.B. 30, Mossman, Qld 4873, Australia; tel: 61-7-4098-9166.

This hostel, two miles (3km) from Cow Bay Beach, has five dormitories (each with 10 bunk beds), eight cabins with private baths, and two double cabins with private baths, all of which are bungalow-style canvas tents on stilts. Activities include guided walks, sea kayak tours, and snorkeling trips. $

Daintree Deep Forest Lodge

Cape Tribulation Road, 20 kilometers north of Daintree ferry crossing, Cape Tribulation, Qld 4873, Australia; tel: 61-7-4098-9162; e-mail: deepforestlodge@internetnorth.com.au

In the shadow of Thornton Peak and less than three miles (5km) from Thornton Beach, this homestead-style lodge has two double rooms and one five-person family room, each with a refrigerator, stove, bathroom, and veranda. $-$$

Heritage Lodge

50 Macrossan Street, P.O. Box 358, Port Douglas, Qld 4871, Australia; tel: 61-7-4099-4488; fax: 61-7-4099-4455.

This cabin-style resort in dense rain forest is at the base of the spectacular Alexandra Falls in the Cape Tribulation region. There are 20 rooms with private facilities (housed in 10 cabins), hiking paths, and a restaurant. Activities include horseback riding and four-wheel-drive safaris. $$-$$$

Mungalli Falls Rainforest Village

Junction Road, Millaa Millaa, Qld 4886, Australia; tel: 61-7-4097-2358; fax: 61-7-4097-2446; e-mail: mfsv@internetnorth.com.au

Set in highland rain forest within easy reach of the Palmerston section of Wooroonooran National Park, this complex includes eight four-person cabins and tent lodges that can house up to 30. Activities include bush walking, wildlife excursions, kayaking, and rafting. $-$$

TOURS AND OUTFITTERS

Daintree Rainforest River Trains

P.O. Box 448, Mossman, Qld 4873, Australia; tel: 61-7-4090-7676; fax: 61-7-4090-7660; e-mail: dntrain@ozemail.com.au

The River Train departs from the Daintree ferry crossing and travels through the Wet Tropics World Heritage Area. The trip includes a guided walk through a mangrove forest.

Jungle Adventures

P.O. Box 117, Port Douglas, Qld 4871, Australia; tel: 61-7-4098-0090; e-mail: treehouse@internet north.com.au

This outfitter runs tours in Daintree and Cape Tribulation rain forests that explore estuarine and freshwater habitats by river ferry.

Kuku-Yalanji Dreamtime Tours

P.O. Box 171, Mossman, Qld 4873, Australia; tel: 61-7-4098-1305; fax: 61-7-4098-2607; e-mail: yalanji@internetnorth.com.au

One-hour guided spiritual and cultural tours near Mossman Gorge focus on the Kuku-Yalanji Aboriginal people's rain-forest lifestyle and traditional use of plants for food and medicine.

Mangrove Adventures

P.O. Box 815, Mossman, Qld 4873, Australia; tel: 61-7-4090-7017.

Morning, day, and night boat tours explore the Daintree River.

Excursions

Cradle Mountain–Lake St. Clair National Park

Cradle Mountain Visitor Centre, P.O. Box 20, Sheffield, Tas 7306; tel: 03-6492-1133; www.tourism.tas.gov.au

Part of the Tasmanian Wilderness World Heritage Area, Cradle Mountain–Lake St. Clair encompasses a majestic, glacier-carved landscape studded with sparkling alpine lakes and bounded by lush temperate rain forest. The park's varied wildlife includes platypuses and pademelons, endemic carnivorous marsupials such as the Tasmanian devil and spotted-tailed quoll, and an array of Gondwanan relict plant species such as pandanus and celery-top pine. Experienced hikers can explore the full range of habitats on the challenging, 53-mile (85-km) Overland Track, one of the best long-distance walking trails in Australia.

Great Barrier Reef

Tourism Queensland, G.P.O. Box 328, Brisbane, Qld 4001, Australia; tel: 61-7-3406-5400; fax: 61-7-3406-5329; www.qttc.com.au

Cairns and Port Douglas are excellent staging posts for excursions to the stunning waters and cays of the Great Barrier Reef, the largest coral reef system in the world. Scuba diving and snorkeling tours, sailing charters, glass-bottomed boats, semi-submersibles, and underwater observatories are among the options to explore the reef's 1,500 varieties of fish, 400 types of hard and soft corals, 4,000 mollusk species, and six turtle species.

Lamington National Park

Lamington National Park, Green Mountains Section, Via Canungra, Qld 4275; tel: 07-5544-0634; env.qld.gov.au

Southwest of Brisbane on the Queensland–New South Wales border, Australia's largest remaining tract of subtropical rain forest cloaks a huge, ancient, and now heavily eroded caldera. With 100 miles (160km) of trails, including a superb canopy walkway, Lamington provides easy access to this lush, primeval world. Amid a cat's cradle of booyong trees, palms, lianas, and strangler figs, visitors can view up to 170 species of rain-forest plants; marsupials such as the red-necked pademelon, sugar glider, ring-tailed possum, and rare brush-tailed phascogale; and intriguing native birds such as rosellas, bowerbirds, and lyrebirds.

Fiordland
National Park
New Zealand

CHAPTER 20

Somber, mist-shrouded temperate rain forest sprawls down the vast and almost vertical rock walls to the tea-colored waters of **Doubtful Sound**. So much rain drenches these great granite mountains that a 10-foot (3-m) layer of freshwater runoff, tannin-stained by the vegetation on the slopes, lies permanently above the denser salt water of the fjord, allowing plants that would normally shrink from the sea to reach right to its edge. ◆ Seemingly alone in this watery wilderness, a tour boat nudges close to the tangled forest face, then cuts its engines. The noise fades. Barely a ripple breaks the surface of the dark water. Huddled in the icy air, hushed passengers peer into the mysterious mosaic of leaf, vine, and frond. Gradually, as their ears adjust, they begin to hear the sounds of the forest wafting toward them – the piping calls of hidden birds, the gurgling of cataracts hurtling unseen beneath the canopy. ◆ Situated in the far southwest of the **South Island**, **Fiordland National Park** is the largest national park in New Zealand and one of the

Extraordinary endemic plant and animal species, including an intriguing array of flightless birds, inhabit this spectacular glacier-carved kingdom.

biggest in the world. Named for the long fingers of water that probe its craggy coastline, it takes in the most rugged and remote region of a rugged and remote land. Its landforms – shaped during ice ages, the last of which ended 14,000 years ago – are on a hugely heroic scale: snaking fjords hemmed in by rock walls up to a mile high; rearing, snow-capped mountains; and mirror-surfaced lakes of exquisite beauty. ◆ But equally fascinating are the primeval-looking temperate rain forests that cling to the sodden slopes and fringe the lakes. Made up predominantly of southern beech

A party of hikers crosses a suspension bridge at Giant's Gate Falls on the Milford Track, one of several trails that lead through Fiordland's temperate rain forests and into the high country.

A **tour boat** (right) cruises the dramatic, glacier-carved fjord of Milford Sound.

Moss (below) grows on and around a stand of beech trees in a section of the park known as the Black Forest.

(*Nothofagus*), they descend directly from the flora of the ancient supercontinent of Gondwana and have their closest relatives far across the oceans in South America, southern Australia, New Caledonia, and New Guinea. When the landmass that became New Zealand broke away 80 million years ago to drift alone across the southern seas, it carried with it the primitive ancestors of the country's distinctive plants, birds, frogs, lizards, and insects (mammals, yet to evolve, missed a berth). Fiordland's forests and their mainly winged inhabitants are the great survivors of this ancient cargo, hanging on through tumultuous ages that saw mighty mountains

forced up and worn down, and lava and glaciers sweep over the land.

Today, the park's more than 2½ million acres (1 million hectares) of evergreen temperate rain forest are fueled by one of the wettest climates on the planet. When moisture-laden air roaring in from the **Tasman Sea** hits the cold hard face of the **Main Divide** (the spine of the South Island), it turns quickly to water – or snow – and in prodigious quantities. Up to 300 inches (760cm) a year falls here, with major storms turning the soaring bluffs into thundering walls of white water. Even on the cooler and comparatively drier eastern slopes, the rainfall is still a soggy 130 inches (330cm) a year.

Although Fiordland's forests have withstood the turmoil of geological upheaval and climatic extremes over millions of years, during the past two centuries they have

faced their greatest threat yet, in the form of animals introduced by European settlers. Predators such as cats and stoats have taken a heavy toll on native species, and deer and possums have wreaked havoc by defoliating trees and preventing regeneration. Minimizing the impact of these introduced species has been the focus of most of the park's conservation programs in recent years.

Enchanted Forest

Fiordland's rain forest is most easily explored from the picturesque township of **Te Anau**, spread along the southern shores of the lake of the same name. An excellent base for excursions to **Lake Manapouri** and Doubtful Sound to the southwest and **Milford Sound** to the north, Te Anau is also a handy departure point for the region's celebrated walks. There are shuttle services to the trailheads of the **Milford, Hollyford,** and **Routeburn Tracks** – all of which climb through rain forest to alpine tussock and back again – and the splendid **Kepler Track** departs from the edge of the township. It can be enjoyed as a four-day, 42-mile (68-km) circuit, including two days on the exhilarating ridges above treeline, or sampled as a day's stroll through lowland rain forest at the lake's edge.

The Kepler starts and ends at the control gates that regulate the flow from Lake Te Anau down the **Waiau River** to Lake Manapouri. Heading north, the easy three-hour return walk to **Brod Bay** leads through dimly lit red-beech forest, following a wide, well-made path thickly padded with countless layers of tiny beech leaves.

Almost as soon as you enter this cool wonderland, a retinue of fearless and friendly birds falls in beside you. Inquisitive fantails feathered in shades of brown and gray lead the way (helpfully hawking sandflies as they go), spreading and refolding their tails as they perform remarkable aerobatics. Bright-eyed black and white tomtits twitter, dart, and flit through the understory, ever alert for tasty leaf-litter morsels exposed by human feet.

Sharp ears will pick up the frequent, high-pitched calls of the forest's tiniest bird, the rifleman, and the chattering of yellow-

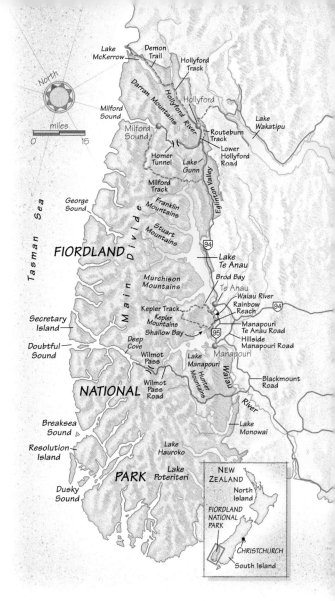

crowned parakeets in the canopy. If you hear a pumping and whirring of wings low overhead, it's most likely to be a kereru, or native pigeon, its gleaming green and mauve head and neck flashing like shot silk above a vest of pure white. The kereru is twice as large as a domestic pigeon and seems to make twice as much noise. Though long-lived, it produces only one egg a year, and in a world transformed by introduced predators this gentle bird is now fighting for survival.

The trail weaves on past rushing streams, their banks crowded with glistening circlets of waist-high crown ferns and thickets of tree ferns. In spring, the nectar-rich yellow

Fearless and Flightless

Isolated and devoid of land mammals for millions of years, New Zealand evolved as a land of birds. Fearless in the absence of flesh-eating predators and blessed with plentiful supplies of food, many abandoned flight, increased in size, and became slow-moving, stout-legged ground-dwellers. This, however, made them vulnerable to hunters and introduced predators following the arrival of humans around 1,000 years ago.

The moa, standing as high as a man, once browsed New Zealand's woodlands, occupying the niche filled by deer, antelope, and kangaroos on other continents. But two centuries after the arrival of human settlers, its numbers had been ravaged, and by the time of European settlement it was doomed, if not already extinct.

The moa's much smaller but similarly flightless relative, the kiwi, is perhaps the world's most unbirdlike bird. It lives in burrows, sniffs about at night using nostrils on the end of its beak, and has loose, hairlike feathers. Though not yet endangered, the species has declined significantly in numbers. The stocky, rooster-sized takahe, the largest living member of the rail family, for millennia grazed subalpine tussock grasslands; it is now reduced to a tiny population in the mountains of Fiordland. The kakapo – the world's only flightless parrot – is heavyweight, owl-like, and prefers to forage on the forest floor by night. With nothing but camouflaging plumage to protect it, the kakapo has become critically endangered and is now restricted to a handful of mammal-free islands.

Only the weka, which looks like a smaller, slimmer version of the kiwi, has held its own, thanks in part to the protection afforded by its strong beak and powerful legs. Inquisitive and acquisitive, it has been known to stride into campsites, snatch a sandwich, roll of toilet paper, or even a watch, then dash for cover to study the spoils.

Kiwis (below) lay very large eggs. Only the size of a chicken, they produce eggs similar in size to those of an ostrich.

Ferns (bottom) carpet the forest floor.

Clouds (right) get snarled on the bare peak of Mount Hart in the mountainous interior.

The Arthur River (opposite, bottom) crashes through a gorge near Milford Sound.

blossoms of the kowhai tree lure bees and bellbirds, and shy orchids scent the air. In fall, fruiting fungi erupt at the feet of beech trees. There are dainty circles of tiny, snow-white toadstools; clusters of glossy, copper-colored miniature cupolas; and crimson, white-spotted saucers arranged on a spongy floor of bright green moss like tables and stools for an elfin tea party.

Heading in the opposite direction on the Kepler Track will take you on a similarly enchanting walk through manuka (tea tree) shrubland and beech forest to a swing bridge above the swirling waters at **Rainbow Reach**. From there, the path continues inland across a kettle bog (a depression left by melting glacial ice) to **Shallow Bay** on Lake Manapouri. This return trip requires a full day, athough you can cut out a section by using the shuttle bus that runs from Te Anau to the control gates and Rainbow Reach and back again.

Waterways and Wilderness

The journey from Te Anau to Milford Sound, Fiordland's major drawcard, is one of the world's great drives and should not be missed. The road climbs through overarching avenues of beech, crosses the tawny flats of the **Eglinton Valley**, skirts **Lake Gunn**, and then traverses the eerie gloom of **Homer Tunnel** to reach the western side of the divide. From there, it zigzags down ice-sculpted slopes to the towering, canyonlike walls of Milford Sound (actually a fjord, as it was gouged out by ice, then flooded by

rising seas), rated by Rudyard Kipling as the eighth wonder of the world.

Yet the trip south from Te Anau to the less-visited Doubtful Sound (also a fjord) is no less awe-inspiring, and permits closer investigation of Fiordland's forests. The first stage involves a ferry journey across island-studded Lake Manapouri. To the north and south rise jagged ranges draped with a blanket of forest that climbs through wreaths of mist to 2,500 feet (760m), where the vegetation changes abruptly to stunted shrubs and low herbs. Stage two consists of a 14-mile (23-km) bus trip over dramatic 2,200-foot-high (670m) **Wilmot Pass**. On the western side of the pass, the road drops steeply to the fern-fringed foreshore of **Deep Cove**, at the head of Doubtful Sound.

Stretching west from here are sheer, rain-forest-clad slopes – an untouched wilderness that can be viewed only from the water. Trees and shrubs grow in dense profusion wherever roots can find purchase. The intriguing mix of species includes silver beech that can tower to 100 feet (30m) and scattered native conifers (*Podocarps*), mainly graceful rimu, emerging here and there above the canopy as pale spires. Broad-leaved rata and kamahi, spiky totara, and long-leaved cab-bage tree add depth and variety to the sub-canopy, and mamaku (black tree ferns) up to 60 feet (18m) high pack narrow gullies.

For all its apparent timelessness, the forest's hold is precarious. Long, pale scars of bare rock are evidence of tree avalanches, natural and regularly occurring catastrophes. Because of the lack of topsoil here, trees rely on an interlocking, matted root system for support. Eventually their weight becomes too great and, often trig-gered by the added burden of a heavy downpour or snowfall, a tree topples, peeling away a long strip of attached vegetation as it falls.

The rock does not remain bare for long. Lichens, able to take hold in the most difficult conditions, are the first to recolonize, followed by liverworts, mosses, and ferns. Together these plants form a recep-tive nursery bed for seeds dropped by nearby trees or spread by fruit-eating kererus, and soon saplings are thrusting skyward.

Within 30 years, the wound will be difficult to discern; a century will see the cycle from bare rock to climax forest com-plete. Left to its own devices, nature will recover. The challenge for humans is to provide the protection that will allow the saplings currently waiting in the shade to reach maturity in this astonishing setting.

TRAVEL TIPS

DETAILS

How to Get There

The international airport closest to Fiordland is in Christchurch, 400 miles (644km) away. Most visitors, however, fly to Auckland, on the North Island, which offers plentiful options for transportation to other parts of the country.

When to Go

Fiordland is battered by up to 300 inches (762cm) of annual rainfall. November through February is the warmest period but also when the heaviest rains – as well as the pesky sand flies – come out in force. For those who don't want to get drenched, May through August is the driest, but coldest, period. During this time, heavy snowfall pounds the high country beyond Hollyford Valley. This means there is the risk of getting snowed in (or out) of Milford Sound, a part of Fiordland reached through subalpine areas. Although trail huts stay open during this period, they are not maintained and have no gas for heat or cooking and no radio.

Getting Around

Good roads, excellent public transportation, and local information centers in most towns make it easy to navigate around New Zealand. Visitors may opt to rent a car in Auckland or decide to get around by train, domestic airlines, or buses. Special flexibility passes are available and are a great value. To soak in the beauty around Fiordland, travelers may hike more than 300 miles (482km) of trails, rent bikes, or take flight-seeing tours by plane or helicopter. There is public transportation around Te Anau to the trailheads of Fiordland.

INFORMATION

Destination Fiordland

P.O. Box 155, Te Anau, New Zealand; tel: 64-3-249-7959; fax: 64-3-249-7949; e-mail: fpai@teanau.co.nz; www.fiordland.org.nz

Fiordland National Park Visitor Centre

Department of Conservation, P.O. Box 29, Te Anau, New Zealand; tel: 64-3-249-7921 or 64-3-249-7924; fax: 64-3-249-7613; e-mail: fiordlandvc@doc.govt.nz

Great Walks Booking Desk

Department of Conservation, P.O. Box 29, Te Anau, New Zealand; tel: 64-3-249-8514 or 64-3-249-7924; fax: 64-3-249-8515.

New Zealand Tourism Board

Level 11, AA Centre, 99 Albert Street, P.O. Box 6727, Wellesley Street Mail Centre, Auckland, New Zealand; tel: 64-9-914-4780; fax: 64-9-914-4789.

CAMPING

Fiordland National Park

Great Walks Booking Desk, Department of Conservation, P.O. Box 29, Te Anau, New Zealand; tel: 64-3-249-8514 or 64-3-249-7924; fax: 64-3-249-8515.

Hikers can stay overnight in the park in either huts or at campsites. Both must be reserved.

LODGING

PRICE GUIDE – double occupancy	
$ = up to $49	$$ = $50–$99
$$$ = $100–$149	$$$$ = $150+

Davaar Country Lodge

R.D. 2, Te Anau, New Zealand; tel: 64-3-249-5838; fax: 64-3-249-8518; e-mail: davaar@teanau.co.nz

Nestled in foothills 20 minutes east of Te Anau, this lodge is on a 2,800-acre (1,133-hectare) sheep and cattle ranch. The self-contained lodge with kitchen accommodates up to five people. Laundry facilities and breakfast are provided. Guests can arrange for a fishing guide. $

Edgewater XL Motel

52 Lakefront Drive, Te Anau, New Zealand; tel: 64-3-249-7258; fax 64-3-249-8099.

Positioned on the lakefront between central Te Anau and the Department of Conservation Visitor Centre, this motel has 16 units with kitchens and private bathrooms. Canoes are available. $

Kepler Cottage

William Stephen Road, R.D. 1, Te Anau, New Zealand; tel: 64-3-249-7185; fax: 64-3-249-7186; e-mail: kepler@teanau.co.nz

Near Te Anau and within walking distance of the Kepler Track, this rural guest house on the edge of Fiordland is also a small farm. Guests have a view of the Fiordland mountains and stay in rooms with private baths. The cottage also provides breakfast and access to mountain bikes and fishing gear. $–$$

Shakespeare House

10 Dusky Street, P.O. Box 32, Te Anau, New Zealand; tel: 64-3-249-7349; fax: 64-3-249-7629.

All the rooms in this bed-and-breakfast, including one double-bedroom suite, have private facilities and sunporches. $$

Te Anau Holiday Park

1 Te Anau-Manapouri Road, P.O. Box 81, Te Anau, Fiordland, New Zealand; tel: 64-3-249-7457; fax: 64-3-249-7536; e-mail: reservations@destinationnz.com

With views of Lake Te Anau and the surrounding mountains, this vacation complex has secluded houses, motel units, cabins with or without kitchens, accommodations for backpackers, and 150 RV/tent sites. Tours can be arranged, and there is shuttle service to all major Fiordland tracks. The Department of Conservation Visitor Centre is across the street. $

TOURS AND OUTFITTERS

Adventure Charters

Waiau Street, Manapouri, New Zealand; tel: 64-3-249-6626; fax: 64-3-249-6923.

Tours in Fiordland include a 12-hour cruise, a four-wheel-drive excursion, and a two-day guided trip to Doubtful Sound.

Fiordland Guides

Kakapo Road, Te Anau, New Zealand; tel/fax: 64-3-249-7832; e-mail: fiordlandguidesltd@nzsouth.co.nz

Nature walks, guided fly-fishing, outfitted hikes and backpacking trips, bird-watching, and natural history lectures are offered. Fiordland Guides also operates a lodge near the park.

Fiordland Travel

P.O. Box 94, Queenstown, New Zealand (head office) or P.O. Box 1, Te Anau, New Zealand; tel: 64-3-442-7509 or 64-3-249-8900; fax: 64-3-442-7365; e-mail: info@fiordlandtravel.co.nz

Full- and multiday cruises and guided excursions tour in and around Fiordland and include a cruise to remote Doubtful Sound.

Hollyford Track

P.O. Box 360, Queenstown, New Zealand; tel: 64-3-442-3760; fax: 64-3-442-3761; e-mail: info@hollyfordtrack.co.nz

As its name suggests, this operator runs three- and four-day "walk-in/fly-out" guided excursions along the Hollyford Track, with accommodations at backcountry lodges.

Sinbad Cruises

15 Fergus Square, Te Anau, New Zealand; tel: 64-3-249-7106; fax: 64-3-249-8293; e-mail: sinbad@teanau.co.nz

Cruises in the Fiordland area vary in duration. Hikers can also use a boat service to the Milford and Kepler Tracks.

Excursions

Mount Cook National Park

Department of Conservation, Mount Cook Visitor Centre, Box 5, Mount Cook, New Zealand; tel: 64-3-435-1819.

This park is named after New Zealand's highest peak, which, at 12,349 feet (3,764m), stands proudly above jagged alpine scenery. Along with Fiordland, Mount Aspiring, and Westland National Parks, it makes up the extensive South Westland World Heritage Area. There are 19 peaks that top 9,800 feet (2,990m) in Mount Cook National Park, and the area abounds with permanently snow-capped mountains and ancient glaciers. Helicopters and ski-equipped planes take visitors on tours of the glaciers.

Stewart Island

Department of Conservation, Box 3, Stewart Island, New Zealand; tel: 64-3-219-1130.

New Zealand's third-largest island, 20 miles (32km) south of South Island, is a serene 650 square miles (1,684 sq km). Largely untouched native forests make it a wonderful hiking excursion. Native birds, including blue penguins, thrive on the island, and twilight kiwi-spotting trips are available.

Westland National Park

Department of Conservation, West Coast Conservancy, Private Bag 701, Hokitika, New Zealand; tel: 64-3-755-8301.

This park backs into its Mount Cook counterpart. While land to the east is in a dry rain shadow, Westland is a lush, wet wonderland of thick rain forest. It rises spectacularly from the rugged coast, through mangroves and forest, to 9,840-foot

(3,000-m) peaks in less than 31 miles (50 km). Two enormous glaciers – Franz Josef and Fox – tumble down valleys, adding to the scenic variety. Bird life abounds in the forest and on the coastal wetlands, home to the elegant kotuku and white heron.

Madagascar

CHAPTER 21

n 1771, an exuberant French naturalist, Jean Philibert Commerson, wrote to his former professor at the Sorbonne: "Madagascar is truly the naturalist's promised land. Here nature seems to have retreated into a private sanctuary to work on models different from those she has created elsewhere. At every step, one meets the most strange and marvelous forms!" ◆ As it was then, so it is now. At every step in Madagascar's rain forests, the observant visitor sees something extraordinary: a spider with legs some 50 times the length of its body, an orange-and-red giraffe-necked weevil like a miniature mechanical digger, purple beetles wearing fuzzy blue tutus, brookesia chameleons impersonating dead leaves to perfection, geckos resembling elongated pieces of moss, the slim fandrefiala snake, which the local people believe can drop from a tree tail-first and **Cast adrift from Africa** spear one of their precious zebu cattle. The **almost 165 million years ago,** vast majority of these creatures are unique to **the world's fourth-largest** Madagascar. Indeed, it is said that of the **island supports a fascinating** 200,000 species on this large island, 150,000 **array of endemic wildlife.** of them live nowhere else on Earth. ◆ To understand the origins of Madagascar's amazing biodiversity and high proportion of endemic species, one must know something of its geological history. Hundreds of millions of years ago, the island was part of a huge southern landmass called Gondwana. This supercontinent began to break up around 200 million years ago, eventually forming the continents of Africa, South America, Asia, Australasia, and Antarctica. About 165 million years ago, further plate movements tore off a small corner of the African continent, creating the island of Madagascar. ◆ This occurred before the evolution of

A well-marked trail leads a visitor into the recesses of Andasibe–Mantadia National Park, home of the indri, a black-and-white lemur known for its distinctive call.

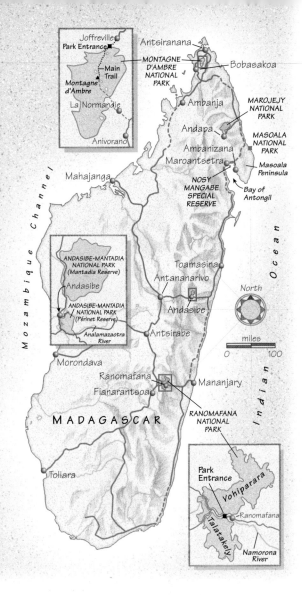

mate includes 300 butterfly species and 4,000 species of moth.

In contrast, the island is home to only five main groups of mammals – primates (lemurs), viverrids (civets and mongooses), tenrecs, rodents, and bats – though these have diversified into numerous species. Lemurs are the island's most distinctive mammals, but the extraordinary tenrecs excite almost as much interest. They come in all shapes and sizes, ranging from little shrewlike creatures to the hedgehog tenrec, which, as its name implies, looks like a European hedgehog.

No one is sure how the first mammals arrived on Madagascar, but it is likely that they hopped aboard a floating island of vegetation, or slept their way through a sea crossing curled up inside a hollow log. Sea crossings were no obstacle to birds, however, and the island is now home to at least 256 species, of which 120 are endemic. There are five endemic families, including the Vangidae, which, like Darwin's finches in the Galapagos, have evolved a range of beak shapes and sizes to deal with different prey.

Land of Contrasts

A range of mountains runs like a spine down the center of Madagascar, creating sharply contrasting regional climates. The east and far north receive regular rainfall, whereas the west is more arid, with the southwestern corner remaining dry for most of the year.

With habitats ranging from mountains and coastline to rain forest and desert, it's little wonder that there are so many native plant species, including around 1,000 orchids, 170 palms (three times the number found in mainland Africa), and seven baobab trees. Eighty percent of the flora is endemic, with a total of around 12,000

mammals, so reptiles and invertebrates would have been the only stowaways as the island drifted eastward to its current position, 250 miles (400km) off the African coast. Today, this is reflected in Madagascar's large number and variety of reptiles and invertebrates and its relatively small number of mammals. There are at least 340 species of reptile, including over half the world's chameleon species, and perhaps 300 kinds of frog. No one knows how many insects there are – entomologists have only just started classifying them – but a conservative esti-

The vivid color of a tomato frog (left) is a signal to predators of its extreme toxicity.

A leaf-tailed gecko (right) at Marojejy National Park relies on camouflage to protect itself from predators.

The striped civet (left) is a nocturnal predator found in the eastern rain forests. It's about the size of a cat and mostly preys upon rodents.

Millipedes (below, right) feed on decaying vegetation and are usually found in the leaf litter on the forest floor.

species. Madagascar's lowland rain forests alone have about 100 tree species per acre.

At one time, the eastern flank of the island was entirely covered with rain forest, ranging from the 100-foot (30-m) trees of the warm coastal zone to the montane forests of the slopes and the stunted cloud forests around the cold peaks. Today, 90 percent of this forest is gone, most of it cleared by a poverty-stricken population desperate for arable land, building materials, and fuel. This has led to a catastrophic decline in certain animal populations, and many species are now on the brink of extinction. Furthermore, the removal of trees has resulted in disastrous erosion, with huge volumes of topsoil being washed into rivers and the ocean. Sadly, while the rate of forest destruction has

slowed, it has not been stopped.

The outlook is not all doom and gloom, however. The 1990s saw the creation of several new national parks as well as a variety of ecotourism ventures that not only generate revenue for protected areas but also encourage local people to preserve their native forests. Visitors to Madagascar now enjoy increasing access to a wide range of reserves that displays an intriguing cross-section of the island's rain-forest ecosystems and wildlife.

The National Association for the Management of Protected Areas (ANGAP) rightly insists that visitors to parks and reserves are accompanied by a local guide.

A stream (left) leaps over a mossy boulder on Nosy Mangabe, an island preserve about three miles (5km) offshore.

Tenrecs (right), primitive, insectivorous, hedgehog-like mammals, are found only on Madagascar.

The giraffe-necked weevil (bottom), surely one of the world's most bizarre insects, uses its long neck to bore into plants and seeds.

Guides in long-established preserves are extremely knowledgeable about wildlife and its whereabouts, but may be less so in newer parks. Likewise, recently established protected areas may have limited facilities, though trails and visitor centers are constantly being developed.

The most accessible and most visited of the country's preserves is **Andasibe–Mantadia National Park**, which lies only three to four hours by car from the capital, **Antananarivo**. It incorporates **Analamazaotra Special Reserve**, which is universally known by its French colonial name, **Périnet**. Andasibe's accessibility is both a plus and a minus. It means you are rarely alone in the forest, but it also ensures that the guides here are the best trained and most knowledgeable of any in Madagascar, and that there are some first-class accommodations right on the edge of the park.

Andasibe is situated at about 3,300 feet (1,000m), so the dominant vegetation is montane forest rather than true rain forest. Unfortunately, the reserve was heavily logged by French colonists; none of the large trees has survived, and, apart from tree ferns and cycads, the vegetation is generally shrubby and rather uninteresting. But the park is still well worth a visit, if only to see

and hear the remarkable song-ster of Madagascar, the indri. With its black-and-white fur, teddy-bear ears, and startled expression, this large tail-less lemur looks rather like a long-limbed panda. For the first few hours of the morning, groups of indris spend their time feeding or sprawling around in the trees; but once warmed by the sun, they raise their heads, open their pink mouths, and begin to yodel loudly. The sound is eerie but wonderful. Like most birdsong, it has a territorial purpose, telling other groups of indris, "Keep out; this is our patch!"

About 150 miles (240km) south of Andasibe lies **Ranomafana National Park**, which opened in 1991. The drive to Ranomafana from the nearest town, **Fianarantsoa**, is wonderful, the eroded hillsides and dry vegetation of the highlands

gradually giving way to lush greenery and colorful flowers, spectacular views of the tumbling waters of the **Namorona River**, and finally, as you approach the reserve, the knobbly green canopy of the virgin forest.

This fragment of mid-altitude rain forest is particularly rich in wildlife. Hidden in the lush and varied vegetation are 12 species of lemur (including the recently discovered golden bamboo lemur), more than 100 species of birds (36 of which are endemic), and numerous reptiles, butterflies, and other insects, among them the extraordinary giraffe-necked weevil.

Coastal Forests

The town of **Maroantsetra** on the northeast coast is the departure point for visits to the delightful **Nosy Mangabe Special Reserve**. This island preserve, perhaps the most rewarding of all the rain-forest parks, is

The female black lemur (above, right) is actually chestnut brown. Only the male is black.

Black-and-white ruffed lemurs (right) are found at Nosy Mangabe and Andasibe-Mantadia National Park.

rich in classic tropical vegetation, including huge, buttress-rooted trees, strangler figs, and flowering shrubs, and is home to two of Madagascar's most bizarre animals: the aye-aye and the leaf-tailed gecko.

It took scientists nearly a century to decide that the aye-aye was a lemur, not a squirrel. This creature of the night seems to be made up of parts borrowed from other animals: a bat's ears, a squirrel's tail, a rodent's teeth. Its hands, however, are like those of no other living creature: long, bony claws with a skeletal middle finger that is used to probe into holes in rotting trees and pull out tasty grubs. In 1966, several aye-ayes were

Leaping Lemurs

Chances are that these endearing creatures, with their soft fur and large, round eyes, top the wish lists of most visiting ecotravelers. Fortunately, lemurs can be seen in almost all of Madagascar's parks and reserves.

Lemurs are primitive primates, or prosimians. That means they evolved during an early stage of primate evolution, beginning around 55 million years ago. In most parts of the world, prosimians were subsequently displaced by more highly evolved primates – monkeys, apes, and, eventually, humans – and only a few isolated groups now remain. They include the bushbabies of Africa and the lorises and tarsiers of Asia, all of which had to become nocturnal to survive.

In Madagascar, however, lemurs had few competitors and diversified solely to take advantage of particular niches within the island's ecosystems. There are currently 51 recognized taxa (including subspecies) of lemur in Madagascar, divided between 33 species, 14 genera, and five families. In the 2,000 years following the arrival of humans, 16 species of lemur became extinct, all of which were larger than those alive today; one was the size of a gorilla.

The remaining species range in size from the tiny pygmy mouse lemur, which weighs only one ounce, to the chunky indri, which is almost as large as a chimpanzee. Smaller lemurs are generally nocturnal, whereas larger species are active by day. Most feed on fruit and leaves and spend all of their time in the trees, using their long tails to help them balance on branches. Only the ring-tailed lemur, with its distinctive black-and-white banded tail, descends regularly to the forest floor.

almost certain that you will walk right past this master of camouflage, whose coloring matches almost perfectly the gray-green bark of its favorite trees. Pressed head down against the trunk, the gecko is virtually invisible. Only if you touch it will it betray its presence by opening its bright pink mouth and flicking up its tail. If you still appear to pose a threat, it may follow this defensive display with another – a high-pitched scream.

East of Maroantsetra, the **Masoala Peninsula** contains one of Madagascar's largest remaining areas of virgin rain forest; such is the variety of wildlife here that scientists are only beginning to classify it. Fortunately, the Malagasy government recently acted to protect the area, creating the 811-square-mile (2,100-sq-km) **Masoala National Park** in 1996. This is currently a destination for adventurous travelers only: the trails are steep and often slippery, there is no lodging, only camping, and reaching the park requires a three-hour boat journey from Maroantsetra across the **Bay of Antongil**.

introduced to Nosy Mangabe to try to save the species from extinction. They are now well established, but visitors must camp overnight to have a chance of seeing them. Although strictly nocturnal, the aye-ayes like to feed in the large trees near the campsite; a flashlight will pick up the tell-tale eye shine and, if you are lucky, the sweep of a bushy tail.

The leaf-tailed gecko, on the other hand, is diurnal and fairly common, so in theory it should be easy to see. However, it's

Masoala is a rare example of coastal rain forest. Bubbling streams rush down to the sea through tall trees with massive buttress roots bordering white-sand beaches. An extraordinarily beautiful place on one of its few fine days – this is the wettest region in

Madagascar – Masoala provides splendid opportunities to view some of the island's rarest wildlife. Perhaps the most sought-after species is a bird, the bizarre helmet vanga, which looks as though someone has rammed a turquoise flower over its beak. Another resident guaranteed to excite birders is the Madagascar serpent eagle, one of the world's most endangered birds of prey. Masoala is also one of the few places in the country where you may come across several species of tenrec snuffling around in the leaf litter and the rare red-ruffed lemur.

Chameleons (opposite, top) have pincerlike claws, prehensile tails, and eyes that swivel 360 degrees.

A brow of clouds (opposite, bottom) drifts below a rock outcrop at Marojejy National Park.

The paradise flycatcher (left) is one of the most colorful birds on the island. Both male and female (seen here) incubate the eggs.

A tree frog (below) perches on a carnivorous pitcher plant at Andasibe–Mantadia National Park.

A flash of chestnut in the bushes may also reveal a flamboyant paradise flycatcher with its long, trailing tail feathers. The jackpot for birders, however, is one of Madagascar's most beautiful birds, the pitta-like ground roller, with its exquisite blue, green, and orange plumage.

Up North

Arguably Madagascar's most visitor-friendly national park is **Montagne d'Ambre**, a 48,000-acre (19,400-hectare) preserve located near the northern tip of the island. Created in 1958 when the French colonial government finally recognized the ecological value of the volcanic massif and its montane forest, the park has a comfortable climate, several waterfalls, fascinating flora and fauna, and 19 miles (30km) of broad trails. In the dry season, vehicles can even drive right up to the main picnic area.

Walking the park's trails, you'll pass magnificent tree ferns, huge bird's-nest ferns perched on high branches, and the tangled lacework of strangler figs hanging from host trees. If you hear a crashing of branches, you may be about to sight a troop of lemurs, usually either Sanfords brown lemurs or the larger crowned lemurs. Though locally common, both are endangered and limited to this small corner of northern Madagascar. The crowned lemur is particularly handsome, with chestnut-colored fur and a neat black crown; the gray female sports a ginger tiara.

From the most visitor-friendly to the most challenging: **Marojejy National Park** lies about 100 miles (160km) southeast of Montagne d'Ambre and is one of Madagascar's newest national parks. Its infrastructure is still being developed, so it is currently a destination for serious naturalists only, although some specialist tours visit. The park is a showcase for Madagascar's diversity, with four main types of forest, 60 species of reptiles, 49 species of amphibians, and 107 bird species. It is also one of the last refuges of a rare lemur, the silky sifaka.

Wildlife watching here can be challenging: the forest is dense and the animals not habituated to humans. But visually Marojejy is stunning – lush forests surround imposing mountains and spectacular craggy cliffs – and few other areas in Madagascar offer such wildness and awesome splendor. The continuing creation of reserves such as Marojejy inspires hope that, despite the ravages of recent times, the island will remain forever "the naturalist's promised land."

DETAILS

How to Get There

Ivato Airport in Antananarivo is Madagascar's only international airport. Air Madagascar and Air France fly to Madagascar, and all flights originate from Paris.

When to Go

The rain-forest reserves in Madagascar are often very wet, and visitors should be prepared for rain at any time of year. The best months to visit eastern Madagascar are April to May and September to November. January through March is the rainiest period, when cyclones may occur. Average midday temperatures in the dry season are 77°F (25°C) in the highlands and 86°F (30°C) along the coast. From June through August it can be unpleasantly cold in high-altitude reserves such as Périnet or Marojejy, and some animals, including tenrecs and dwarf lemurs, hibernate.

Getting Around

Travelers should coordinate visits to the reserves with a tour operator unless they have a lot of time and patience. Most reserves are accessible only by a domestic flight combined with a taxi ride. Buses and bush taxis are unreliable and uncomfortable.

INFORMATION

Malagasy Embassy

2374 Massachusetts Avenue, N.W., Washington, DC 20008; tel: 202-265-5525.

National Association for Management of Protected Areas

B.P. 1424, Antananarivo 101, Madagascar; tel: 261-20-224-1554; fax: 261-20-224-1539; e-mail: angap@bow.dts.mg

This is the government conservation body in Madagascar.

Tours Operateurs Professionnels

Espace DERA de l'Université, BP 8308, Antananarivo 101, Madagascar; tel/fax: 261-20-227-8859; e-mail: topmad@dts.mg; www.madagascar-guide.com/top/index.html

CAMPING

Camping is allowed and may be the only form of accommodation in many of the reserves. Tour operators can provide equipment.

LODGING

Because of limited infrastructure in many parts of Madagascar, it's advisable to arrange lodging, rental cars, and other logistics before your arrival.

PRICE GUIDE – double occupancy	
$ = up to $49	$$ = $50–$99
$$$ = $100–$149	$$$$ = $150+

Hotel Domaine Nature

Destinations Mada, 32 Rue Andrianary Ratianarivo, Ampasamadinika, B.P. 8335, Antananarivo 101, Madagascar; tel: 261-20-31072; fax: 261-20-31067; e-mail: desmada@dts.mg

This hotel, halfway between Ranomafana village and Ranomafana National Park, has six bungalows with shared facilities, hot water, and good food with vegetarian options. $

Hotel Vatosoa

B.P. 46, Andapa 205, Madagascar (Reaching this hotel by phone is possible only by calling the international operator and indicating its local number in Andapa, which is 39.)

Rooms with hot water, a good restaurant, and a very helpful owner are all pluses at this hotel near Marojejy National Park. $

Las Palmas

B.P. 120, Sambava, Madagascar; tel: 261-20-88-92087.

Bungalows have air-conditioned rooms and hot water at this lodging on the beach near Marojejy National Park. $

Le Club Plage

B.P. 33, Sambava, Madagascar; tel/fax: 261-20-88-92064.

This hotel, near Marojejy National Park, has two-person bungalows overlooking the sea. $

Relais du Masoala

16 Rue Stephanie, Amparibe, Antananarivo, Madagascar; tel: 261-20-22-34993; e-mail: relais@simicro.mg

Ten palm-thatched bungalows have bathrooms and covered verandas overlooking the Bay of Antongil. The hotel operates a number of tours, including trips to Nosy Mangabe Special Reserve, bird-watching on the Masoala Peninsula, and river excursions. $$

Vakôna Forest Lodge

B.P. 750, Antananarivo, Madagascar; tel: 261-20-21394; fax: 261-20-23070; e-mail: izouard@bow.dts.mg

Located in Andasibe village just outside Andasibe National Park, this luxury lodge has 14 bungalows, good food, horseback riding, and its own small reserve. $–$$

TOURS AND OUTFITTERS

Boogie Pilgrim

Villa Michelet, Lot A11, Faravohitra, Antananarivo, Madagascar; tel: 261-20-25878; fax: 261-20-62556; e-mail: bopi@bow.dts.mg

Guides lead adventure and camping safaris, overland tours, special-interest trips, customized itineraries, and tours by light aircraft.

Cortez Travel Services

124 Lomas Santa Fe Drive, Solana Beach, CA 92075; tel: 619-755-5136 or 800-854-1029; fax: 619-481-7474; e-mail: info@cortez-usa.com

Naturalists and anthropologists

lead tours focusing on natural history, lemurs, culture and anthropology, botany, bird-watching, trekking, and other subjects.

Field Guides

9433 Bee Cave Road, Building 1, Suite 150, Austin, TX 78733; tel: 800-728-4953 or 512-263-7295; fax: 512-263-0117; e-mail: fgileader@aol.com

This bird-watching tour company offers a 22-day itinerary through Madagascar with expert guides, featuring extensions to either the Masoala Peninsula wilderness or the Indian Ocean islands of Mauritius, Réunion, and the Seychelles.

Madagascar Airtours

33 Avenue de l'Indépendance, B.P. 3874, Antananarivo, Madagascar; tel: 261-20-24192; fax: 261-20-64190.

This agency has offices in most major towns. Specialized tours cover natural history, ornithology, trekking, river trips, and sailing.

Malagasy Tours

Lot VX29, Avaradrova, Antananarivo, Madagascar; tel/fax: 261-20-35607.

Specialized tours on a variety of subjects, including ethnobotany, use local people to convey Malagasy cultural complexities. Explorations off the beaten track are also available.

Mountain Travel-Sobek

6420 Fairmount Avenue, El Cerrito, CA 94530; tel: 888-687-6235; fax: 510-525-7710; e-mail: info@mtsobek.com

A 19-day tour visits many of the country's protected areas.

Za Tours

Lot ID 33 BIS, Ambohitsorohitra, Antaninarenina, Antananarivo 101, Madagascar; tel: 261-20-65648; fax: 261-20-65647; e-mail: za.tour@dts.mg

Itineraries suit a wide range of interests, including botany, bird-watching, culture, and geology.

Excursions

Comoro Islands

Ministere des Transports et du Tourisme, B.P. 97, Route de la Corniche, Moroni; tel: 269-74-42-43; fax: 269-74-42-42.

The most interesting island in this archipelago, at least for naturalists, is Anjouan. This is the home of the very rare Livingstone's fruit bat, a bizarre, black, pterosaurus-like creature with a wingspan of more than a meter. There are only about 60 left, all inhabiting the island's dwindling rain forest.

Réunion Island

Office de Tourisme de Saint Denis, 48 rue Sainte Marie 97400, Saint Denis, Réunion Island; tel: 262-41-83-00.

There's a gem of a forest on this French volcanic island – one of the most exciting places in the Mascarenes. The Bebour Forest is in the high center of the island and is more of a cloud forest than a rain forest. The boughs of the trees are festooned with mosses and epiphytes, their reddish coloring giving the whole scene a golden tinge. Orchids abound and endemic birds such as the Réunion bulbul are easily seen here.

Seychelles

Seychelles Tourist Office, 32 rue de Ponthieu, 75008 Paris, France; tel: 33-1-42-89-97-77; fax: 33-1-42-89-97-70.

United Kingdom: 111 Baker Street, Second Floor, London W1M 1FE, UK; tel: 44-171-224-1670; fax: 44-171-486-1352.

On the island of Praslin is an ancient and unique forest, the Vallée de Mai. This is a true rain forest, with all the usual inhabitants – tree frogs, chameleons, and other reptiles – but the trees themselves are astonishingly different. The forest is dominated by the coco-de-mer, endemic to Praslin, whose enormous and suggestive fruit so excited General Gordon that he named the place the Garden of Eden and the coco-de-mer the Tree of Good and Evil.

Bwindi Impenetrable Forest National Park
Uganda

CHAPTER 22

The first glimpse of a wild mountain gorilla is nothing short of spine-tingling. Anybody who has tracked gorillas will confirm the primal thrill attached to standing deep in the heart of an African rain forest, separated from the most magnificent of the great apes – a creature who shares some 98 percent of its genes with humans – by nothing more than a few feet of lush undergrowth. The sheer bulk of a fully grown male gorilla is awesome. Of the three races of gorilla, the mountain gorilla is only marginally the largest, weighing up to 450 pounds (204kg), but its imposing presence is greatly exaggerated by a luxuriant coat acquired over generations of living in a relatively high, cool climate.   ◆   Mountain gorillas are exceedingly rare. Confined to the **Virunga Mountains** and Bwindi rain forest, both of which lie on the eastern rim of the **Albertine Rift Valley**, they were first seen by a European as recently as 1902, and they have probably always been rather scarce in

A tangled wilderness in the highlands of central Africa is one of the last refuges of the endangered mountain gorilla.

comparison to the two more widespread lowland gorilla races of west-central Africa (combined population 40,000–50,000). Nevertheless, mountain gorilla numbers have shrunk dramatically in historical times. Only 500 years ago, the Virunga and Bwindi forests were linked by an uninterrupted belt of choice gorilla territory. Today, they are isolated pockets of rain forest, separated by 20 miles (32km) of cultivation. Just as habitat loss has taken its toll, so too has poaching; the most optimistic estimate of the combined mountain gorilla population of these two rain forests is 600.   ◆   All of which makes **Bwindi Impenetrable Forest National Park**, whose 128 square miles (331 sq km) harbor roughly 320 mountain gorillas, as precious a

Mountain gorillas live in family troops of up to 30 individuals under a dominant, or silverback, male. They live nomadically within a range of about 10 to 15 square miles (26–39 sq km), feeding and resting as they move.

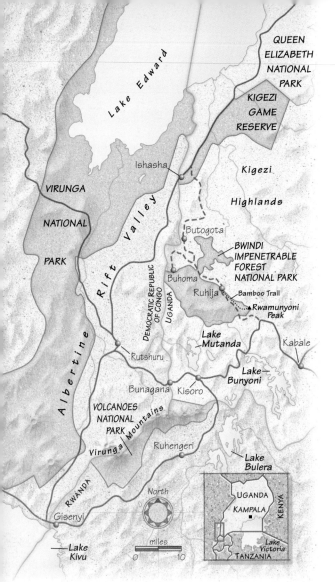

Golden Cats and Blue Monkeys

Pretty much everything that happens in Bwindi is focused around park headquarters at the **Buhoma** gate. Gorilla tracking trips leave from Buhoma, as do a number of other walking trails, and this is also where most of the accommodations and facilities are clustered. Visitors who take a guided forest walk out of Buhoma will soon realize that spotting rain-forest mammals is rather more challenging than game viewing in savanna reserves such as nearby **Queen Elizabeth National Park**.

In any case, Bwindi scarcely qualifies as classic safari material – of the so-called Big Five, lions and rhinoceroses are generally absent from forests, buffalo and leopards appear to be locally extinct, and the forest's small elephant population rarely frequents areas visited by tourists. An alluring list of resident forest specialties includes African golden cat, serval, giant forest hog, black-fronted duiker, yellow-backed duiker, Lord Derby's flying squirrel, and tree pangolin, but the only large terrestrial mammal likely to be encountered by a casual visitor to Bwindi is the common bushbuck.

On the plus side, Bwindi is something of a primate nirvana. Mountain gorillas hog the limelight, but the forest is home to 10 other primate species, including a substantial population of chimpanzees (these fascinating apes, more closely related to humans than to any other living creature, are not readily observed in Bwindi, but they have been habituated to tourists in several other accessible Ugandan forests). Most visitors will come across the largely arboreal black-and-white colobus, red-tailed, and blue monkeys, as well as the semiterrestrial olive baboon. Meanwhile, a short nocturnal drive with a spotlight has been known to yield a rare glimpse of a potto, a large slothlike creature distantly related to the lemurs of Madagascar.

Bwindi is a highlight of Uganda's superb birding circuit. Of the 1,008 species recorded in Uganda, roughly 100 are West African forest birds at the eastern limit of their range and more than 20 are endemic to the mountains of the Albertine Rift. Bwindi is

chunk of ecological real estate as there is in Uganda. Yet, paradoxically, while it is the mountain gorillas that attract tourists to Bwindi, it is the gorillas, too, that tend to distract from the broader ecology of what is a truly spectacular environment. Ranging in altitude from 3,805 to 8,551 feet (1,160–2,606m), Bwindi protects a continuum of environments from tropical lowland forest to Afro-montane forest, a diversity reflected in its checklist of 93 mammal species, 200 kinds of tree, 350 bird species, and more than 200 types of butterfly.

the best place to see a good selection of high-altitude forest birds, along with most of the Albertine Rift endemics, and birders whose rain-forest experience is limited to South America or Asia will marvel at the ease

Black-and-white colobus monkeys (left), also known as guereza, can eat up to a third of their weight in leaves a day. They spend most of their time in the canopy.

Forest flowers (opposite) rely on color and scent to attract pollinators.

Tree ferns (below) pioneer gaps in the forest left by fallen trees.

with which their quarry can be located. Armed with nothing more elaborate than light binoculars and a field guide, a casual bird-watcher might reasonably expect a morning walk from park headquarters at Buhoma to yield close to 50 bird species, many of which are unlikely to be seen elsewhere in East Africa.

Few visitors to Bwindi stray far from Buhoma, but the tiny fraction who have the time, means, and temperament – in other words, a couple of days to spare, a sturdy four-wheel-drive, and a pioneering spirit – will find that a visit to **Ruhija** pays ample dividends. Ruhija functioned as an informal base for gorilla tracking in the forest before Bwindi Impenetrable Forest National Park was established in 1992, and the colonial-

era stone cottage that serves as a rest house provides a commanding view over a series of extravagantly forested ridges to the jagged volcanic peaks of the Virunga Mountains. Ruhija lies at a higher altitude than Buhoma, which means the surrounding Afro-montane forest has a markedly different species composition. The gorgeous black-and-white colobus is common here, often seen swinging gracefully from branch to branch, shaggy white tail in tow.

Using Ruhija as a base, visitors can follow the three-hour **Mubwindi Swamp Trail** or six-hour **Bamboo Trail**. The former trail, which leads to a swamp at an altitude of 6,797 feet (2,072m), offers a good chance of encountering elephants as well as a number of birds absent from the Buhoma area; at

least 20 birds recorded near Mubwindi are either endemic to the Albertine Rift or else rare or threatened species. The latter trail, also good for birding, leads through dense bamboo forest to **Rwamunyoni Peak**, the highest point in the national park.

Gorilla Treks

For all Bwindi's diverse attractions, gorilla tracking remains the core tourist activity. Most visitors come solely to see gorillas, and few return home disappointed, provided that they arrived clutching one of the six tracking permits that are issued for any given day. The trekking party leaves Buhoma

every morning in the company of an experienced armed ranger on a round-trip that usually lasts from three to eight hours, depending on the proximity of the habituated gorilla troop.

Gorilla treks generally start along the barely passable track that serves as a main road through Bwindi. Hiking along this road is unqualified bliss. The forest is lush and shady, and alive with bird calls, while colorful butterflies flutter above small roadside puddles, and monkeys rattle and shriek in the canopy. All this changes when the trekking party abandons the road at a point

The Woman Who Loved Gorillas

Dian Fossey was a controversial figure, though few would question her courage or resolve. Never formally trained as a biologist, she persuaded paleontologist Louis Leakey to sponsor her research on mountain gorillas in the Congo and later in Rwanda, where she founded the **Karisoke Research Centre** at **Volcanoes National Park** in 1967.

Fossey's achievements include a landmark study of gorilla behavior based on the gradual habituation of the animals to her presence, a technique that is detailed in her best-selling book *Gorillas in the Mist*, later made into a movie. The focus of her work changed from research to "active conservation" in 1978, after the slaying of Digit, a beloved gorilla she had studied for a decade.

Fossey's grief was compounded six months later when three members of the same troop, including the dominant silverback, were also slaughtered. Never strong on diplomacy, she became overtly confrontational in her dealings with poachers, ineffective park officials, bureaucrats – and anybody else who got in her way. While Fossey's passion certainly saved the lives of many mountain gorillas, it won her few friends locally, split her supporters in the West, and almost certainly led to her brutal murder at the hands of an unknown assassin on the night of December 26, 1985. She was buried next to Digit under a simple marker that reads: "No one loved gorillas more."

Since Fossey's death, Rwanda has been racked by a succession of genocidal civil wars, and Karisoke has been evacuated on several occasions. The mountain gorillas remain, however – largely through the efforts of the organization founded by Fossey in 1978, originally called the Digit Fund, and posthumously renamed the Dian Fossey Gorilla Fund.

Dian Fossey (above) gained the acceptance of mountain gorillas by gradually habituating them to her presence and adopting such behavior as social grooming. Fossey is buried in Rwanda near the grave of her beloved subject Digit (left).

Mushrooms (top) thrive on rotting vegetation on the forest floor.

A Virunga tree frog (opposite, top) hides in the undergrowth.

A gorilla's diet (opposite, bottom) is almost entirely vegetarian, consisting of wild celery, nettles, bamboo, and a variety of fruits.

close to where the gorillas were seen on the previous day. Walking off-road, it becomes abundantly clear why Bwindi is known as the Impenetrable Forest. Tangled vegetation, steep hills, and high rainfall combine to make the slopes dangerously slippery, while the dank valleys are buried in a blanket of leaf litter thick enough to engulf the leg of anybody who misjudges the leap from one exposed root to the next.

No matter how tough the going, when the ranger finally locates fresh gorilla nests, all fatigue is washed away by anticipation. Gorillas are the most terrestrial of the great apes, typically covering less than one mile (1.6km) in the course of a day's wandering, which means that once the most recent nests have been located, the troop won't be far away. Adrenaline starts flowing in earnest when the muted noises of the deep forest are rent apart by the sound of a gorilla beating his fists against a tree trunk or his chest – a convincing reason, if you needed one, to listen closely to the ranger's spiel about the finer points of gorilla etiquette.

Despite their fearsome appearance, gorillas are essentially "gentle giants," and the habituated troop at Bwindi is remarkably relaxed in the presence of humans. The animals live in family troops of up to 30 individuals, who spend most of the day grazing peacefully. The dominant silverback male will occasionally assert himself over potential challengers, but outright conflict is avoided and mock charges are far more common than the real thing.

To spend time with these rare creatures in their forest home is a bittersweet privilege. The mesmerizing hour allocated for any encounter passes all too quickly; during the long walk back to Buhoma you can't help but be haunted by those gentle, liquid brown eyes, possessed of such humanity and gravity. Then comes the sobering realization that only 600 pairs of mountain gorilla eyes remain on the planet. For this reason alone, Bwindi is not merely precious but priceless.

TRAVEL TIPS

DETAILS

How to Get There

Several carriers fly into Entebbe International Airport, 19 miles (30km) from Kampala, the capital city. From Kampala, Bwindi is a day's drive, partly on dirt roads. Driving yourself is possible, but the last part of the journey through mountainous, cultivated lands can only be driven slowly, so be sure to leave Kampala early. The route can be especially difficult during the rains.

When to Go

Uganda's equatorial climate, tempered by altitude, is pleasant year-round, rarely exceeding 80°F (27°C) or falling below 55°F (13°C). From March to May and from October to November, however, the rain can feel relentless and may make some dirt roads impassable or at least confine their use to four-wheel-drive vehicles.

Getting Around

The only convenient way to visit the gorillas is with an organized tour. There are currently two habituated groups of gorillas in the park and, with only six people allowed to visit each group on any one day, the waiting list tends to be long. Book your place well before leaving home and pay the deposit of $30 per person (the full cost is $250 per person). The tour can be strenuous, with up to nine hours of walking on steep hillsides that are slippery with mud and rotting vegetation. You will need a good pair of walking boots and rain gear.

Travel advisory: Security is an issue due to political unrest. The government is mindful of the value of tourism and is making every effort to ensure the security of visitors to Bwindi, sometimes sending army personnel out with gorilla trackers. However, rebels have attacked tourist camps in the past, and visitors are urged to consult their embassies or the U.S State Department (www.travel.state.gov/travel_warnings.html) for the latest advisories before making their plans. Visitors should also be aware of an outbreak of the deadly ebola virus in northern Uganda in October 2000. According to the Centers for Disease Control (CDC), general travelers are unlikely to contract the disease, but they are advised to consult the CDC (www.cdc.gov/) for the latest recommendations.

INFORMATION

Uganda Embassy

5911 16th Street, N.W., Washington, DC 20011; tel: 202-726-7100 or 202-726-7101; fax: 202-726-1727.

Uganda Tourist Board

336 East 45th Street, New York, NY 10017-3489; tel: 212-949-0110; fax: 212-682-5232.

Uganda Wildlife Authority

Plot 3, Kintu Road–Nakasero, P.O. Box 3530, Kampala, Uganda; tel: 256-41-346-287 or 256-41-346-288; fax: 256-41-346-291.

CAMPING

Independent camping is not permitted in the park. However, there is a community campsite within a few hundred meters of park headquarters at Buhoma.

LODGING

PRICE GUIDE – double occupancy

$ = up to $49 $$ = $50–$99
$$$ = $100–$149 $$$$ = $150+

African Pearl Homestead

P.O. Box 4562, Kampala, Uganda; tel: 256-41-233-566, fax: 256-41-235-770.

This compound near park headquarters offers self-contained cottages and rooms with communal facilities. $$–$$$$

Backpackers' Hostel and Campsite

P.O. Box 8643, Kampala, Uganda; tel: 256-41-258-469; fax: 256-41-272-012; e-mail: backpackers@infocom.co.ug

A good place to meet other travelers and pick up current information, this hostel has dormitory rooms, a large campsite, and double rooms. $

Gorilla Forest Camp

P.O. Box 7799, Kampala, Uganda; tel: 256-41-266-700; fax: 256-41-266-702.

This safari camp, run by Abercrombie and Kent, consists of eight self-contained, private standing tents. $$$$

Kampala Sheraton

P.O. Box 7041, Kampala, Uganda; tel: 256-41-344-590; fax: 256-41-356-696.

This hotel has four restaurants and either single or double rooms with private balconies and bathrooms. $$$$

Mantana Tented Camp

10818 McComas Court, Kensington, MD 20895; tel: 202-244-4395; fax: 202-244-4676; e-mail: mantanausa@juno.com

Bwindi Camp, about one mile (1.6km) from park headquarters, offers a central dining tent and seven fully furnished tents with verandas, twin bedrooms, and private baths. $$$$

TOURS AND OUTFITTERS

Abercrombie and Kent

1520 Kensington Road, Oak Brook, IL 60523; tel: 630-954-2944 or 800-323-7308; fax: 630-954-3324; e-mail: info@abercrombiekent.com

This outfitter's Uganda packages include a week-long primate-watching tour in Bwindi and Queen Elizabeth National Parks, and five days of gorilla-tracking in Bwindi.

Afritours and Travel

P.O. Box 5187, Kampala, Uganda; tel: 256-41-344-714; fax: 256-41-344-855; e-mail: afritours@swiftuganda.com

Several packages are available, including gorilla treks, seven- to 14-day countrywide tours, and three-week bird-watching trips.

Gametrackers

Parliament Avenue, P.O. Box 7703, Kampala, Uganda; tel: 256-41-258-993; fax: 256-41-244-575, or P.O. Box 62042, 1st Floor, Kenya Cinema Plaza, Moi Avenue, Nairobi, Kenya; tel: 254-2-338-927; fax: 254-2-330-903; e-mail: game@africaonline.co.ke

Safaris throughout East Africa include mountain biking, canoeing, mountaineering, wildlife excursions, customized packages, and nine-week overland tours from Nairobi to South Africa.

International Expeditions

One Environs Park, Helena, AL 35080; tel: 205-428-1700 or 800-633-4734; e-mail: nature@ietravel.com

A 16-day "Wildlife Frontier" trip in Uganda includes visits to Bwindi and Queen Elizabeth National Parks.

Mountain Travel-Sobek

6420 Fairmount Avenue, El Cerrito, CA 94530; tel: 888-687-6235; fax: 510-525-7710; e-mail: info@mtsobek.com

A 12-day Uganda trip focuses on nature and wildlife and includes a trek in Bwindi.

Wild Frontiers

P.O. Box 844, Halfway House, Gauteng, South Africa, 1685; tel: 27-11-702-2035; fax: 27-11-468-1655; e-mail: wildfront@icon.co.za

Specialized birding tours and other excursions explore Uganda and neighboring Kenya and Tanzania.

Excursions

Kibale Forest National Park

Uganda Wildlife Authority, P.O. Box 3530, Kampala, Uganda; tel: 256-41-346-290; fax: 256-41-236-291.

This large and accessible area of equatorial rain forest, about 200 miles (320km) west of Kampala, is said to contain the world's highest concentration of primates. Its 11 species include black-and-white colobus monkeys, red colobus monkeys, galagos, and more than 500 chimpanzees. You stand a good chance of seeing a group of these habituated chimps during a guided forest walk. Also watch for elephants and admire the park's giant rain-forest trees.

Mgahinga Forest National Park

Uganda Wildlife Authority, P.O. Box 3530, Kampala, Uganda; tel: 256-41-346-290; fax: 256-41-236-291.

This park, about the same size as Bwindi, borders both the Congo and Rwanda and protects Uganda's section of the important Virunga Volcanoes area, inhabited by just over half of the world's population of mountain gorillas. High-altitude savanna woodland, montane forest, and bamboo clothe the slopes, while dwarf heath vegetation is found near the summits. Visits to the gorillas are subject to the same strictures as in Bwindi, with the added proviso that visits cannot take place if no habituated groups are in Uganda's section of the Virungas. Security is still a major consideration in this area.

Murchison Falls National Park

Uganda National Parks, Plot 31, Kanjokya Street, Kamwokya-Kololo, P.O. Box 3530, Kampala, Uganda; tel: 256-41-256-534.

Uganda's largest conservation area is best known for the powerful waterfall after which it is named. Highlights include a launch trip to the base of the waterfall, which follows a stretch of the Nile teeming with hippos, crocodiles, and various waterbirds. Murchison Falls is the best place in Africa to see the shoebill, a bizarre storklike bird with an outsized bill. Game drives in the north of the park are likely to produce elephants, giraffes, antelope, and possibly lions or leopards, while the Budongo Forest fringing the southern boundary of the park offers superlative forest birding and chimpanzee tracking.

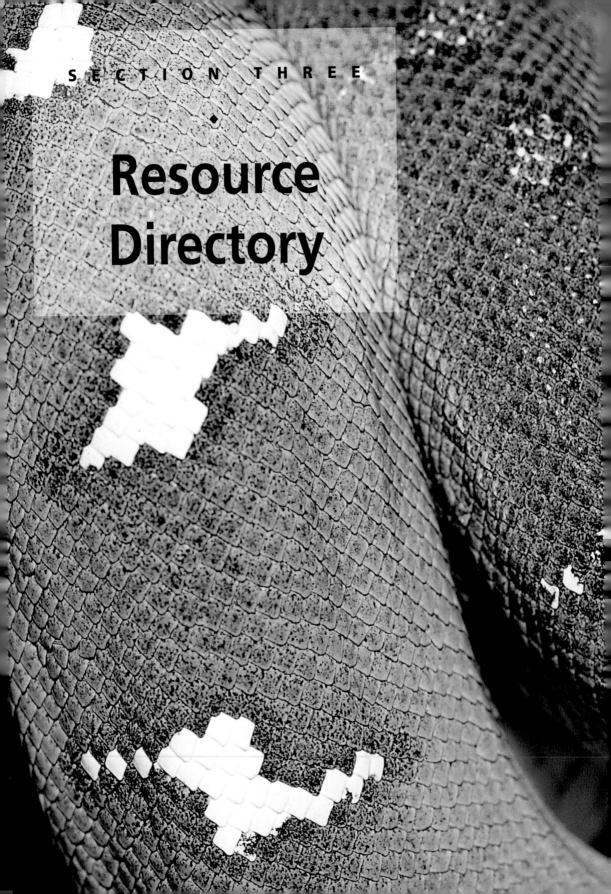

Resource
Directory

FURTHER READING

Rain-Forest Ecology

The following titles present a wide range of information on the natural history of rain forests, with an emphasis on evolution and biodiversity.

The Amazon River Forest: A Natural History of Plants, Animals, and People, by Nigel J. H. Smith (Oxford University Press, 1999).

Australian Rainforests: Islands of Green in a Land of Fire, by D. M. J. S. Bowman (Cambridge University Press, 2000).

Australia: Reef, Rainforest, Red Heart, by Darren Jew (New Holland, 1999).

Costa Rica Natural History, Daniel Janzen, ed. (University of Chicago Press, 1983).

Diversity and the Tropical Rainforest, by John Terborgh (Scientific American Library, 1992).

The Diversity of Life, by Edward O. Wilson (Belknap Press, 1992).

The Food Web of a Tropical Rain Forest, Douglas P. Reagan and Robert B. Waide, eds. (University of Chicago Press, 1996).

Four Neotropical Rainforests, Alwyn H. Gentry, ed. (Yale University Press, 1991).

Hawaii: A Natural History, by Sherwin Carlquist (National Tropical Botany, 1980).

How Monkeys Make Chocolate: Foods and Medicines from the Rainforests, by Adrian Forsyth (Owl Communications, 1995).

In the Rainforest: Report from a Strange, Beautiful, Imperiled World, by Catherine Caufield (University of Chicago Press, 1986).

An Introduction to Tropical Rain Forests, by Timothy Whitmore (Oxford University Press, 1998).

Lessons of the Rainforest, Suzanne Head and Robert Heinzman, eds. (Sierra Club Books, 1990).

The Monkey's Bridge: Mysteries of Evolution in Central America, by David Rains Wallace (Sierra Club Books, 1997).

A Neotropical Companion: An Introduction to the Animals, Plants, and Ecosystems of the New World Tropics, by John C. Kricher and Mark Plotkin (Princeton University Press, 1997).

New Zealand: Mountains to the Sea, by Warren Jacobs (New Holland/Struik, 2000).

Olympic National Park: A Natural History, by Tim McNulty (Sasquatch Books, 1999).

Origin and Evolution of Tropical Rain Forests, by Robert J. Morley (John Wiley & Sons, 2000).

Portraits of the Rainforest, by Adrian Forsyth, Patricia Fogden, and Michael Fogden (Camden House, 1995).

The Rainforests: A Celebration, Lisa Silcock, ed. (Chronicle Books, 2000).

Rainforests of the World: Water, Fire, Earth & Air, by Art Wolfe and Ghillean T. Prance (Random House, 1998).

Tropical Nature, by Adrian Forsyth and Kenneth Miyata (Scribner's, 1987).

Wild Fiordland: Discovering the Natural History of a World Heritage Area, by Neville Peat and Brian Patrick (University of Otago Press, 1996).

Field Guides

An informative, well-illustrated field guide is essential on any wilderness adventure and is critical in rain forests, where flora and fauna is unfamiliar to many visitors. Hundreds of guides and reference books are available. This is a short list of some of the most popular and reliable titles.

Belize and Guatemala: The Ecotravellers' Wildlife Guide, by Les Beletsky (Academic Press, 1998).

Birds of Australia, by Ken Simpson et al. (Princeton University Press, 2000).

Birds of Chile, by Sharon R. Chester (Wandering Albatross, 1995).

Birds of the Indian Ocean Islands, by I. Sinclair and O. Langrand (Struik, 1999).

Birds of New Guinea, by Bruce M. Beehler, Thane K. Pratt, and Dale Zimmerman (Princeton University Press, 1986).

The Birds of South America, vols. I and II, by Robert S. Ridgely and Guy Tudor (University of Texas Press, 1989/1994).

The Butterflies of Costa Rica and Their Natural History, by Philip J. Devries and Jennifer Clark (Princeton University Press, 1997).

Costa Rica: The Ecotravellers' Wildlife Guide, by Les Beletsky. (Academic Press, 1998).

Field Guide to the Birds of Australia, by Ken Simpson and Nicolas Day (Princeton University Press, 1996).

A Field Guide to the Birds of Borneo, Sumatra, Java, and Bali, by John Ramsay MacKinnon et al. (Oxford University Press, 1993).

A Field Guide to the Birds of Hawaii and the Tropical Pacific, by H. Douglas Pratt, Phillip L. Bruner, and Delwyn G. Berrett (Princeton University Press, 1987).

Field Guide to the Birds of New Zealand, by Barrie Heather and Hugh Robertson (Oxford University Press, 1997).

Field Guide to the Mammals of the Indian Subcontinent: Where to Watch Mammals in India, Nepal, Bhutan, Bangladesh, Sri Lanka and Pakistan, by K. K. Gurung and Raj Singh (Ap Professional, 1998).

Guide to the Birds of Alaska, by Robert H. Armstrong (Alaska Northwest Books, 1995).

Guide to the Birds of Costa Rica, by F. Gary Stiles, Alexander F. Skutch, and Dana Gardner (Cornell University Press, 2000).

Guide to the Birds of Madagascar, by Olivier Langrand (Yale University Press, 1990).

A Guide to the Birds of Mexico and Northern Central America, by Steve N. G. Howell and Sophie Webb (Oxford University Press, 1995).

A Guide to the Birds of Peru, by James F. Clements (Ibis, 2000).

Guide to the Birds of Southeast Asia: Thailand, Peninsular Malaysia, Singapore, Myanmar, Laos, Vietnam, Cambodia, by Craig Robson (Princeton University Press, 2000).

Insight Guides: Amazon Wildlife (Apa Publications, 1998).

Insight Guides: Southeast Asia Wildlife (Apa Publications, 1998).

Madagascar Wildlife, by H. Bradt, D. Schuurman, and N. Garbutt (Bradt Publications, 1996).

Mammals of Australia, Ronald Strahan, ed. (Smithsonian Institution Press, 1996).

Mammals of Madagascar, by Nick Garbutt. (Yale University Press, 1999).

National Geographic Field Guide to the Birds of North America, Third Edition, by Jon L. Dunn (National Geographic Society, 1999).

Neotropical Rainforest Mammals: A Field Guide, by Louise Emmons (University of Chicago Press, 1997).

A Photographic Guide to the Mammals of Australia, by Peter Rowland and Ron Strahan (Chelsea Green Publishing, 1998).

Plants and Flowers of Hawaii, by S. H. Sohmer and R. Gustafson (University of Hawaii Press, 1987).

The Reed Field Guide to New Zealand Birds, by Geoff Moon (Stackpole Books, 1999).

The Safari Companion: A Guide to Watching African Mammals Including Hoofed Mammals, Carnivores, and Primates, by Richard D. Estes, Daniel Otte (illustrator), Kathryn S. Fuller (Chelsea Green Publishing, 1999).

Seabirds: An Identification Guide, by Peter Harrison (Houghton Mifflin, 1985).

Wild Flowers of East Africa, by M. Blundell (HarperCollins, 1994).

Wild India: The Wildlife and Scenery of India and Nepal, by Gerald Cubitt and Guy Mountfort (MIT Press, 1991).

Travel Guides and Literature

Regional guidebooks will help you find your way around a destination, provide you with information on lodging and dining, and direct you to other attractions in the region. Travelogues offer a personal view of a destination and give readers an opportunity to learn from the authors' experiences – both positive and negative.

Adventuring in Central America: A Sierra Club Adventure Travel Guide, by David Rains Wallace (Sierra Club Books, 1995).

Adventuring in New Zealand: A Sierra Club Travel Guide to the Pearl of the Pacific, by Margaret Jeffries (Sierra Club Books, 1993).

The Amazon: The Bradt Travel Guide, by Roger Harris and Peter Hutchison (Bradt Publications, 1998).

Amazon Up Close: The Passionate Adventurer's Guide to the Brazilian Amazon and the Pantanal, by Pamela Bloom (Hunter Publications, 1997)

Australia's Wet Tropics: Rainforest Life, Including the Daintree Region, by Clifford and Dawn Frith (Frith and Frith Books, 1992).

Australia's Wet Tropics and North-Eastern Outback: The Driving Guide, by Ian Read (Cimino Publishing Group, 1998).

Belize: Adventures in Nature, by Richard Mahler (John Muir Publications, 1999).

Chile and Argentina: Backpacking and Hiking, by Tim Burford (Bradt Publications, 1998).

The Cloud Forest: A Chronicle of the South American Wilderness, by Peter Matthiessen (Penguin USA, 1996)

Costa Rica: A Traveler's Literary Companion, Barbara Ras, ed., (Whereabouts Press, 1994).

Costa Rica Handbook, by Christopher P. Baker (Moon Travel Handbooks, 1999).

Costa Rica's National Parks and Preserves, by Joseph Franke (The Mountaineers, 1999).

Daintree: Jewel of Tropical North Queensland, by Lloyd Nielsen (Lloyd Nielsen, 1997).

Discovery Travel Adventures: African Safari, Melissa Shales, ed. (Discovery Communications/Insight Guides, 2000).

Discovery Travel Adventures: Alaskan Wilderness, Tricia Brown, ed. (Discovery Communications/Insight Guides, 1999).

Discovery Travel Adventures: Australian Outback, Scott Forbes, ed. (Discovery Communications/Insight Guides, 2000).

Hawaii Handbook: The All-Island Guide, by J. D. Bisignani (Moon Publications, 1999).

Hiking Olympic National Park, by Erik Molvar (Falcon Publishing, 1996).

Insight Guides: Australia (Apa Publications, 1998).

Insight Guides: Belize (Apa Publications, 1998).

Insight Guides: Brazil (Apa Publications, 1999).

Insight Guides: Chile (Apa Publications, 1998).

Insight Guides: Costa Rica (Apa Publications, 1998).

Insight Guides: Hawaii (Apa Publications, 1998).

Insight Guides: Malaysia (Apa Publications, 1998).

Insight Guides: New Zealand (Apa Publications, 1998).

Insight Guides: Peru (Apa Publications, 1998).

Insight Guides: Puerto Rico (Apa Publications, 1999).

Insight Guides: Vietnam (Apa Publications, 1999).

Insight Pocket Guides: Sabah Borneo (Apa Publications, 1996).

Into the Heart of Borneo, by Redmond O'Hanlon (Vintage Books, 1987).

Islands in the Clouds: Travels in the Highlands of New Guinea, by Isabella Tree (Lonely Planet, 1996).

Lonely Planet New Zealand, by Peter Turner, Jeff Williams, and Nancy Keller (Lonely Planet, 1998).

Lonely Planet Papua New Guinea, by Adrian Lipscomb. (Lonely Planet, 1998).

Madagascar: The Bradt Travel Guide, by Hilary Bradt (Bradt Publications, 1999).

Madagascar Travels, by C. Dodwell (Hodder & Stoughton, 1995).

My Wilderness: The Pacific West, by William O. Douglas (Comstock Book Distributors, 1989).

The New Zealand Bed & Breakfast Book: Homes, Farms, B&B Inns, by J. J. Thomas (Pelican Publishing, 1999).

New Zealand Handbook, by Jane King (Moon Publications, 1999).

North Queensland Wet Tropics: A Guide for Travellers, by Rod Ritchie (NSW Rainforest Publishing, 1995).

Passage to Juneau, by Jonathan Raban (Pantheon, 1999).

Sastun: My Apprenticeship with a Maya Healer, by Rosita Arvigo (Harper San Francisco, 1995).

South America's National Parks: A Visitor's Guide, by William C. Leitch and Bill Leitch (Mountaineers Books, 1990).

Travelers' Tales Brazil, Annette Haddad and Scott Doggett, eds. (Travelers' Tales, 1997).

Travels in Alaska, by John Muir (Houghton Mifflin, 1998).

Travels in a Thin Country, by Sara Wheeler (Modern Library, 1999).

Trekking in Nepal: A Traveler's Guide, by Stephen Bezruchka (Mountaineers Books, 1997).

Uganda: The Bradt Travel Guide, by Philip Briggs (Bradt Publications, 1998).

Under the Mountain Wall: A Chronicle of Two Seasons in Stone Age New Guinea, by Peter Matthiessen (Penguin USA, 1996).

Visitors' Guide to Madagascar: How to Get There, What to See, Where to Stay, by Marco Turco (Menasha Ridge Press, 1998).

Wild Alaska: The Complete Guide to Parks, Preserves, Wildlife Refuges, and Other Public Lands, by Nancy Lange Simmerman (Mountaineers Books, 1999).

Where Masks Still Dance: New Guinea, by Chris Rainier and Meg Taylor (Bulfinch Press, 1996).

History and Conservation

It's impossible to discuss rain forests without addressing the history of exploitation and conservation that bears so profoundly on their future. The following books are a good introduction to the various issues involved.

Borneo in Transition: People, Forests, Conservation, and Development, Christine Padoch and Nancy Lee Peluso, eds. (Oxford University Press, 1996).

Chile's Native Forests: A Conservation Legacy, by Ken Wilcox, Lisa Beck, and Galen Rowell (North Atlantic Books, 1997).

Cockscomb Basin Wildlife Sanctuary: Its History, Flora and Fauna for Visitors, Teachers and Scientists, by Katherine Emmons (Community Conservation Consultants, 1996).

The Fate of the Forest: Developers, Destroyers, and Defenders of the Amazon, by Susanna Hecht and Alexander Cockburn (Verso, 1989).

The Final Forest: The Battle for the Last Great Trees of the Pacific Northwest, by William Dietrich (Penguin, 1993).

Gorillas in the Mist, by Dian Fossey (Houghton Mifflin, 2000).

The Hidden Amazon: The Greatest Voyage in Natural History, by Richard L. Lutz (Dimi Press, 1998).

Jaguar: One Man's Struggle to Establish the World's First Jaguar Preserve, by Alan Rabinowitz (Shearwater Books, 2000).

Monteverde: Ecology and Conservation of a Tropical Cloud Forest, Nalini Nadkarni and Nathaniel T. Wheelwright, eds. (Oxford University Press, 2000).

The Nature of Southeast Alaska, by Rita M. O'Clair. (Graphic Arts Center Publishing, 1997).

Of Men and Mountains, by William O. Douglas (Chronicle Books, 1990).

One River: Explorations and Discoveries in the Amazon Rain Forest, Wade Davis (Simon & Schuster, 1996).

Rainforest: Ancient Realm of the Pacific Northwest, by Wade Davis (Chelsea Green Publishing, 1999).

Trees of Life: Saving Tropical Forests and Their Biological Wealth, by Kenton Miller, Laura Tangley, and Gus Speth (Beacon Press, 1991).

With Broadax and Firebrand: The Destruction of the Brazilian Atlantic Forest, by Warren Dean (University of California Press, 1995).

Woman in the Mists: The Story of Dian Fossey and the Mountain Gorillas of Africa, by Farley Mowat (Warner Books, 1988).

Ecotourism and Travel Advice

The following books chronicle the development of ecotourism and lay down guidelines for environmentally sound travel. They also offer advice to handicapped travelers and help readers prepare for journeys to ecologically sensitive destinations around the globe.

Around the World Resource Guide, by Patricia Smither (Access For Disabled Americans Publishing, 2000).

Backcountry First Aid and Extended Care, by Buck Tilton (Globe Pequot Press, 1998).

Comprehensive Guide to Wilderness & Travel Medicine, by Eric A. Weiss, Rod Nickell, and Butch Collier (Adventure Medical Kits, 1998).

Easy Access to National Parks: The Sierra Club Guide for People with Disabilities, by Wendy Roth and Michael Tompane (Sierra Arts Foundation, 1992).

Eco-Journeys: The World Travel Guide to Ecologically Aware Travel and Adventure, by Stephen Foehr (Noble Press, 1992).

Ecotourism: Impacts, Potentials and Possibilities, by Stephen Wearing and John Neil (Butterworth-Heinemann, 1999).

The Green Travel Sourcebook: A Guide for the Physically Active, the Intellectually Curious, or the Socially Aware, by Daniel Grotta and Sally Wiener Grotta (John Wiley & Sons, 1992).

Nature Travel, by Dwight Holing, Susanne Methvin, David Rains Wallace, and Ben Davidson (Time Life/Nature Company, 1995).

Rethinking Tourism and Ecotravel: The Paving of Paradise and What You Can Do to Stop It, by Deborah McLaren (Kumarian Press, 1997).

Traveling Smart: The Know-Before-You-Go Guide to International Travel, Carolyn Hayes Uber and Patricia Woy, eds. (Dragonflyer Press, 1999).

Wheelchair around the World, Patrick D. Simpson (Pentland Press, 1998).

World Travel: A Guide to International Ecojourneys, Christopher P. Baker et al. (Time Life/Nature Company, 1996).

Magazines

Alaska
619 East Ship Creek Avenue, Suite 329, Anchorage, AK 99501; tel: 800-288-5892.

Audubon
700 Broadway, New York, NY 10003; tel: 800-274-4201.

National Parks
1776 Massachusetts Avenue, N.W., Washington, D.C. 20036; tel: 800-628-7275.

National Wildlife
8925 Leesburg Pike, Vienna, VA 22184; tel: 815-734-1160.

Natural History
American Museum of Natural History, Central Park West at 79th Street, New York, NY 10024; tel: 212-769-5100.

Outside
400 Market Street, Santa Fe, NM 87501; tel: 800-678-1131.

Outdoor Photographer
12121 Wilshire Boulevard, Suite 1220, Los Angeles, CA 90025-1175; tel: 310-820-1500.

Sierra
Sierra Club, 85 Second Street, San Francisco, CA 94105; tel: 415-977-5653.

ORGANIZATIONS

The organizations listed below serve both travelers and the environment by advocating rain-forest protection, supporting research, offering volunteer opportunities, and, in some cases, providing travel information. Contact them for advice on getting involved in conservation.

American Disability Association
2201 Sixth Avenue South, Birmingham, AL 35233; tel: 205-328-9090; www.adanet.org

Australian Rainforest Conservation Society
19 Colorado Avenue; Bardon, QLD 4065, Australia; www.rainforest.org.au/index.htm

Biodiversity Group of Environment Australia
G.P.O. Box 636, Canberrra, ACT 2601, Australia; tel: 61-2-6250-0200; www.biodiversity.environment.gov.au

Conservation International
2501 M Street, N.W., Suite 200, Washington, DC 20037; tel: 202-429-5660; www.conservation.org

The Ecotourism Society
P.O. Box 755, North Bennington, VT 05257; tel: 802-447-2121; www.ecotourism.org

Environment Australia
G.P.O. Box 787, Canberra, ACT 2600, Australia; tel: 61-2-6274-1111; www.environment.gov.au

Friends of the Earth
1025 Vermont Avenue, N.W., Suite 300, Washington, DC 20005; tel: 202-783-7400; www.foe.org

National Audubon Society
700 Broadway, New York, NY 10003; tel: 212-832-3000; www.audubon.org

National Fish and Wildlife Foundation
1120 Connecticut Avenue, N.W., Suite 900, Washington, DC 20036; tel: 202-857-0166; www.nfwf.org

National Wildlife Federation
8925 Leesburg Pike, Vienna, VA 22184; tel: 703-790-4000; www.nwf.org

The Nature Conservancy
4245 North Fairfax Drive, Suite 100, Arlington, VA 22203; tel: 703-841-5300; www.tnc.org

Rainforest Action Network
221 Pine Street, Suite 500, San Francisco, CA 94104; tel: 415-398-4404; www.ran.org

Rainforest Alliance
65 Bleecker Street, New York, NY 10012; tel: 212-677-1900 or 877-693-2784; www.rainforestalliance.org

Rainforest Conservation Fund
2036 North Clark Street, Suite 233, Chicago, IL 60614; tel: 773-975-7517; www.rainforest conservation.org/

The Rainforest Foundation, UK
Suite A5, City Cloisters, 196 Old Street, London, EC1V 9FR UK; tel: 207-251-6345; fax: 207-251-4969; www.rainforestfoundationuk.org

Sierra Club
85 Second Street, San Francisco, CA 94105; tel: 415-923-5630; www.sierraclub.org

U.S. Fish and Wildlife Service
4401 North Fairfax Drive, Arlington, VA 22203; tel: 202-857-0166 or 800-344-9453; www.fws.gov

The Wilderness Society
900 17th Street, N.W., Washington, DC 20006; tel: 202-833-2300; www.wilderness.org

World Rainforest Movement
Maldonado 1858, Montevideo 11200, Uruguay; tel: 598-2-403-2989; fax: 598-2-408-0762; www.wrm.org.uy/index.html

World Wildlife Fund
1250 24th Street, N.W., P.O. Box 97180, Washington, DC 20037; tel: 800-225-5993; www.worldwildlife.org

TOUR OPERATORS

The companies below offer a variety of organized rain-forest tours, from trips that emphasize natural history and wildlife watching to those that special-ize in outdoor adventures such as kayaking, backpacking, and mountain biking. Additional

tour operators are listed in Travel Tips at the end of each destination chapter.

Abercrombie & Kent International, Inc.
1520 Kensington Road, Oak Brook, IL 60523-2141; tel: 800-323-7308; fax: 630-954-3324; www.abercrombiekent.com/

Asia Transpacific Journeys
2995 Center Green Court, Boulder, CO 80301; tel: 303-670-2406 or 800-642-2742; fax: 303-443-7078; www.southeastasia.com/

Earthwatch Institute
3 Clock Tower Place, Suite 100, Box 75, Maynard, MA 01754; tel: 978-461-0081 or 800-776-0188; fax: 978-461-2332; www.earthwatch.org/

Field Guides
9433 Bee Cave Road, Building 1, Suite 150, Austin, TX 78733; tel: 800-728-4953 or 512-263-7295; fax: 512-263-0117; www.fieldguides.com/home.html

Focus Tours
103 Moya Road, Santa Fe, NM 87505; tel: 505-466-4688; fax: 505-466-4689; www.focustours.com

International Expeditions
One Environs Park, Helena, AL 35080; tel: 800-633-4734; www.ietravel.com/

Journeys International, Inc.
107 April Drive, Suite 3, Ann Arbor, MI 48103; tel: 734-665-4407 or 800-255-8735, fax: 734-665-2945; www.journeys-intl.com/

Mountain Travel-Sobek
6420 Fairmount Avenue, El Cerrito, CA 94530; tel: 888-687-6235; fax: 510-525-7710; www.mtsobek.com/

Nature Expeditions International
7860 Peters Road, Suite F-103, Plantation, FL 33324; tel: 954-693-8852 or 800-869-0639; fax: 954-693-8854; www.naturexp.com/

Outer Edge Expeditions
4830 Mason Road, Howell, MI 48843-9697; tel: 517-552-5300 or 800-322-5235; fax: 517-552-5400; www.outer-edge.com/

Zegrahm Expeditions
192 Nickerson Street, Suite 200, Seattle 98109; tel: 206-285-4000 or 800-628-8747; www.zeco.com/

TRAVEL ADVISORIES

The following resources provide travelers with up-to-date infor-mation on medical issues, polit-ical stability, crime, and person-al safety. Consult them before making your travel plans.

Centers for Disease Control
1600 Clifton Road, Atlanta, GA 30333; tel: 877-394-8747 or 800-311-3435; www.cdc.gov/travel

The CDC provides comprehensive information on vaccinations and other travelers' health issues.

Foreign and Commonwealth Office Travel Advice Unit
1 Palace Street, London SW1E 5HE, England; tel: 44-20-7238-4503; fax: 44-20-7238-4545; web: www.fco.gov.uk

This site has security updates from around the world.

Medical Advisory Services for Travellers Abroad (MASTA)
tel: 44-906-8224-1000; web: www.masta.org

MASTA offers a massive online database with up-to-the-minute information on 250 countries. For a small fee, the telephone information service will provide you with a medical plan of action for your trip.

U.S. Department of State
Office of American Citizens Services, Washington, DC 20520; tel: 202-647-5225; web: www.travel.state.gov/travel_warnings.html

The state department posts its current travel warnings on this site.

World Health Organization
Headquarters Office, Avenue Appia 20, 1211 Geneva 27, Switzerland; tel: 41-22-791-2111; www.who.int/ith

This site provides current infor-mation on health conditions and recommended vaccinations in destinations around the world.

PHOTO AND ILLUSTRATION CREDITS

Tim Acker/Auscape 32B

Theo Allofs 176, 180T

Bill Bachmann 188B, 191T

Erwin & Peggy Bauer/Auscape 128B, 131T

D. Donne Bryant/DDB Stock Photo 53B

John Cancalosi/Peter Arnold, Inc. 117B

John Cancalosi/Auscape 170B, 185B

Corbis 92, 97m, 111T,

Nigel J. Dennis 194, 199T

Tui De Roy/Auscape 163T

Michael DeYoung/Alaska Stock 69M

Dian Fossey Gorilla Fund International 208M

Michael J. Doolittle/Peter Arnold, Inc. 158-159B, 163B

Michael Durham/ENP Images 196

Gerry Ellis/ENP Images 18T, 22, 27T, 49, 53T, 58-59, 66B, 74B, 100, 102T, 113B, 129T, 132, 136T, 152B, 166, 169T, 171T, 197T, 208B, 209T

Bruce Farnsworth/Place Stock Photography 26B, 32T, 39T, 40B, 43TL, 43TR, 48T, 48B, 54B, 56T, 57B

Jean-Paul Ferrero/Auscape 46T, 147M, 160B, 173B, 178, 181T, 183, 185M

Mason Fischer/Fischer Photography 102B, 105B, 110B, 160T

Michael & Patricia Fogden 108TL, 108ML, 109T, 109B, 113M

Jeff Foott/Auscape 69T

Jeff Foott/Jeff Foott Productions 62T, 67T, 67B

Robert Fried/DDB Stock Photo 97T

Don Fuchs 179T

Nick Garbutt 197B, 198B, 199M, 200B, 201T

François Gohier 118T, 120T, 120B

Dennis Harding/Auscape 185T

Gavriel Jecan/Art Wolfe Inc. 72T, 101T, 147B

Michael Jones/Alaska Stock 69B

Wolfgang Kaehler 44, 63, 79T, 79B, 86, 87T, 97B, 123T, 135, 136B, 137T, 145T, 145B, 165T, 165M, 169B, 175M, 200T, 203T, 203M

Steve Kaufman 90

Thomas Kitchin/Tom Stack & Associates 12-13, 70

Kitchin & Hurst/Tom Stack & Associates 9B

Bob Krist 83B, 85T, 87M, 89B, 93T, 111B, 168, 172T, 190B, 191B, 193T

Mike Langford/Auscape 188T

Frans Lanting/Minden Pictures 156

Wayne Lawler/Auscape 46B

Luiz C. Marigo/Peter Arnold, Inc. 212-213

Joe McDonald/Tom Stack & Associates 30B, 110T, 127T

Colin Monteath/Auscape 139M, 186

Jock Montgomery 155M

Randy Morse/Tom Stack & Associates 105M

Suzanne Murphy-Larronde/DDB Stock Photo 94T

D. Parer & E. Parer-Cook/Auscape 170T

Brian Parker/Tom Stack & Associates 89T

Douglas Peebles 80, 87B

Don Pitcher 64B, 106, 134B, 137B, 140, 144T

Carol Polich 201B

Fritz Polking/Peter Arnold, Inc. 75B

Tony Rath 103

Larry Rice 79M

Galen Rowell 134T

Kevin Schafer 6-7, 24B, 25B, 34T, 50, 54T, 55, 57T, 65T, 74T, 94B, 95T, 105T, 113T, 116, 117T, 127B, 128T, 129B, 131M, 131B, 139B, 193B, 198T, 199B, 211B, back cover top

Kevin Schafer/Peter Arnold, Inc. 52B, 89M

Roland Seitre/Peter Arnold, Inc. 144B

Wendy Shattil & Bob Rozinski 98

Bill Silliker, Jr. 85B

Barry Skipsey 182

SuperStock 128M, 180B, 190T

J. Sweeney/Trip Photo Library 142

Tom Till 66T, 75T, 82, 84, 93B, 95B, 123M, 155T

Ariadne Van Zandbergen 211T

Ingrid Visser/Innerspace Visions 193M

Tom Walker 64T

Martin Wendler/Peter Arnold, Inc. 47B

S. Wilby & C. Ciantar/Auscape 175B

Duncan Willetts/Camerapix 203B

Art Wolfe/Art Wolfe Inc. front cover, 1, 2-3, 4, 5T, 5B, 8L, 8T, 9T, 10-11, 14-15, 16, 18B, 19, 20-21, 24T, 25T, 26T, 27B, 28, 30T, 31T, 31M, 31B, 33, 34B, 35, 36, 38T, 38B, 39B, 40T, 41T, 41B, 42, 43B, 47T, 52T, 60, 62T, 65B, 72-73B, 73R, 76T, 76B, 77, 83T, 101B, 108BR, 114, 118B, 119T, 119B, 121T, 121B, 123B, 124, 126, 143B, 147T, 148, 150, 151T, 151B, 152T, 153T, 153B, 155B, 158, 159T, 161M, 161B, 162T, 162B, 165B, 171B, 172B, 173T, 175T, 179B, 181B, 197M, 204, 206, 207T, 207B, 208T, 209B, 211M, back cover bottom, spine

Alison Wright 143T

Gunter Ziesler/Peter Arnold, Inc. 161T

Design by Mary Kay Garttmeier

Layout by Ingrid Hansen-Lynch

Maps by Karen Minot

Indexing by Elizabeth Cook

*T-top, B-bottom, M-middle,
R-right, L-left*

INDEX